WHO DO YOU THINK YOU ARE ?

TRACE YOUR FAMILY HISTORY BACK TO THE TUDORS

WHO DO YOU THINK YOU ARE ?

TRACE YOUR FAMILY HISTORY BACK TO THE TUDORS

ANTON GILL & DR NICK BARRATT

HarperCollins*Publishers*

HarperCollins*Publishers*
77–85 Fulham Palace Road,
Hammersmith, London W6 8JB

www.harpercollins.co.uk

Published by HarperCollins*Publishers* 2006
1

A CIP catalogue record for this book
is available from the British Library

ISBN-10 0 00 723008 7
ISBN-13 978 0 00 723008 2

Printed and bound in Great Britain by
Butler and Tanner, Frome

Wall to Wall Media Ltd
Series Producer – Lucy Carter
Executive Producer – Alex Graham.

CONTENTS

A WORD TO BEGIN WITH ...

If you are looking at this in a bookshop or a library somewhere, the chances are that you are already interested in the noble art of genealogy, and you may even be some way along the path of tracing your family tree. If not, you are probably intrigued as to your family history and wondering how to embark on such a search. Either way, we want you to read on, because this is your chance to delve even further into your family's history – back through six centuries of dynamic history. It is reasonably easy these days to trace your family back through to the beginning of official records, in the mid-nineteenth century, but this book will enable you to follow your family back much further, through the history of the preceding centuries.

Of course genealogy isn't an exact science, and the further back you go, the more challenging it can become, but that's what makes it all the more intriguing. Let's start by giving an overview of how the recording of our existences and those of our ancestors became established, and how it works.

Every ten years in the late spring, in the first year of the decade, a census takes place. Nowadays each household receives a form which it is required to complete, though nobody double-checks on the accuracy of the answers returned: those answers, however, are meant to give an indication of who was in the home in question on the night of the census, their occupations, and their relationship to one another.

The first formal national census took place in 1801, and one has taken place every decade since then except for 1941, when a skeleton census only was taken on account of the Second World War. At the same time, identity cards were issued in Britain after a national registration programme. They were discontinued after the war and we remain one of the few countries fortunate enough not to have them. (Note that records for 1931 were destroyed in Second World War German air-raids.) Census records are confidential for a century, to protect the privacy of those who took part in them until such time as it may reasonably be deemed that they are dead. The next census returns to be made accessible to the public, those of 1911, will be available from January 2012.

The first censuses taken, in 1801, 1811, 1821 and 1831, aren't of much use to the family historian, because the only information required for them was simply the number of people in any given area, their sexes and age-groups, but no more than that. It's not entirely barren ground, because some of the census-takers (enumerators) did take down names of heads of households and their families. But for this period the family historian will be better off consulting parish records.

The modern system of registering births, marriages and deaths was not introduced until 1 July 1837. From that date, they had to be reported to a local registrar (England and Wales were divided into slightly over 600 administrative districts for this purpose). Records were retained locally, and copies were sent quarterly to the Registrar General at the General Register Office in London. We'll deal with this in detail later.

It's fairly straightforward to trace your forebears back to the early nineteenth century. Spelling was pretty well standardised, information was centralised, registrars' handwriting was reasonably legible, and for the modern family historian there is the advantage that census records from 1841 are available online, so that a large amount of research can be done without even leaving home. The challenges begin when you decide to go further back. This book is designed to help you take up that challenge.

The Blitz destroyed large portions of London, including the buildings containing the census records of 1931.

When working on family history, however far back you aim to go, it's always worth starting with yourself. Always work back from there. Define how far sideways you want to go as well – as far as siblings? As cousins? As second cousins? As first cousins once removed? As second cousins once removed? As second cousins twice removed? As great-aunts and -uncles? And what line do you want to pursue? Your father's forebears or your mother's? It's probably best to concentrate on one line at a time – and you'll probably find that more than enough of a handful. Be aware that this is a fascinating and rewarding task – but be prepared to be patient and to have a reasonable amount of time and money to spend.

There are some quick ways in. Before you embark, talk to your relatives. What do they know? What do they remember? You'll probably find that older relatives will be delighted to reminisce, though it may take a bit of gentle prodding sometimes. Oral history is a vital part of our heritage. Find out from them about their parents and grandparents. Most families never talk about such things because most of us are more concerned with day-to-day matters. Take the trouble: it is enormously rewarding, but beware of family myths. These are usually far too intriguing to ignore and can lead you in entirely the wrong direction in your family research, so corroborate details as much as possible and hopefully some interesting facts will emerge.

You should also check that other family members haven't already researched the family tree. I was lucky: on my mother's side, a first cousin once removed (that is, the son of one of my great-uncles), Donald Smart, had researched his family back to my great-great-great-

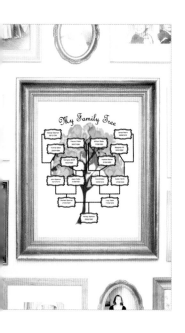

Information on your family tree can be found in the strangest of places.

grandfather, who was born about 1800. John Smart lived in Bristol and was a glass-blower and bare-knuckle fighter. On my father's side, my aunt Kunigunda has traced the Messerschmitt family of Bamberg back to 1340; but that wasn't so hard. They were a prominent local family (my father's branch were barge-masters and even had a coat of arms) and never moved from the town. My aunt however, born in 1910, is the last member of the family in Bamberg, and she will die without issue, though the line continues through cousins in Ludwigsburg and New York. As for me, my father changed his name to Gill when he came to live in England, where he married my mother and where I was born: Gill is an anglicisation of my German grandmother's maiden name, Giehl, but my father changed his name by deed poll after I was born, so that my name on my birth certificate is Anton Messerschmitt. I have no children and shall have none, so that the dynasty of the Gills of Ilford and London is a very short one indeed!

I mention all this just to show the kind of things you are likely to find out within even a few generations. After all, being 'English' is a very relative thing. King Charles II was half French, a quarter Danish, and a quarter Scots. The early Georges were 100 per cent German. George I, and to a lesser extent George II, had to converse with Robert Walpole, then the government's chief minister, in Latin, as it was the one language they had in common. Queen Victoria was also German by blood, and she and her husband would have spoken German to each other in private. The Battenberg family, so close to the Royal Family, changed its name to Mountbatten in 1917 because the German connection had become undesirable on account of the Great War. Similarly, King George V, in the same year, dropped all his German titles and changed the family name from Saxe-Coburg-Gotha to Windsor. Our current Queen Elizabeth is part Scottish and part German; and the Heir Apparent is a mixture of German, Greek and Scots. The last more-or-less reliably English monarch, and coincidentally our greatest, was Elizabeth I.

If all this daunts you, you can always hire an expert to trace your ancestry. This may set you back a few grand for the whole job, however, and you'll have none of the personal satisfaction of doing it yourself. After all, you'll learn a lot more than just your family history if you do the job properly. But if you need someone to research either the lot or just particulars, consult the classifieds in *Family Tree Magazine*, *The Genealogists' Magazine*, or contact your local family history society.

To help you through the minefield, this book is split into three parts:

Part One gives an outline of how what we call early modern records began, with the establishment of parish records in 1538 in England and Wales (rather later in Scotland and Ireland), and touches on the earliest-known records in this country. In Part One also you'll find a description of modern records (from 1837) up to the present and some details of the historical background to them. The bulk of this part of the book is dedicated to the question of how to trace your ancestors prior to 1837. This section aims to guide you back in your research as far as the mid-sixteenth century, to when parish records began.

The cornerstone of family history is knowing how your ancestors lived – not only what they earned, what they ate, how they dressed, what sort of houses they lived in and how they kept clean (if they did at all), but the events and changes that shaped their lives. Not a few of us will find as we go back that our families were divided against themselves by such things as conflicting loyalties in the Civil War of the 1640s and by religious convictions. Others will trace forebears who left these shores to escape prejudice and persecution, or simply to seek a better life, and those who came here for precisely the same reasons.

Part Two of the book is divided into five chapters, each dealing with a half-century or so of our history, social, political, military and cultural, as we go back in time. These chapters cover the period approximately between the advent of parish records towards the middle of the sixteenth century and the first national censuses of the early nineteenth. Interspersed with them are the profiles of the celebrities whose ancestries have been traced by Dr Nick Barratt and his team in the BBC TV series, which this book accompanies.

The third and final part of the book is a reference section. Here are all the tools you need to get started and some for more advanced research as well. You'll find an international directory of organisations you may need to contact and a list of publications you may want to consult as your search extends; a list of principal websites; a concise bibliography, not only listing the essential books to aid you in your quest but also leading more intrepid souls to further and more sophisticated areas of discovery. Last but not least, you will find a check-list of monarchs and chief ministers for the period approximately 1550–1800, as well as a timeline of important events at home and abroad.

Throughout the book, I've occasionally modernised spelling and grammar in old texts quoted, but only to clarify meaning. Where quotations are translations from Latin, Anglo-Saxon or any other languages I have wherever possible credited the translator when the translations are not my own. Unusual or obsolete words are briefly explained where they crop up. In dealing with money, I have used contemporary sums and not attempted to give modern equivalents, as values are relative (tea in the late seventeenth century, for example, was more expensive relatively than Dom Pérignon is today) and change from century to century. Decimal currency was not introduced to the United Kingdom until 1971, all sums prior to that being expressed in terms of pounds, shillings and pence. A pound retains its relative value. A shilling, of which there were twenty to the pound, is equal to five decimal pence; an old penny is equal to much less than half a new one, since there were 240 to the pound (twelve to the shilling). Where appropriate, I have given 'new' decimal expressions of sums of money in brackets after the old, but not always. Pounds, shillings and pence are expressed thus: £ remains the same; one shilling is expressed as 1s.; a penny is expressed as 1d. – 'd' because the old word used for a penny was Latin 'denarius', and it stuck until we modernised. You should also be aware of coins current until the 1950s and 1960s – the far-thing (one quarter of an old penny), the halfpenny, the threepenny bit, and the sixpence. A florin was a coin worth two shillings; a half-crown was worth two shillings and sixpence. You will find such sums expressed as 2/-, 2/6 etc. in certain documents. As you go back, you will encounter the guinea, the sovereign, the crown, the silver threepenny bit, and, earlier still, the groat (about 4d.). But you've probably had enough of this by now, and more arcane denominations needn't bother us for present purposes.

In conclusion, remember that you are not alone: researching family history ranks just after pornography and personal finance in popularity on the Internet (which may say something about how 'far' civilisation has come!), and you will find the institutions and organisations you visit as you make progress with your research are often very busy. Don't be afraid to ask for help, either from staff members, who will be glad to lend their expert-ise, or even from fellow-researchers. Or get other members of your family involved and work on the project together. One word of warning though before you start: this can get seriously addictive.

A pile of old English money, including pound notes, shillings and pence.

DISCOVERING YOUR EARLY ANCESTORS

In the Beginning...

UNTIL VERY RECENTLY, COMMUNICATION HAS ALWAYS TAKEN TIME. BEFORE THE ADVENT OF THE RAILWAY ENGINE, LAND TRAVEL WAS AN ARDUOUS, TIME-CONSUMING AND OFTEN DANGEROUS UNDERTAKING. IT'S HARD TO IMAGINE, IN AN AGE WHERE TRAVEL ANYWHERE IS QUICK, OFTEN INEXPENSIVE, AND EASY, AT LEAST FOR THOSE OF US LUCKY ENOUGH TO HAVE BEEN BORN IN THE DEVELOPED NATIONS, JUST HOW LENGTHY A PROCESS COMMUNICATION COULD BE, EVEN AS RECENTLY AS TWO HUNDRED YEARS AGO.

An early typewriter from the 1870s.

OPPOSITE TOP
Papyrus showing hieroglyphics from c. 1250 BC: this semi-literate form of communication stems from c. 4000 BC.

The amassing and storing of knowledge were also onerous tasks. Although the first patent for a typewriter was granted to an engineer named Mills, in England, on 17 January 1714, no viable machine appeared until Charles Thurber's in 1843, and no typewriters appeared commercially until the first Remingtons thirty years later. Hard as it may be to imagine now, as recently as 1995 relatively few people had home computers, which were in any case pretty primitive by comparison with what we have now, mobile phones were not common, laptops unknown, and the Internet and e-mails, which we already take for granted, were in their infancy. (Not forgetting that most of the people in the world still have no access to such privileged equipment, and that most of our fellows in Africa and Asia continue to lead lives that would be far more recognisable to our remote ancestors than our own.)

Mankind's early attempts at documentation

Nevertheless, man has always been interested in recording the events around him – those that happen to him and those that he causes to happen. The earliest evidence we have of this are the cave paintings of such places as Lascaux in France. The animal scenes depicted there are over 15,000 years old. The earliest writing is a cuneiform (wedge-shaped) script from Mesopotamia (part of modern Iraq), dating back to 3500 BC; though claims have been made for a pictographic script found on tortoise-shell fragments in Henan, China, which predate the Mesopotamian form by 2500 years.

The Sumerian culture of Mesopotamia can lay claim to being the first urban civilisation, but more familiar to us is that of Ancient Egypt. The pyramids, not only monuments but historical documents in themselves, date from about 2500 BC. For the Egyptian elite, writing was a precious craft and literacy a priceless gift: giving them the ability to record their existence. Masses of material in their hieroglyphic script, and the scripts deriving from it, survive. Much of it is historical, and much is concerned with who lived where and what they did. On papyrus (for important documents) and shards of pottery (which they used in the way we use notebooks or scrap paper) they recorded everything from legal disputes

to the price of corn, from family rows to family trees. In this way we have been able to build up a vivid picture of what life was like for them. And later civilisations, such as those of Greece and Rome, followed suit.

Recording our existence is not only a matter of smoothing administration in a sophisticated and complex society; it is a means of defining ourselves. No doubt that is one of the reasons why so many people today are interested in genealogy.

The *Chronicle*

Among the earliest English annals we have are seven manuscripts and two fragments collectively known as *The Anglo-Saxon Chronicle*. We don't know for sure when they were started. They were probably begun in the ninth century, and we know they ceased to be added to at the time of the coronation of Henry II in 1154, though we don't know why this was. The *Chronicle* was the work of the clergy, at the time the only literate class, at least amongst its elite; which in turn accounts for the power of the Church for so many centuries.

King Alfred was once thought to be the instigator of the *Chronicle*, though in fact there's nothing to link him with it. But it's a hugely important document, partly because it provides material from which to construct genealogies, at least of the noble houses of England, partly because it is written in Anglo-Saxon (Old English), not Latin, which was by then in

ABOVE

Papyrus showing hieroglyphics from c. 1250 BC: this semi-literate form of communication stems from c. 4000 BC.

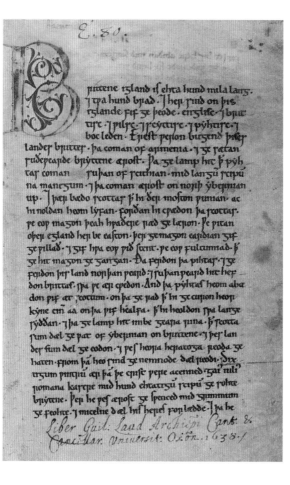

A page of the Anglo-Saxon Chronicle c. 891: the Chronicle is now available in translation in books and on the internet, along with explanatory material.

decline; and partly because it is one of the first attempts at a complete history of Britain, from the birth of Christ. Here's an account of Alfred the Great seeing off the Danes at the Battle of Edington in 878 (the translation is by Anne Savage – see Bibliography):

The force (i.e., the Danes) stole in midwinter, after Twelfth Night, to Chippenham. They rode over Wessex and occupied it, and drove many of the people over the sea; the other, greater part they overcame, except King Alfred with a little company, which with difficulty went through the woods onto the inaccessible moors. The same winter Iwar's brother Healfdene was in Wessex, in Devon, with twenty-three ships; he was killed there and eight hundred men with him and forty men of his retinue. There the standard was taken, which they call the Raven. At Easter, King Alfred, with a little company, built a fort at Athelney, and from the fort kept fighting the force, with the help of those of Somerset who were nearest. In the seventh week after Easter he rode to Ecgbryht's Stone, east of Selwood. All those of Somerset came to meet him, and those of Wiltshire, and Hampshire, the part this side of the sea; they were glad of his coming. After one night he went from that camp to Iley oak, and after a night to Edington, and there fought with the whole force and put them to flight. He rode after them to the fort and besieged it for fourteen nights. Then the force gave him hostages, and great oaths that they would go from his kingdom; they also promised that their king would receive baptism.

Alfred the Great, who ruled Wessex (Wessex covered the whole of modern south-western England, for in those days the country was not united but divided into several kingdoms, as well as some territory controlled by the Danes), was a liberal king, interested in education, and the founder not only of the first navy but of the first legal code. He reigned from 871 to c. 901, and is credited with encouraging the translations of works from Latin, some of which he undertook himself, as well as halting the progress of the Danes.

By tradition Alfred was also the translator of a book which pre-dates the *Chronicle* and is at least its equal in importance. Written in Latin and completed in 731, it is called *A History of the English Church and People*. It was composed by a Northumbrian monk named Bede, and it traces the history of Britain from its conquest by Julius Caesar in 55 BC to Bede's own day. It is a mixture of myth and legend as well as genuine history, but it is an invaluable book for anyone who wishes to understand the infancy of our nation and remains an important historical source to this day.

The *Chronicle* and the *History* were known in copied form (think of all those monks beavering away) throughout the country, and it's worth remembering that while travel was difficult it was by no means unusual, and traffic between England and mainland Europe was common. Bede's own bishop had studied in France and been to Rome, and St Augustine, the first Archbishop of Canterbury, had arrived in England from Italy on the mission of conversion entrusted to him by Pope Gregory I in 597. Of course only the privileged and literate members of the population had these options, as well as some journeymen and others in their entourages, and that's why early records don't concern themselves with ordinary people, who were born, lived and died in total anonymity.

Alfred the Great established a court school as an example of his desire to halt the loss of literacy and the knowledge of latin following the influence of the Danes.

LEFT
Saint Bede – the scribe who became known as 'The Father of English History' for his *Ecclesiastical History of the English People*

FAR LEFT
Julius Caesar's invasion of Britain is recorded in the *Chronicle*.

RIGHT

The Domesday Book –
located at the Public
Record Office in London
and now available via the
National Archives website
for Internet searches.

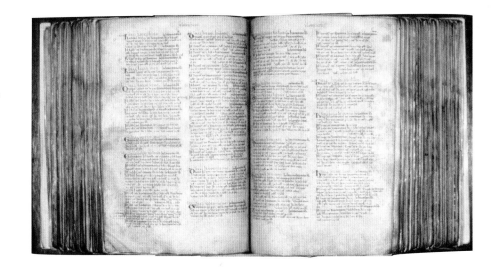

Domesday Book

The long period during which the *Chronicle* was composed is punctuated by another significant instrument of English record. This is the *Domesday Book*, compiled in 1085 and 1086 by order of William the Conqueror, and so called because it was held that its findings were as final and irrevocable as those of Doomsday itself. William was in the sixtieth year of his age in 1086, and the twentieth (and penultimate) year of his reign. The Book was intended as a record of his rights – that is, the income to which he was entitled. Unfortunately for the bulk of the population, who lived in rural communities based on the village or manor, power fell increasingly into the hands of landlords, and taxation and rents were harsher the further down the social scale you went. William himself was guilty of sub-letting his lands to tough landlords, who exploited the farm labourers tied to the land they controlled.

Some men were free and owned the land they worked, but even they were obliged to pay a nominal rent to the lord of the manor and to help bring in his harvest. Most people held land to farm for themselves, but had to work the lord's land for two or three days a week on top of paying rent; and there was no such thing as a weekend in those days. Any holiday came at Christmas, conveniently located at the back end of the farming year. The first Monday after Twelfth Night was Plough Monday. The local priest blessed the ploughs, and then it was back to work.

Craftsmen such as thatchers, masons, smiths and carpenters (note those four trades as modern surnames by the way) as well as specialised farmworkers like shepherds (another surname – though no one today seems to be called swineherd or cowherd) had small plots of their own and were not obliged to work such long stints on the lord's land. At the bottom of the pile were the serfs, tied to the estate and forbidden to leave it. Farming was primitive and land was parcelled out by the estate manager, the reeve. Most of the land was arable. There were few herds of livestock as yet; though pigs were numerous, as they could look after themselves, foraging in the extensive woodland and forest which covered most of the country. By the end of the 11th century work

BELOW

The Four Seasons – from
an early 11th Century
manuscript of *De
Temporibus* by the
Venerable Bede.

IN EACH VILLAGE OR
MANOR WILLIAM'S
INVESTIGATORS
INTERROGATED THE
PRIEST AND FOUR
LOCAL MEN. THE
ANSWERS THEY GAVE
WERE ENTERED INTO
ROLLS, FROM WHICH
THE BOOK WAS
COMPILED.

had begun on clearing the forests for more farmland, and, in the east, on draining the fens and marshes. But these projects would take many centuries.

England after the Conquest was not a merry place. The Normans had taken over the old estates and devastated much of the common land to subdue any possible Saxon resistance. This led to a fractured society, and to chaos and starvation, especially in the north. The northern counties are not covered by *Domesday Book*, the first general survey of the land of England. The information it contains was gathered by sending officials into each county. In each village or manor William's investigators interrogated the priest and four local men. The answers they gave were entered into rolls, from which the Book was compiled. Though not a complete review, it was an impressive undertaking, requiring sophisticated organisational skills. The result, as was intended, gave William an overview of how much each part of his kingdom could and should pay the state, either by rents, land taxes or *geld* (a form of tax payable to the Crown by landholders).

In each county the first entries are those of William's own lands. These are followed by details of the lands held by the Church, a vastly rich and powerful organisation in those days. Next come the holdings of major lay landowners, and after them those of smaller estates. Most entries give details of what the land was worth in 1066, the time of the Conquest, together with its value when the present owner acquired it, and finally its current value. Each entry gave details of the acreage, in terms both of arable and grazing land, as well as the number of cottars (cottage-tenants), villeins (a peasant occupier and/or cultivator entirely subject to the lord of a manor – *Domesday Book* lists 100,000 of them), notes of the numbers of oxen and other livestock, and details of churches, watermills, fisheries and fishponds. (Though no one is more than a hundred kilometres from the sea in England, that was a long distance to cover once, and fish had to be available to provide food on Fridays and other holy days, and during Lent.)

Here is a typical entry, for Westminster, London – then a rural area. The population of London proper in 1086 was about 18,000.

In the villa, where is situated the church of St Peter, the abbot of the same place holds 13½ hides. There is land for eleven plough teams. To the demesne belong nine hides (an ancient land measure: about 100 acres – deriving from the idea of the amount of land one team could plough in a year) and one virgate (another land measure: about 30 acres), and there are four plough teams. The villeins have six plough teams, and one more might be made. There are nine villeins with a virgate each, one villein with a hide, nine villeins with half a virgate each, one cottar with five acres, and forty-one cottars rendering a shilling

BELOW
An engraving of a simple
Anglo-Saxon home.

BELOW RIGHT
A 14th-century artwork of
William the Conqueror
hunting.

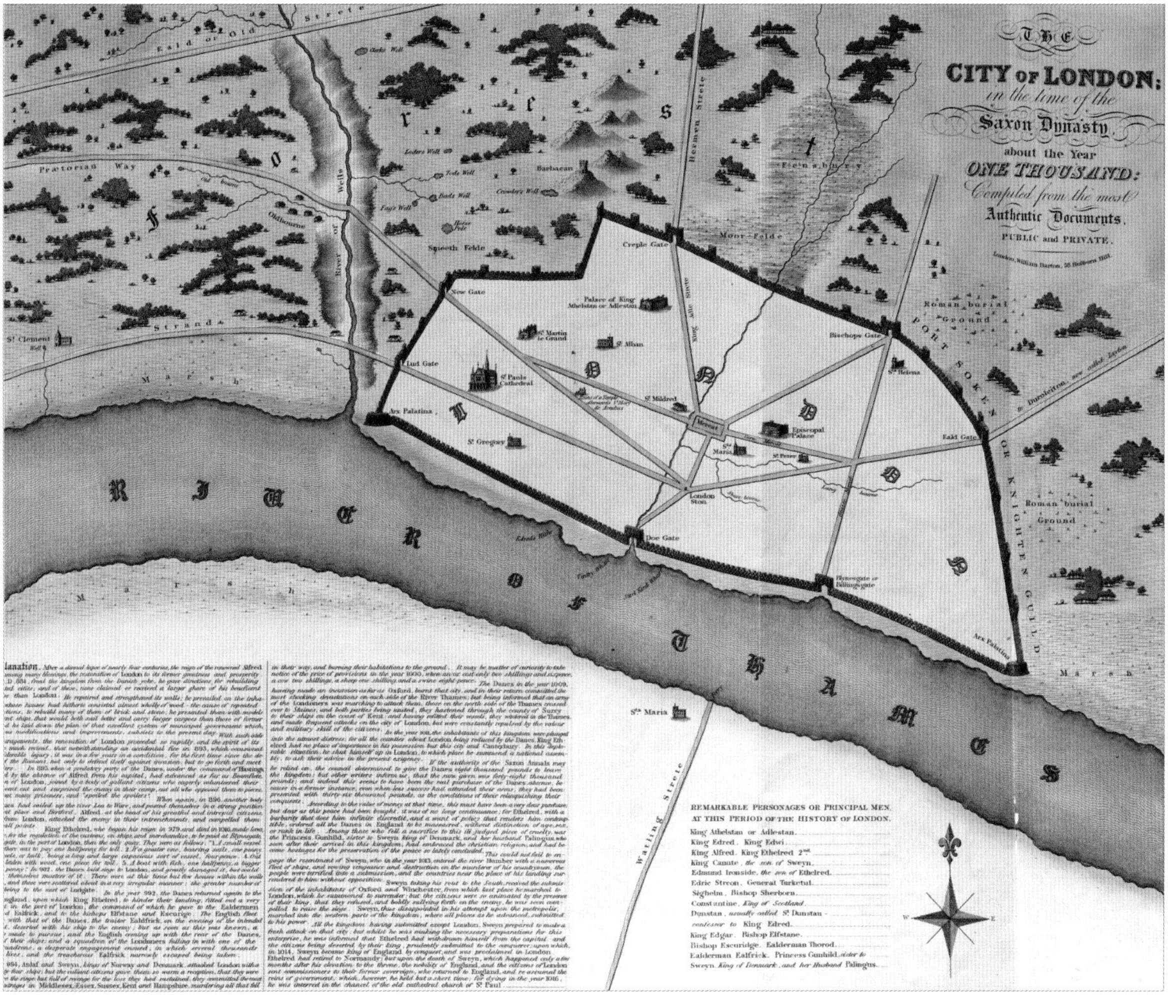

each for their gardens. There are twenty-five houses of the abbot's soldiers and of other men, who render one shilling a year or ten pounds in all ...

ABOVE

The City of London in the time of the Saxon Dynasty, about 1000 AD.

Domesday Book is also important for the incidental information it contains concerning local customs, almost all of which have long since vanished, some indeed within the last few decades. Above all, it provides a vital time-photograph of life in England in the early medieval period.

Originally kept in Winchester, for a long time England's capital, *Domesday Book* is now part of the National Archives at Kew. It was first printed and published in 1783, and facsimiles of the original for each county are available. Be warned though: the manuscript is clear enough for the most part but the Latin isn't easy. It's probably best, if you want to consult the document, to refer to a modern translation. And don't forget that there is no individualisation: you won't find ordinary people identified by name, though landowners holding land from the king are. If you want to consult *Domesday Book*, use the Phillimore edition, in 38 volumes, with parallel original text and a translation by J. Morris. Obviously this is not a book you will necessarily want to buy, but specialist libraries like the National Archives carry copies.

John Aubrey – the writer and English Antiquary.

John Aubrey

No further attempts were made at national surveys for centuries, though the idea cropped up from time to time. Political upheaval, wars, lack of money, difficulties of communication, increasingly shifting populations, all may have militated against the practicability of such schemes. One man who did make a detailed proposal, well ahead of his time, was the antiquarian and biographer John Aubrey, who wrote in 1684 a plan which described 'a Register Generall of People, Plantations and Trade of England ... to gett an Office for such a Registrie for the collecting the Accounts for the severall particulars following, viz:'

1. Of all the Births, Marriages, Burialls throughout all England: and to see them duly kept: that his Majestie may have a yearly account of the increase and decrease of his subjects.
2. An account of the Hearths, and Houses in England: as also of the People, by their Age, Sex, Trade, Titles, and Office.
3. An account of the Trade is to be deduced from the Customs-house Bills, and prices currant (upon the Exchange).
4. A particular account of the Excise, according to the last collections of subfarmes (sub-lets, I think).
5. An account of the severall payments that have been made by Land-taxes, Polls, Subsidies, Benevolence, and particular Imposts.
6. An account of all the Church Revenues.

7. A Village Anglicanum, sc. (scilicet, = 'to wit') an account of all the Cities, Townes, Villages, great Houses, Roads, carriages, principal Innes and Families of England, with the Post-stages of the same.
8. An account of all the Scholars in the Universities: and public schools.
9. An account of all the prisoners from time to time, and of all Executions.
10. A particular account of all the Shipping of England, and all Foreign parts: and the Sea-men resident in each port.
11. The prices currant of the principall Commodities in each Market of England.
12. The true number of irish cattle imported.
13. The number of Attorneys in each Countie: now: and what heretofore.

Aubrey's aim was simple and obviously useful: 'to have Abstracts of all the above particulars in order to compare them with one another, so as to give the King a true State of the Nation at all times.' Unfortunately, the scheme was one of sixty-odd projects this supreme dilettante had on the boil at one time or another, and he simply didn't push it hard enough. Even if he had, it's doubtful if Charles II, in the closing year of his reign, would have been inclined to invest in such a scheme. He was without issue, and his younger brother James, who would inherit the throne, was an ardent and inflexible Catholic. The state of the nation was tense. Charles would have had other things on his mind than a census.

Although a Census Bill was put before parliament in 1753, it gained no support, and Aubrey's ambitious project had to wait another century or so before it was applied, at least partially, in practice.

Getting information together about private individuals on a national scale didn't get started until the summer of 1837, when, just to recap quickly, a national system of registering births, marriages and deaths was set up. Before that, the early censuses had been brought in amid a good deal of controversy, because plenty of people believed that they represented an infringement of personal privacy, and even of their human rights. (The same arguments were put forward in the 1820s when Robert Peel proposed the idea of a proper professional police force.) It's probably as a result of this antipathy that the first three censuses (1801–1831) are no good to anyone interested in their family tree, since all they reveal is, as has already been said, the size of the population.

The first census to give personal detail was that of 1841, covering the number of people living in England, Wales, the Isle of Man, the Isle of Wight, the Scilly Isles and the Channel Islands. (Ireland and Scotland later conducted their own censuses.) It was taken by the recently instituted General Register Office. Since then, one has been taken in the spring every decade (except for 1941). Its format has been subject to certain changes and refinements, but essentially it has concerned itself with who was where on the specific night it was taken, and thus provides a valuable research tool. Again, as we have seen, to protect the privacy of the individual, census details are not made public until one hundred years after the census was taken.

Because of these records and thanks to modern technology, it's possible to use the Internet through a variety of sites to trace your ancestors back to 1841, though even here don't accept everything at its face value so follow through and double-check the information you do get online. For example, it's been estimated that between 1837 and 1875, especially in south-east England and Shropshire, up to 15 per cent of births simply weren't registered.

ALTHOUGH A CENSUS BILL WAS PUT BEFORE PARLIAMENT IN 1753, IT GAINED NO SUPPORT, AND AUBREY'S AMBITIOUS PROJECT HAD TO WAIT ANOTHER CENTURY OR SO BEFORE IT WAS APPLIED, AT LEAST PARTIALLY, IN PRACTICE.

Using research sources

The next question is, what do you do if you want to dig deeper, go back further? That is what we are going to try to outline in the following pages. It's worth reiterating that you should be prepared to be patient, and to have a reasonable amount of time and money to spend, because although there are websites to help you, a lot of your work now is going to be in libraries, county record offices, and even among parish records. The documents held in these places (on microform in most cases in the record offices) take us back a good deal further.

Something to take on board from the start if you don't already know this is that record offices don't permit pens. Take pencils, a pencil sharpener, a rubber and a good supply of paper – lined for these purposes is best – with you. In certain places laptops and power-points are available, and in certain circumstances you may be allowed to photograph manuscripts/books or have them photocopied. Quite often you will find that resource centres you visit are crowded. It's as well to check in advance and/or avoid weekend or evening opening hours. Above all, go as well prepared in advance as you can – you'll save an enormous amount of time, and the sheer slog otherwise can sometimes be disheartening.

Making the most of early records

In 1538, King Henry VIII's vicar-general, Thomas Cromwell, ordered that all local parishes in England and Wales should keep a written record of christenings, marriages and burials performed in their churches, giving names and the dates. In Scotland, a few registers can be

An early Parish Register at Holy Trinity Church. William Shakespeare's birth and death are listed in these pages.

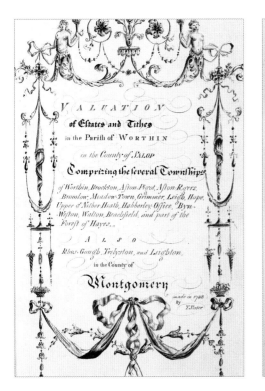

WE CAN GO BACK
WITH WRITTEN
RECORDS (AND WITH
A GOOD DEAL OF
DETERMINATION)
NEARLY 500 YEARS

LEFT
Signatures on a Register of
Grievances in the Parish
Records of Taverny parish
in 1789.

FAR LEFT
An early Valuation of
Estates and Tithes
document from the Parish
of Worthen in Salop.

found from 1553 on, but in neither part of the realm did the system really get going until about 1600, in Scotland actually ninety years later when the country united under Presbyterianism. In Ireland it was, effectively, even later.

Still, we can go back with written records (and with a good deal of determination) nearly 500 years. But pitfalls abound. Not all clergy were literate, many more were not remotely conscientious, the Civil War of 1642–49 created a great disruption, when priests were replaced in their parishes by the Puritan adherents, and in general the arduousness of transport, the intervention of the plague, the long-lasting Catholic/Anglican stand-off, and the complexity of communication mean that it's a miracle that anything coherent emerged. And in any age when divorce was next to impossible for most people, desertion and bigamy were common. Often by mutual consent, countrymen 'sold' their wives at fairs set up for the purpose.

The Black Death of the 1340s reduced the population of Britain by one third, and a lasting result is that although the population of our country now is well over ten times greater than it was then, there are fewer surnames today. And unfortunately surnames seem to group by region, so be prepared for dozens of similar or identical family names in any one set of records. A rare or unusual surname is a distinct advantage. Be prepared too for a plethora of men called William or Thomas or Henry or John, and of women named Ann or Susan or Elizabeth. And as if that wasn't bad enough, don't forget that spelling wasn't standardised until the eighteenth century, and earlier than 1650 it could be quite flamboyant! See What's in a Name on page 228 to look up some specific surnames and their meanings.

But there are always books and people to help you, and with a little practice you will find old manuscripts easier and easier to decipher. And we hope that as you progress you will find the rewards of your work more and more satisfying.

Robert Lindsay (real name: Robert Lindsay Stevenson) is one of our best-loved actors, both for his starring appearances in popular TV sitcoms like *Citizen Smith* and *My Family* and for his roles in the classical theatre, such as Benedick in Shakespeare's *Much Ado About Nothing* and Edmund in *King Lear*. Little did he imagine, when he set out in search of his family's past, that he would uncover a melodrama of his own, complete with hidden skeletons, and explode a family myth.

Now in his mid-fifties, Robert comes from a working-class family which, on both sides, has lived for generations in the small Derbyshire mining town of Ilkeston. Several relatives, including his widowed father Norman, still live there. Robert himself, needless to say something of a celebrity in the town, has never forgotten his roots and visits frequently, though he now shares his life with Rosemarie Ford and their two sons, Sam and Jamie, and his daughter Sydney.

Norman Stevenson was a joiner before he retired, and Robert's mother, Joyce, worked in a stocking factory; but together with John Lally, the art master of his school, Gladstone Boys' (where D.H. Lawrence once taught), they recognised Robert's talent for dramatic art and encouraged him to pursue it. He left Ilkeston for a place at the Royal Academy of Dramatic Art, London, in 1968.

Sadly, Joyce, to whom Robert was very close, died suddenly of a heart attack in 2000. Robert remembers family life in the early years as being about hard work and play in a close-knit community where everyone lived cheek-by-jowl in houses built and owned by the town's principal employer, Stanton's Ironworks, where generations of the family worked.

Robert began by talking to his father about the family's history. Norman had a family photo album compiled for him for his 80th birthday, and that proved a useful starting-point. Norman showed Robert photos of his maternal grandparents, Hannah and Raymond, both of whom Robert knew as a child. Raymond had served on the battleship *HMS Prince of Wales* during the First World War and had seen action during which he sustained injuries which made him deaf. There was a family story that he'd been in a big naval battle – possibly the Battle of Jutland – and had been wounded then. The *Prince of Wales* had apparently sunk.

Robert didn't know his paternal grandfather, Jesse, though he knows what he looked like from photos in Norman's album. Jesse, like his son, was a stoical, hard-working man who also saw action in the First World War, fighting with the Sherwood Foresters Regiment as a private and losing a finger in action at Armentières in 1916. Robert gathered these details from the Archivist of the Sherwood Foresters and from the National Archives, where service records that were not destroyed in the 1941 London Blitz are preserved. It came as news to Norman, who only got sparse information from his father, another man of few words where the war was concerned.

Invalided out, Jesse returned to Ilkeston to work at the ironworks, where, as local rates records revealed, he'd also worked before joining up. He was an iron-fettler, meaning that he filed off the rough edges of iron parts once they'd been removed from the casting-moulds and cooled. The loss of a finger in the war would have been

ABOVE
Robert and his father, Norman.

RIGHT
Baby Robert with his mother, Joyce.

OPPOSITE
Robert's paternal grandfather, Jesse Stevenson.

no hindrance since many workers were missing a digit or two as a result of industrial accidents. Health and safety regulations belonged to the future. Conditions were scarcely less dangerous than at the front, and when Jesse returned to Ilkeston he was put to work manufacturing bombs.

Jesse and his family lived at 111 Crompton Street, one of many terraces built by the company to house their workers. The house no longer exists, nor does Stanton Ironworks but local historian Danny Corns worked at the factory for twenty years, and his family lived at 109 Crompton Street, so he was able to fill Robert in on what life was like in those days. The houses were basic 'two-up-two-downs' (referring to the number of rooms) with no bathroom, kitchen or electricity, and an outside loo at the end of the yard known as a midden, which would be emptied after dark by night-soil workers, since the flush toilet was an unknown luxury to the working classes then. It was a tight community, so everyone knew everything about everyone else.

Jesse died suddenly of pneumonia in February 1938. He left three sons – Harry, Cyril and Norman. Norman married Robert's future mum Joyce Dunmore, a local girl, in 1948. Robert came along in December the following year. It was a happy and secure marriage for its fifty-two years. Not all Robert's forebears enjoyed the same harmony, however.

The first clue to this was that when Norman announced his intention of marrying Joyce, his own mother, Mary, tried to dissuade him. She told her son that his would-be wife's family had a dark side. Norman shrugged it off and went ahead, but Robert was intrigued to know the details. Research revealed that his mother was one of four sisters, the daughters of Hannah (*née* Hallsworth) and Raymond Dunmore, the hero of Jutland.

Hannah was a large, dark, beautiful woman with a fiery temperament. Raymond was small – just over 5 feet tall – and quiet, with an artistic bent: he was a capable painter in oils of landscapes and birds. To find out more about this apparently unlikely relationship, Robert visited his mother's surviving sisters, Grace and Elsie, who also still live in Ilkeston. They confirmed that Hannah and Raymond were totally mismatched – a large, loud woman with a small, quiet man. They also told him they had had a sister Beryl, who died at 11 months, and another, Patricia, who died at the age of 3, both from pneumonia, a common killer of the very old and very young among the poor in the 1930s. There was no National Health Service, and often no easy access to a doctor. Grandfather Raymond would mix medicines for the kids himself. Because of the high infant mortality of the time Beryl and Patricia were buried in common graves, a fact which saddened Robert.

Even more intriguingly, Grace and Elsie recalled that they had a half-brother, Bert, who presented Robert with a different challenge. At Ilkeston Register Office, Robert established that Bert was born Herbert Dawson Hallsworth in 1919. Evidently the baby wasn't Raymond's. As no father's surname was given in the register, it was impossible to establish where Bert might be today, if he is still alive.

There was more to come: Hannah and Raymond split up late in life, in the early 1960s. And research revealed that Hannah's own parents, Henry and Ada, also separated – giving another twist to the family tree. Norman knew all about this and told Robert that Henry was a real womaniser and may have been the inspiration for the

ROBERT'S EARLIER FAMILY TREE LOOK LIKE A VICTORIAN MELODRAMA ... NO WONDER, ROBERT CONCLUDED, THAT HIS FATHER'S FAMILY HAD OPPOSED HIS MARRIAGE INTO JOYCE'S!

ABOVE
Roberts maternal grandmother, the charismatic Hannah Dunmore.

RIGHT
Raymond Dunmore, Robert's maternal grandfather, who served on the battleship HMS *Prince of Wales* during the First World War.

gamekeeper Mellors in D.H. Lawrence's sexually explicit novel *Lady Chatterley's Lover*.

Henry and Ada had four daughters, some of whom, according to the 1901 census, would have been too old to have been Ada's children. It emerged that at least one of them was Henry's daughter by an earlier liaison, not apparently a legal one, though the mother's name is given as Hallsworth in the register. It's a complicated story, but it demonstrates that, because divorce was still so difficult in those days, couples who separated either entered into illegal liaisons and lied to the authorities about them, or began bigamous relationships – quite often both partners would do this.

Robert managed to establish that, between them, Ada and Henry had thirteen children, some not Ada's, and that after their split Henry had a further two, making Robert's earlier family tree look like a Victorian melodrama. And there were great-great-grandparents too, who led equally tangled lives – evidence suggests they too

were bigamists. No wonder, Robert concluded, that his father's family had opposed his marriage into Joyce's!

Returning to paternal grandfather Raymond, a family myth was unravelled. The ship he served on in the Great War, *HMS Prince of Wales*, wasn't engaged in the Battle of Jutland. At the time it was in port in Italy and later stationed off the shores of Turkey. It was involved in the disastrous landings at Gallipoli in 1915, and it was there that grandfather Raymond, working on the boats that towed the landing-craft carrying the ANZAC troops to shore, was injured. It was his tow-boat that had sunk, not the battleship herself, though the injuries he sustained were real enough.

From all he learned, Robert says he was impressed by how lucky his parents and grandparents had been to survive, and how lucky he himself has been not to have lived through such testing times.

CHAPTER TWO

Finding Out

THOMAS CROMWELL WAS HENRY VIII'S CHIEF MINISTER AS WELL AS HIS VICAR-GENERAL. NOT A PARTICULARLY ATTRACTIVE MAN, HE WAS PARTLY RESPONSIBLE FOR ABETTING HENRY VIII IN BREAKING THE POWER OF THE ROMAN CATHOLIC CHURCH IN ENGLAND, AN ACT WHICH WAS TO LEAD TO A CENTURY AND A HALF OF UPHEAVAL AND THE DOWNFALL OF SIR THOMAS MORE. BUT HE'S INTERESTING, AND WORTH A MOMENT'S INTRODUCTION.

Thomas Cromwell, born in Putney the son of a blacksmith.

The English Middle Ages, it could be argued, came to an end with the defeat and death of Richard III, the last of the Plantagenets, at the Battle of Bosworth Field in 1485. The next king, the Welshman Henry VII, founded the Tudor dynasty. Through marriage he united the warring factions of the great aristocratic houses of Lancaster and York, and during his reign he stabilised the power of the Crown, as well as its control over parliament. He also gained domination over all fractious elements of the nobility by crushing resistance, forbidding the nobles to maintain retainers, and imposing heavy fines and confiscations of property. At the same time he avoided foreign wars and promoted commerce. When he died in 1509, leaving the throne to his son Henry, he left England prosperous and strong. He had also in a sense ushered in the modern age, and his son, who was just short of eighteen when he became king and who ruled for 38 years, continued his work.

Henry VIII's reign saw the rise of self-made men. They had existed before now, especially in the fields of the arts and the humanities, and often rose through the ranks of the Church, but now they began to appear in the arenas of business and politics, areas hitherto largely the domain of the aristocracy. Thomas Cromwell (a very remote ancestor of Oliver, by the way) was an exemplar of this trend. A glance at his life shows how a man could be very mobile both geographically and socially, if he set his mind to it.

Thomas Cromwell and the decline of the Catholic Church

Cromwell was born in 1485 in Putney, the son of a blacksmith who also worked as a cloth-cutter, brewer and innkeeper. (If you can trace ancestors who were in trade, your chances of following through successfully are greater than if your roots are in the peasantry. Traders could be identified as individuals, and guilds and trade organisations kept records.) From the age of nineteen or thereabouts, young Thomas crossed the Channel and spent the next eight or nine years out of the country, at one point serving as a footsoldier, possibly in one of the mercenary armies which plied for hire on the Continent. This was nothing new. The English soldier-of-fortune Sir John Hawkwood, immortalised by Uccello in an equestrian portrait in Florence cathedral, was active abroad as a *condottiere* in the fourteenth century!

Thomas later crops up as a friend of the Florentine banker, Frescobaldi, as a clerk working in Antwerp, and doing the same job in Venice, both cities important trade centres. He seems to have visited Rome, and later to have set up in business in Mittelberg, about 60 kilometres east of Lake Konstanz.

By 1513 he was back in England where he earned his living variously as a scrivener, a wool-merchant, a money-lender and a lawyer (he evidently had some training in the law). He was successful, and through the influence of Cardinal Wolsey, Henry's right-hand man in the early years of his reign, and himself something of a self-made man, found his way into court circles and into parliament, making himself useful in the suppression of some of the smaller monasteries, and working as Wolsey's secretary. When Wolsey overreached himself, fatally prevaricating over Henry's divorce from the Catholic Catherine of Aragon (his first wife) and having the cheek to build at Hampton Court a far grander palace than anything Henry himself had, Cromwell stepped adroitly into his former master's shoes, taking care not to ruffle the feathers of the aristocracy by behaving in the haughty, *arriviste* manner of the Cardinal, That son of an Ipswich butcher hadn't stopped with Hampton Court, he'd founded a college at Oxford and a school at Ipswich as well, and his retinue and his power – admittedly largely conferred by Henry – rivalled the monarch's.).

Once in with the king, Cromwell directed the break with the Roman Church, counselling Henry to create himself Head of the Church in England and thus empowering himself to divorce his no-longer-desirable queen, who (as he believed) was unable to provide him with a male heir. The dissolution of the monasteries followed in the last years of the 1530s, and under Cromwell's direction a Protestant reign of terror descended on the country. He became Privy Councillor, Chancellor of the Exchequer, Master of the Rolls, Vicar-General and Lord Privy Seal, and those were not the last of his honours – he ended up a Knight of the Garter, Lord Great Chamberlain, and Earl of Essex.

But he didn't do all this without attracting many enemies and as a commoner he probably never wholly gained Establishment acceptance. He'd earned the hatred of the still-powerful Catholics (the Church of England was after all a purely political expedient to begin with) who remained in a majority; but his zeal for the suppression of Roman rule led to his fall. He was the arranger of Henry's marriage to his fourth wife, Anne of Cleves, a good new Protestant from northern Germany, and only 25 when she married the English king in 1540. But they didn't like each other, Henry found her plain and called her 'the Flanders mare', and the marriage collapsed after six months.

Now Cromwell's enemies saw their chance to topple him. Within two months of Anne's return home Cromwell was arrested at the council table on a charge of treason. Despite rather pathetic appeals from the Tower for his life to be spared, he was executed on Tower Hill on 28 July 1540, aged 55. The headsman botched the job rather messily, taking several strokes to get the head off. (This was not uncommon, by the way. Death by beheading was far from an exact science. Everybody knew that, which makes people's behaviour on the block doubly brave. Henry VIII apparently imported a specially skilled headsman from Calais, who used a sword, to finish off Anne Bullen [Boleyn] – a backhanded gesture of regard, if you like.) Before his death, Cromwell declared that he would die a Catholic. An interesting stance, and one which proves how much more political than doctrinaire was the split from Rome.

BELOW
Henry VII founder of the Tudor dynasty.

BOTTOM
Cardinal Wolsey, Cromwell's mentor, fell out of favour with Henry VIII.

The 1538 mandate

For family historians, Cromwell is remembered with gratitude since as we have seen it was he who produced the mandate by which, in 1538, parishes the length and breadth of England were obliged to keep a record of baptisms, marriages and burials. (It's quite important here to be aware of the distinctions between 'birth' and 'baptism', and 'death' and 'burial' – the dates are not the same. Sometimes children were baptised long after their birth, and both baptisms and burials could take place in parishes other than those in which the person was born or died.)

Parishes were the centre of what would now be regarded as local government. The Church at that time played a far more important role in the temporal as well as the spiritual lives of people, and parish churches were social centres as well as places of worship. In fact, for most people they were more important in the former role than the latter. Our ancestors weren't in general much more God-fearing than we are.

The records of the approximately 11,000 parishes of England and Wales were to be kept, according to Cromwell's instructions, in a stout chest, along with the church plate, parish constables' accounts, and any other relevant documentation. Scotland, which had about 900 parishes, was still a separate country and although various enactments were passed to introduce a similar system, and a few registers start as early as 1553, for general purposes little was regularised until the late seventeenth century. In Ireland, which had 31 dioceses, ministers (for the official Church in that Catholic country was the Anglican Church of Ireland until 1869) were required to keep records only from 1634, and most surviving registers date from the late eighteenth century.

The system was difficult to enforce and for the first sixty years responsible following of it was patchy, so that in 1598 an injunction was passed to reinforce the original mandate, requiring additionally that existing records be copied on to parchment in order the better to preserve them. It should be re-emphasised immediately that these early records are of baptisms, marriages and burials, *not* births, marriages and deaths, so that the dates of the first and last entries will *not* give us an exact chronology of our remoter ancestors; but we are fortunate that they exist at all.

From 1598, each parish priest had to send a copy of the year's records to his bishop. This gives us a first centralised source; but in the process of copying mistakes could and did appear, so when dealing with such material it is a good idea to cross-check with the earlier record if it is available.

County Record Offices

Almost all surviving parish records a century old or more are now held in their original form and/or on microfiche or microfilm in County Record Offices, where staff will be able to help with the handwriting, vagaries of spelling, and dog-Latin of our ancestors, though there are plenty of books available to teach you to guide yourself through these. It's always worth visiting a County Record Office whose holdings are relevant to your research, because they house a rich variety of information, from police records to election results, from local tax details to local newspapers, from transport to military to civil law to estate and manorial archives. A real Aladdin's cave. If the place you're after is miles away, you can always engage a local researcher, but there's no real substitute for doing the job yourself, time and money always permitting!

County Record Offices can be useful, too, if you think you have a criminal in your ancestry; for example, it's worth checking the records of Petty, Borough or Quarter Sessions in the relevant record office. Assize records are in the National Archives. But it's fair to say that if an ancestor was a vagrant or villain before police records began it's unlikely that you'll ever find him or her. If you suspect an ancestor was pushed from village to village as one community after another ducked the responsibility of paying him or her dole, it'll be hard, but you needn't lose heart. Your best chances lie in identifying where they were born, and then going to see if there is any documentation on them.

BELOW
County Record Offices hold original records of election results, local tax details and even manorial archives.

BELOW LEFT
Many records are held in their original form.

Once you've found the parish that interests you, you should refer to a specialist publication, to be found in good reference libraries, called *The Phillimore Atlas and Index of Parish Registers*, edited by Cecil Humphery-Smith. The map section of this book will give you the boundaries of the parish, its location, its diocese, and the date of its earliest parish records. The text section of *Phillimore* will provide you with a number of references to the most important genealogical sources and resources for you to follow up. If it all looks a bit daunting, it's important to remember that you're not alone. With the help of the Society of Genealogists or a local family history group, you may be able to locate copies of the registers you're interested in without making a long journey (which could result in disappointment).

Associated with parish records are the records of the Vestry, the group of local men elected to run the parish, the records of the churchwardens, of the parish constable, and those of the Overseers of the Poor. These where available complement each other and can deepen one's knowledge and understanding.

Once you've got what you're looking for, remember always to keep a record. If you go a certain distance down the track and then find you need a reference which you've forgotten because you didn't write it down, you'll have to start at square one again, which, given that you've embarked on one of the most painstaking quests known to man, might make you swear a bit.

Are you related to a Lord of the Manor?

Members of the aristocracy always wanted to maintain the status quo. It was all right for the son of a noble house to marry the daughter of a rich banker or merchant to salvage the family fortunes, but for a high-born daughter to marry a commoner was almost always unthinkable. The Duchess of Buckingham was appalled by the doctrines of the Methodists: 'It is monstrous,' she said, 'to be told that you have a heart as sinful as the common wretches that crawl on the earth. This is highly offensive and insulting and at variance with high rank and good breeding.' Another noblewoman said of the workers on her estates, 'I'd like to converse with them, but pigs can only understand grunts.'

Given such attitudes, it's a mark of British forbearance that we didn't follow the example of the French and have another revolution. However, unless you are lucky enough (from a genealogical point of view) to have been born into a noble house, in which case tracing your family history should be a breeze, it's a plus if you can track down an ancestor who worked for, or held land from, a great estate or a lord of the manor. Land is registered, and through land registers it's possible to find out who owned or worked it. Manorial records are another means of finding your earlier forebears. Conveniently, a Manorial Documents Register has been compiled and is available at the National Archives at Kew. That part of it relating to Wales is even available online.

So, given that your search is in very many cases likely to lead you back to country roots, you can be certain of having strong lines to follow as you look for them, at least in terms of locating where your ancestors lived. But don't forget either that, tied to the land as many of our ancestors were, there was also a lot more mobility, especially among craftsmen and traders, and much earlier, than one might at first think.

Good research begins at home

This section of the book is concerned with helping you trace your ancestors before modern records began, but you have got to get that far back first. The golden rule is to start with yourself. Most of us know who our grandparents were and what they did, and where they came from, but beyond that I think it's fair to say that only a few do. Yet you may be surprised at what documents have been kept by others, especially older members of your family. Of course there will be birth and marriage certificates, school reports and records, details of financial, investment and other business transactions. Someone somewhere may have stored death certificates, and there may be papers relating to funeral and memorial services.

I know it sounds gloomy, but I found out a huge amount about my own parents, and was able to explode a few family myths (and discover some fairly dramatic family secrets), when I had to go through their papers after their deaths (they died within ten days of each other, so I was able to get a complete picture very quickly). I was lucky in that my parents were absolute squirrels and threw nothing away (I even found cheque stubs from the 1930s and a clip of live rifle ammunition!), so there was a mass of letters and other informal documentation to help, as well as a huge number of photographs, many of them of people I had no knowledge of and who were not identified in the albums.

Photographs can be a great source, but remember that even as recently as the 1930s photography was still a relatively rare thing. Apart from stiff family portraits, you may find few records of holidays, travels, birthdays and weddings. I was lucky, for my grandfather and my uncle on the English side were great amateur photographers. But I still needed cousins and second cousins, some of whom I barely knew, to help identify people. The family isn't the tight-knit extended unit it once was, and as a resource it isn't always available these days.

If your close forebears kept a journal, then that is an amazing plus. Failing that, the nature of their work may give you some clues. Was anyone ever an apprentice? Did anyone

Family photographs are a great place to start your search.

THE NATIONAL
ARCHIVES HOLD
RECORDS OF
PASSPORTS OR THEIR
EARLIER FORMS BACK
TO 1795

belong to a trade union? Are there any records from the armed forces? (It was only after his death that I discovered a couple of medals my father had been awarded, shoved in the back of a drawer. I hadn't a clue what they were and he'd never mentioned them.)

If any of your recent ancestors were, for example, civil servants, in the police, in the medical profession, in the merchant navy or in the Church there may be ways of checking details of their professional lives through official channels. Even such mundane things as passports and driving licences can set you off on a trail. (It was noticing a clumsy 'edit' on my mother's passport, followed by a bit of detective work, that led me to a very deeply buried family secret and the answer to something that had bothered me since I was sixteen.)

Passports, it should be noted, though they have existed in various forms, such as safe-conducts, since the Middle Ages, were not made compulsory for foreign travel until 1914. Great Britain has a liberal passport policy, allowing people of dual nationality to have a British passport as well as the other country of which they are nationals. This is not true, however, of certain other European nations. The National Archives hold records of passports or their earlier forms back to 1795.

School and university records can also be mined as a source of information, as well as a guide to subsequent employment. Try consulting trade directories, for example. Where to find these, and books to guide you in the precise detail of how to conduct your research in these fields, are listed in Part Three. Your family may have fallen on hard times. Poor Law Union records have been compiled, as have workhouse registers. You may also wish to consult the *Poor Law Union Gazette.* If you suspect that you have forebears who led a life of crime, you are fortunate in that there is more likely to be particular documentation on them (if they were caught!) than there will be on law-observing ancestors.

Similar records exist in relation to mental illness and, if you can trace divorces in the family, the divorce courts keep records which can be consulted.

Be aware, however, that some of these resources will only take you back reliably to about the middle of the nineteenth century, and that those concerning divorce, adoption and

Look in local newspapers and local photographic archives.

mental illness may be subject to certain viewing restrictions. Divorce papers for example cannot be consulted unless they are more than 75 years old.

Something else my family had, which is now in my possession, is a family Bible. These are useful because traditionally each generation the Bible passes through records their names and dates of birth. (Deaths are also recorded.) Mine is from my mother's side and goes back to John and Sarah Grocott who were born respectively on 21 September 1845 and 2 June 1843, and died on 19 May 1915 and 21 October 1918. Since I knew where my maternal grandmother's family came from, and since Grocott is a distinctive local surname, this simple bit of information gave me quite a jumping-off point in research not covered by other members of my family.

Also, especially if you hope to go a long way back, be aware of the value of wills. You may have some in your family papers, or you may be able to trace copies in the records of the various ecclesiastical courts. Wills can not only tell you something of the character of the testator, quite apart from what he or she owned, but introduce you to other 'characters' who may form part of your family's history in the persons of the legatees.

LOOK OUT IN PAPERS FOR LAW REPORTS, COURT CIRCULARS, PERSONAL ANNOUNCEMENTS, AND OBITUARIES

Read the papers

Be aware, too, of the value of contemporary written sources. Newspapers began around the beginning of the eighteenth century, though some publications go back earlier. A vast resource is the Newspaper Library of the British Library, located at Colindale in north London. Local papers can be a mine of information – don't forget the personal announcements columns. The first real newspaper, apart from handbills, was *The London Gazette*, which actually started life as *The Oxford Gazette*, since it was founded in 1665 when the Court had removed to Oxford on account of the Great Plague. Early editions contain such treasures as eye-witness accounts of the Great Fire of London. Among other early newspapers and magazines worth consulting are *The Gentleman's Magazine*, which ran from 1731 to 1868; *The Times*, founded in 1785, which was until recently *the* British national newspaper, and the newspaper of record – its obituaries, anthologies of which have been published, are of great interest; *The Illustrated London News*; and, as a curiosity, *Old Moore's Almanack*, founded by Francis Moore, a doctor, astrologer and Whig politician, in 1700, who in that year published his *Vox Stellarum, an Almanac for 1701 with Astrological Observations*.

Look out in papers for law reports, court circulars, personal announcements, and obituaries – all can provide valuable clues provided your search is focused. And should you be lucky enough to be looking at life in London towards the end of the seventeenth century, nothing can give you a more delightful introduction to the day-to-day activities of the period than Samuel Pepys' *Diaries*.

What's in a name?

Names can turn out to be trump cards and they can take you back a long way. Sometimes first names run in families for generations, and it was a Huguenot tradition for the first-born son to be named after his father. Saints' names have always been very popular for boys and girls, and a saint's name is, or was until recently, more or less obligatory among observant Catholics in countries such as Italy, Poland and Spain. There are fashions for names which can help you date their owners sometimes, especially if there was a trend for naming one's offspring after a famous personality or public figure. A number of men born soon after November 1948 have 'Charles' as one of their first names, for example. Women's first names like Ivy, Gladys, June or April are not current now, but would have been in the first half of the last century. Georgian names like Emma and Charlotte have become fashionable again recently, as well as Victorian names such as Emily and Daisy. The choosing of first names also follows class, cultural, and ethnical background trends.

Another batch of first names that may provide clues for you are those either from the Old Testament or compound names reflecting moral stances – names which were favoured by non-conformists such as Methodists and Baptists. The famous Barebones Parliament, which sat in the latter half of 1653, after Oliver Cromwell had expelled the Rump Parliament, was named after one of its members, a Fleet Street leather-seller called Praisegod Barbon. His brothers' first names were: Jesus-Christ-Came-Into-The-World-To-Save, and If-Christ-Had-Not-Died-For-Thee-Thou-Hadst-Been-Damned. The most popular book in the country after the Bible in the late seventeenth and early eighteenth century, *The Pilgrim's Progress,* was by a Puritan, John Bunyan. The names of his characters, though consciously didactic, make interesting reading and some had an influence. Note also that Puritan 'moral' names were open to mockery, as with 'Zeal-Of-The-Land Busy' – the pompous, hypocritical Puritan in Ben Jonson's play *Bartholomew Fair.*

There may simply be a distinctive name that crops up down the generations. My middle name is Egbert. Don't laugh. It was also my English uncle's name and my great-uncle's, and it's Anglo-Saxon – we've already read the name 'Ecgbryht' in the *Anglo-Saxon Chronicle* earlier. He was Egbert the Great, King of the West Saxons, who died in 839. The name means 'bright-edged' or, in our parlance, 'dead sharp'. Not that I'm claiming any descent from him, but the name's useful when I track back, and you may find similar unusual family names which will make your forebears stand out in lists and make them easier to find. There may be several names to follow. I've also got Edwin, Victor, Louis and Herbert, which run back generations. It's worth bearing them in mind. (I wish my mum had chosen one of them instead of Egbert, though it made even school bullies feel sorry for me once they'd tortured it out.) It could have been worse: a popular first name for the sons of Low-Church members in the nineteenth century was 'Abishag'.

Surnames (unless you've a confection like mine, because 'Gill' is a north-eastern English surname in its pure form) can be even more useful if they are unusual, but bear in mind that spelling didn't begin to become standardised until around the mid-eighteenth century, so any name can be subject to a variety of forms, which indeed continue to this day. The variant spellings of 'Catherine' are well known and easily distinguishable, as are those of 'Marjorie'; but surnames can lead you astray: Ruddle, Ruddal, are easy, but the distinguished genealogist John Titford lists 47 variant spellings of his surname, which differ wildly: 'Titfield, Tissord, Tidmarsh, Twyford, Pickford and Mitford' are six examples that are graspable, but what of 'Thord and Lidgard'? Be aware that the further you go back, and consequently the more you have to adjust to early forms of handwriting, you will have to cross-question every finding. That's where unusual first names (in older annals referred to as 'Christian names') may come in handy.

The current location of the owners of unusual surnames can sometimes be traced through telephone directories (you may need to find a major library that keeps a national set; or try typing it into a search engine on the Internet and see what you come up with). Or consult a specialist book, *The Homes of Family Names*, by H. B. Guppy (published 1890).

There's also the Guild of One-Name Studies (GOONS) who live at the same address as the Society of Genealogists (see Part Three for contact details).

Despite the 'death' of many surnames during the pandemic bubonic plague in the fourteenth century which I've mentioned, there are still plenty to go round. They fall into four basic categories. The most obvious is the Richardson, Thompson, Johnson, Johnston, Smithson, Jefferson-type of surname which simply indicates 'son-of' John, Smith, Jeffrey and so on. Note that Icelanders today continue a surname tradition on these lines: Magnus Magnusson is Magnus the-son-of-Magnus. But Gudrun Magnusdottir is Gudrun the-daughter-of-Magnus. Her son or daughter would take the male or female child-form from the patronymic. If Gudrun married Einar, and had a daughter Inga, she'd be Inga Einarsdottir. The population of Iceland is tiny compared with ours; but keeping track of changeable surnames must be a difficult business. Still, it gives an indication of how patronymics can be traced.

The second type of surname has to do with professions. We've already seen how Thatcher, Carter, Shepherd, Archer and so on came about as surnames to identify people by their jobs. Surnames didn't put in an appearance until about the turn of the twelfth and thirteenth centuries, at about which time the population was growing big enough (the choice of first names remaining relatively narrow) for people sharing a first name in a town or even village to need to be identified individually. Professions or jobs or trades were an obvious way to do this, if the 'son/daughter' of the father hadn't been opted for. Look carefully at surnames and you will quickly discover how many derive from occupations. Some survive from occupations long gone: Reeve, for example, or Wainwright, or Crowther, or Latimer. These might still give a clue to tracing ancient ancestors. Others are obvious but quite common: Miller, Cook, Smith, Clerk (Clarke, Clark, Clerke etc.). Beware of what we might call false friends – 'Coe' is a name found in Essex and Suffolk, and comes from a local word for a jackdaw. 'Cohen' is a Jewish form for 'priest'. Some rare names, such as Ewence, are probably variations of familiar names like Evans.

Place or location names provide a third category: Ford, Sands (Sandys), Barrow (Borrow, Barrie), Waterford, Bridge, Castle are obvious ones; Leicester, Bristol, Carlisle, Kendal, Ramsbottom are others. You should also be aware of surnames that stick to certain geographical areas: it's common knowledge that Evans, Jones and Price suggest a Welsh background (and the name Onions/O'nions may mean 'son of Einion'); look too at the large number of surnames that indicate Irish or Scottish ancestry. And there are many names which indicate Jewish forebears. Some common German-Jewish names (Rosensaft, Rosenbaum, Rosenzweig, for example) may come from names conferred for ease of administration by Prussian officials on Jewish refugees fleeing Russian pogroms in the nineteenth century. African and Asian names are more recent arrivals and tend to be ethnically authentic. However, a friend of mine is descended from African slaves who were shipped to the Caribbean, and her surname – Llewellyn – derives from the name conferred on her forebears by their slavemaster, whose own name it probably was. This was not an unusual practice.

Place-related surnames can give important clues about foreign ancestry. Look particularly at anglicisations of Norman or old French forms, which may not be obvious, like Dando or Dangerfield. And be aware of names deriving from Old English, Old Norse, Old German, and Gaelic.

Finally there are the surnames which indicate personal attributes, and probably originated as nicknames. Keep in mind the way monarchs in olden times were identified,

BUT THE DISTINGUISHED GENEALOGIST JOHN TITFORD LISTS 47 VARIANT SPELLINGS OF HIS SURNAME, WHICH DIFFER WILDLY

sometimes in delightfully graphic ways: Pedro the Cruel, Pepin the Fat, Charles the Bold, Demetrius the Spurious, to name but a few; and our own Ethelred the 'Unready' (so called because he would not take advice – *rede* – not because he was caught with his trousers down). Names like Redhead and Truman are obvious, Benbow (an archer or bowman) less so; more obscure still perhaps are Annear (tall and thin) and Belcher (pretty and cheerful). Smollett means 'pinhead', Spink is a corruption of 'chaffinch'.

Double-barrelled names often indicate a marriage; and occasionally you will come across names like D'eath and B'stard. Illegitimacy wasn't always frowned on – it took the hypocritical Victorians to usher in such attitudes. Children born out of wedlock were acknowledged and looked after. Surnames beginning 'Fitz-' (the prefix derives from Old French *fiz*, which became Modern French *fils*, 'son') denote illegitimacy originally. Williamson or Fitzwilliam. Take your pick! There are plenty of books to help you through the labyrinth of surnames and their origins. Some of them are listed in the Bibliography in Part Three.

Common problems

Although births, marriages and deaths have been recorded officially since the middle of 1837, to begin with it was the responsibility of the local registrar to locate births and deaths and record them, while in the case of marriages the officiating clergy were supposed to report to the Registrar General. (Registration of marriages was initially further complicated by the fact that some non-conformist chapels were not officially licensed.)

Despite the fact that registrars seem to have been very efficient, many births and deaths – especially births, as high as 15% – were still going unregistered, so in 1874 a new Act of Parliament provided that individuals should report such events in their families to the local registrar themselves. But people remained suspicious of what they viewed as undue interference in their personal affairs by the authorities. (Something which to a certain extent endures to this day.) The pool is further muddied by infant mortality. Although it's believed now that English families weren't that much larger in earlier centuries than they are today, nevertheless infant mortality was high, and often a family first name was used repeatedly. A first-born son called John, for example, might have died as an infant, and a subsequent male child would be given the same name. This kind of thing requires very careful checking when going through old registers.

Irish families could be very large – even into modern times. I have a friend in his fifties whose first wife was the youngest of seventeen. For those of you reading this who have Irish ancestry, the sheer number of your forebears even within the immediate family group (outwards only to siblings, uncles, aunts and cousins) may provide you with quite a lot of paperwork! The Catholic Church has a lot to answer for!

Where to look

Where are records kept? There are two main repositories in England. The first is the National Archives at Kew, London. It's worth knowing that until very recently this was called the Public Record Office (PRO) because you will find older but still valid reference books using this name. Remember too that the PRO's branch in Chancery Lane is now closed and its archive subsumed within the National Archives. Also contained there now is the Historical Manuscripts Commission.

The National Archives is a wonderful resource, open to all, in a beautifully organised research environment which puts the new British Library (for which you will have to apply for a Reader's Ticket) to shame. It's worth making the journey just for the experience, but if you can't, some contact can be made via Internet. The National Archives can provide information where local resources have failed you, and can fill you in with first-hand documentary information on the historical background to your ancestors, especially legal matters. There are also available records in printed and book form, as well as indexes to guide you through the sheer volume of treasure that is here.

You can also find specific information on, for example, births, marriages and deaths of British subjects abroad; genealogical records relating to the whole of the United Kingdom, the Isle of Man and the Channel Islands, as well as the Republic of Ireland; changes of name by Deed Poll; Naturalisation; details of employees of the state – the police, the civil service, the education service; the law; medicine; the Church, the armed forces, and so on – even down to such specifics as debtors and bankrupts.

Remember that any personal detail, any false move, divorce, fraud, mistake committed by an ancestor may have found its way into the records. If your trail runs cold when following official lines – think laterally. A reprobate in the family is more likely to have left tracks than an honest citizen! And apart from anything else, the thrill of holding in your own hands documents that are more than 300 years old, for example, is indescribable!

The second major resource (which has its equivalent offices in Belfast, Dublin and Edinburgh) is the Family Records Centre. Again this has gone under other names before the mid-1990s. People will still talk of 'Somerset House' (where family records were first lodged) and 'St Catherine's House', on the corner of Kingsway and The Strand, where they were subsequently stored, so beware of references in older books and sources.

The Family Records Centre in Islington is where you need to go now. There you will find all the General Register Office's records for births, marriages and deaths in England and Wales (from 1837). You can also, within certain limitations, trace people who died or

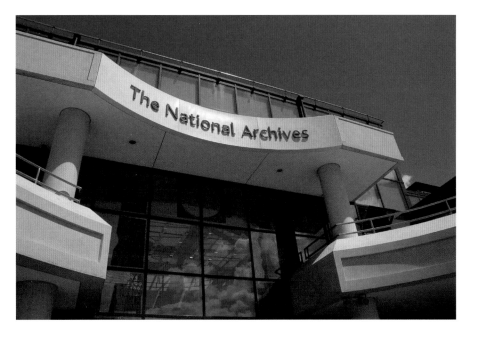

The National Archives at Kew, London, previously known as the Public Records Office.

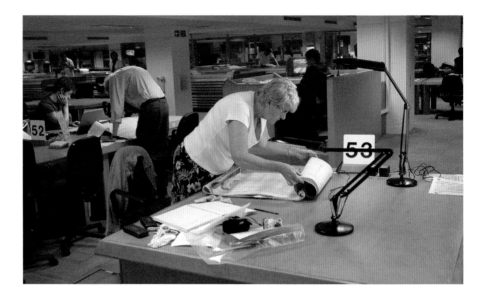

The internet can take you back just so far. There's no better thrill than unfolding the actual historical record.

were born on ships or aeroplanes, and use resources to trace still-born babies, to track adoptions. Be aware however that such records in general will not take you further back than the early nineteenth century.

The FRC and the GRO have websites and can be contacted by telephone and by post with respect to specific requests (for all details, see Part Three). Copies of certificates, and searches conducted on your behalf, will cost modest sums of money. Ring for details. Alternatively, contact your local register office. You'll find staff friendly on the whole, and interested in their work. But be prepared to be patient.

Scotland started its official registration programme at the beginning of 1855, and for the first year a great deal of personal information was required, providing a rich vein for the researcher. Sadly this was reduced on account of the amount of work required to process it, and a further reduction in detail came in 1861. Nevertheless Scottish records are still more comprehensive than those for England and Wales.

Centralised Irish Republic (Eire) records date from 1864, though on account of the continued repression of the Catholic faith in Ireland by Great Britain, and the oppression of the Irish by the English until the early 20th century, only Protestant marriages can be found registered earlier (to 1845). All marriages are detailed from 1922, the date of the foundation of the Irish Free State. (Northern Irish marriage records from 1922, the year of partition, are to be found in Belfast.) Unfortunately, a disastrous fire in the same year destroyed many Dublin census records. In a nutshell, indexes and registers for the whole of Ireland to 1921 and for Ireland (Eire) are in Dublin. Indexes and registers for Northern Ireland for births and deaths from 1864 and for marriages from 1922 are in Belfast.

Your researches may also lead you to the record/register offices of Jersey and Guernsey (with Jethou and Herm, Alderney and Sark) – they are to be found in St Helier and St Peter Port respectively – and to the General Registry in Douglas, on the Isle of Man. Note that births on Lundy Island were treated as 'foreign' in days gone by; but they can be traced in the National Archives.

Another resource you will find useful is maps. Old maps can show you boundaries and even estates that no longer exist. A number have been reprinted, and the Ordnance Survey, begun in the late 18th century, has produced extremely detailed maps of the country.

We have already touched on the census. Censuses are nothing new. In ancient times they were often used as a means of finding out what resources there were for recruiting soldiers or for imposing taxes. Censuses can also be useful for finding out demographics. For example, the 1901 census tells us that even as late as that, 30% of the population were still based in the countryside. If you wish to consult census records (available currently up to 1901), they are available online or at the Family Records Centre, or at the National Archives, in each latter case on microfilm. The records are also available at some major provincial libraries and at some county record offices. Check locally for the whereabouts of these, and/or get in touch with your local family history or local history society as well. When going through census records, always double-check your findings, as they are not infallible. People would sometimes, innocently or by design, submit incorrect information; and in the 1841 census people's ages were rounded down to the nearest half-decade.

A huge extra aid is an enormous record compiled by The Church of Jesus Christ of Latter-day Saints (the Mormons). One of their tenets is that new converts should be able to admit their forebears to the sect retrospectively. This has led to their undertaking a vast genealogical research project covering millions and millions of people. The archive itself is stored in a hollowed-out mountain near Salt Lake City, where the Mormons have their headquarters, but much information is available online. The archive is called the International Genealogical Index (IGI). It not only covers censuses, but parish records, and its scope is worldwide. For our purposes, note, however, that deaths and burials are not very fully covered, though births, baptisms and marriages are.

SCOTLAND STARTED ITS OFFICIAL REGISTRATION PROGRAMME AT THE BEGINNING OF 1855, AND FOR THE FIRST YEAR A GREAT DEAL OF PERSONAL INFORMATION WAS REQUIRED

Working with parish records

As you go further back, you will, as we've seen, need to depend more and more on parish records. These, and the so-called 'bishops' transcripts', which are the copies of individual church records copied out and sent to each diocesan centre, are the first line of enquiry. They are available on microfilm or microfiche at your local record office, though for some documentation you may have to go to the bishopric or even the individual parish, especially if they are less than one hundred years old. This in turn may be no bad thing, because there is a lot you can learn from tombstones and monuments, provided you know what or whom you are looking for. But don't just turn up: make appointments, and be prepared to pay consultation fees. You may not have to travel. You may find that there are copies of records in local libraries; and it is always worth checking with the Library of the Society of Genealogists.

Parish records are not always complete. As was stressed earlier, not all local priests were conscientious, though some were more so than others. You will encounter challenging handwriting and vagaries of spelling, and you will even encounter Latin. The Latin is usually pretty basic, but it's good to equip yourself with a Latin–English dictionary and a guide to the study of old forms of handwriting, or palaeography. Useful books are suggested in Part Three.

One pitfall here is provided by the Commonwealth, as we call the period of interregnum between Charles I and Charles II, when Oliver Cromwell ruled as Lord Protector of a British Republic. If you look at some parish records you will find that a priest is replaced abruptly by a Puritan preacher (the former incumbent sometimes reappears in or soon

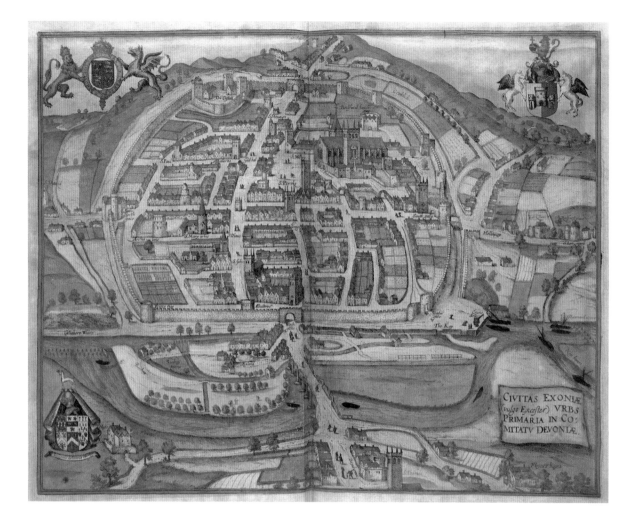

Old maps are useful in identifying parish or estate boundries which no longer exist.

after 1660). Records will almost certainly be affected by the Commonwealth. They may be interrupted altogether, or there may be a serious discontinuity. From 1653 only civil marriages were allowed, which also affects the smooth progress of parish records. Finally, after the Restoration, some returning incumbents destroyed the records of the intervening Puritans. Where records are continuous, be prepared for dramatic changes, often for the worse, of handwriting.

Another difficulty, about a century later, is something you must be aware of. This is the change in the calendar. You will probably already have noticed that old records and books often give two year-numbers. This affects dates from 1 January to 24 March. For example, you may find that your ancestor Thomas Ipswich was born on 25 February 1670/71. This means effectively that he was born on 15 February 1671. The problem is that England, lagging well behind Scotland and the rest of Europe, clung to the Julian Calendar until 1752. The year according to the Julian Calendar starts on Lady Day, 25 March.

From 1 January 1753 you are all right – we are in line with the rest of the world and have adopted the Gregorian Calendar. The shift occurred in 1752. In that year, we had to make the adjustment from 'Old Style', as it is called, to 'New Style'. It was effected in the following way.

In 1582, Pope Gregory XIII reformed the Julian Calendar by suppressing ten days (5 October became 15 October), and introducing the leap year together with an extra day in every centennial year divisible by four. The reform was adopted by most Roman Catholic countries immediately, but by the time we fell into line eleven days needed to be docked from 1752, as 1700 had been a leap-centennial year. As the legal year before 1752 began on 25 March 1751, that year is notionally at least bereft of 1 January to 24 March; while 1752 had to lose eleven days – in that year, 3–13 September inclusive went by the board. This upset a lot of people, who took to the streets shouting, 'Give us back our eleven days', which they believed had been snatched from their lives. A longer-lasting effect was on people who'd been born under the 'Old Style' within the crucial September calendar dates. When exactly should they celebrate their birthdays thereafter? Wouldn't the anniversaries of their lives from now on be 'out' eleven days?! For the family historian who goes back earlier than 1753, it is of vital importance to grasp the implications of this adjustment. All dates in this book are adapted to New Style.

Hardwicke's Marriage Act

Another innovation, in 1753, brought a bit more order with it. This was the Marriage Act, introduced by Lord Hardwicke and effective from the following year. This provided that banns should be read before a marriage. Records of these can confirm the parishes of origin of our ancestors as they prepared to continue the family line. Licences originated in the Middle Ages but very few survive earlier than the seventeenth century, and none were issued during the Commonwealth, when all marriages were civil. But records of marriages, wherever you find them, can be a rich source of information, since they can contain not only the names, but the ages and occupations of the bride and groom, as well as the names and occupations of parents, guardians, and other witnesses.

Hardwicke's Act brought more or less to a close the picturesque but confusing business of clandestine and other irregular marriages. In an age when divorce was almost impossible for ordinary people, and yet relationships were just as difficult as they can be today, getting hitched with no questions asked was very convenient. Imagine Reno, the world capital of quickie divorces, in reverse. The Mayfair Chapel was a popular venue; and bankrupt parsons, confined in the Fleet Debtors' Prison in London, could get day-release in return for a fee to their gaolers and make a bit of money marrying any couple who sought their services. Even so, some records were kept and some still exist; and there were provincial centres of clandestine marriage as well.

The Marriage Act obliged everyone to toe the line except Jews and Quakers, who were allowed to follow their own rules; so eloping couples had to head north to Scotland, where Hardwicke's writ didn't run, if they wanted to get married in the face of either the law or parental disapproval. Conveniently just across the border was Gretna Green, where a veritable cottage industry grew up, and from where many records survive.

Specialist publications you may wish to consult are Boyd's *Marriage Index* and Pallot's *Marriage Index*. Boyd's, compiled in the 1920s, is available at the Society of Genealogists, and the Guildhall Library has a microfiche copy. It is a vast record covering perhaps 12% of all marriages in England between 1538 and 1837. The Pallot Index covers marriages in the City of London and some in what is now Greater London from 1780 to 1837. The IGI, the National Archives, and the Society of Genealogists are also very valuable sources.

RECORDS OF MARRIAGES, WHEREVER YOU FIND THEM, CAN BE A RICH SOURCE OF INFORMATION, SINCE THEY CAN CONTAIN NOT ONLY THE NAMES, BUT THE AGES AND OCCUPATIONS OF THE BRIDE AND GROOM

Boyd's Marriage Index, a vast archive of marriages between 1538 and 1837.

Useful tips

When working with early documents, check to see if printed transcripts and/or translations exist, as these can make life a lot easier. Also, never assume that people sharing the same name are related. Try to narrow your field as much as you can, and don't hesitate to abandon the normally golden rule of 'always working backwards' – you may find yourself in a position to follow some interesting side-tracks, which can lead to valuable results. If you go a long way back, you'll need careful preparation before you tackle what's available in the National Archives. There isn't room here to do more than make you aware of such resources as the Records of Chancery, containing the Charter Rolls, which pertain to lands, rights, titles and privileges granted by Royal charter; the Patent Rolls, which are a collection of public documents; Close Rolls – private instructions from the king to his officers; and Fine Rolls, which are records of offers to the king of money in exchange for privileges – not bribes, but transactions! Then there are the Records of the King's Exchequer, and many other medieval documents.

Remember always, and especially when dealing with older documents, to go as well prepared as you can. There is a book available to help you very thoroughly. It's called *Tracing Your Ancestors in the National Archives* by Amanda Bevan. It has appeared this year (2006) in a seventh revised edition and is one of the four essential books for your research library, which you'll find listed at the beginning of the Bibliography in Part Three.

Finding 'non-conformist' ancestors

It's possible that you've got nowhere with parish registers. If your people don't show up in the records, don't panic. Do you know if they may have been non-conformists? If so, there may be other ways of getting to them. 'Non-conformist' conjures up the idea of the Low Church; but the term can embrace anyone outside the Established Church – Roman Catholics have remained a minority in the UK since Henry VIII broke their power, despite the best efforts of Queen Mary I and King James II. And other religions, some relative newcomers to these Isles, like Buddhists and Muslims, some here for a long time but militated against, like Jews, retain their own records.

Jews present an interesting case: they thrived in England and enriched our culture and our exchequer. But the advent of Lombard bankers (from Italy) in the late thirteenth century, who took over finance, allowed Edward I to banish Jews from England in 1290. They weren't officially allowed back until Oliver Cromwell saw the political advantage of re-opening Britain's doors to the Jews. In doing this Cromwell gave us a great blood transfusion (it was also an astute commercial move), but anti-Semitism was a worm in the bud that wouldn't go away.

The first to come, in the years following 1655, tended to be wealthy Sephardic Jews from Italy, Spain and Portugal, but greater numbers followed, especially in the late nineteenth century, when they arrived as refugees from pogroms in Russia, and again when the Nazi persecution began.

The Jews' cause wasn't helped by one or two members of the small, unofficial Portuguese community that clung on in London during the years of their banishment.

Disastrously significant among these was Dr Roderigo Lopez. He'd fled to England in 1559 and rose to become physician to Queen Elizabeth I. However, Lopez also appears to have been a spy, even a double-agent, who peddled information between England and Spain. His machinations were uncovered by the Earl of Essex in 1594, who believed he had evidence enough to prove that Spain was paying Lopez to poison the queen. Though that is very doubtful in fact, Lopez was arrested, tried and executed, despite Elizabeth's refusal to believe in his guilt.

The case fuelled resentment. In 1590, Christopher Marlowe's anti-Semitic play *The Jew of Malta* had already portrayed its protagonist, Barabas (a not insignificant name), as a murderous, treacherous Jewish fiend who meets his end in a gruesome fashion. William Shakespeare bravely presented a wronged Jew in humane terms six years later. Shylock pre-figures Lear in some ways. He is also a man 'more sinned against than sinning'. But Shakespeare also had to toe the line, and in *The Merchant of Venice* Shylock's opponents, anti-Semitic as they are, emerge as heroes. Even Shylock's daughter joins them, though it's clear that Shakespeare was employing an irony over the heads of his public. Percipient members of the audience at The Globe Theatre would, however, remember and reflect on the humanitarian appeal of Shylock's greatest speech: 'I am a Jew. Hath not a Jew eyes? Hath not a Jew hands, organs, dimensions, senses, affections, passions fed with the same food, hurt with the same weapons, subject to the same diseases, healed by the same means, warmed and cooled by the same winter and summer, as a Christian is: if you prick us, do we not bleed? If you tickle us, do we not laugh? If you poison us, do we not die? And if you wrong us, shall we not revenge? If we are like you in the rest, we will resemble you in that.'

Apart from the built-in anti-Semitism which derived from purist early Christian teachings, and the belief that the Jews were exclusively responsible for the cruel death of Jesus, and to blame for not recognising Him, a fault we shared with many other European states, the English were always good at welcoming refugees from more tyrannical powers, because we could see the expertise foreigners brought with them. Italian bankers? Most gratifying. International loans? Of course! (It's interesting to note in passing that when our own King Edward III (reigned 1327–1377) defaulted on an Italian loan of one million florins on account of one of his wars with France, it caused two banks in London to crash and all but led to a run on the banks in Florence.)

Jewish marriages were recognised under the Hardwicke Marriage Act of 1753 but records across the board weren't deposited with the Registrar General. Your first ports of call for enquiries should be the Office of the Chief Rabbi, the Jewish Historical Society of Great Britain, and the Jewish Genealogical Society of Great Britain.

The Church of England began life as a non-conformist sect itself. Henry VIII and Thomas Cromwell took their cue from Martin Luther and used his recent doctrinaire arguments against the Roman Catholic hegemony as a political vaulting-horse to push through the divorce from Henry's detested first wife. England's own Church would in future owe nothing to Rome. However, once the Church of England was established as the official religion, as we've seen, the term 'non-conformist' came to be applied to Quakers, Baptists and Methodists, as well as Roman Catholics –- you will sometimes come across the terms 'recusant' and 'dissenter' used in a similar context. If you can't find evidence of your ancestors in parish records and you are sure you're looking in the right place geographically, then it's likely that they were or became non-conformists and you will have to look for records elsewhere.

Roman Catholics started to keep their own records from the 1560s but their survival is

YOUR FIRST PORTS OF CALL FOR ENQUIRIES SHOULD BE THE OFFICE OF THE CHIEF RABBI, THE JEWISH HISTORICAL SOCIETY OF GREAT BRITAIN, AND THE JEWISH GENEALOGICAL SOCIETY OF GREAT BRITAIN

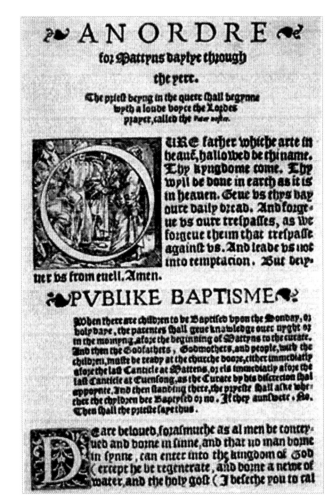

The Act of Uniformity 1662, required all worshippers to use The Book of Common Prayer.

patchy on account of the prejudice against and even persecution of Catholics which continued into the eighteenth century. Low-Church members, who had flourished under Oliver Cromwell, fared less well after the Restoration. Charles II was privately sympathetic to the Catholics and his brother James was openly a member of that branch of Christianity. In an attempt to unify the English Church an Act of Uniformity was passed in 1662 which required all worshippers to use the Book of Common Prayer. A couple of thousand dissenting prelates refused to and were promptly relieved of their livings. Sterner Acts of Parliament followed, penalising any who diverged from the required Church of England tenets.

But non-conformism wasn't crushed. It went underground. Lay preachers (John Bunyan was one) conducted services in private, and Low-Church clerics were protected by communities which formed around them. Traces of their activities can be found in official church records of them, when their illegal worship was uncovered. Relief came only after James II had been driven into exile in 1688. His all but fanatical attempt to re-impose Catholicism on the country had come as a shock, and though once again Catholics were to go through a period of mistrust, and being barred from various public offices, Britain ensured its Protestant succession by inviting the nephew of Charles and James, William of Orange, a Protestant, to succeed his uncle. William was married to Mary, the Protestant daughter of James and his Protestant first wife. In the year of their accession, 1689, the Toleration Act gave freedom of religious expression to all who accepted at least 36 of the 39 Articles of Religion. This meant that most non-conformists could come out of hiding and from 1689 on tracing of ancestors who were Low Church becomes significantly easier. The Family Records Centre and county record offices should be your first ports of call. In the National Archives you will also find a large batch of papers called collectively The Non-Parochial Registers. These include all the principal sects in England and Wales from 1567 as well as Catholic registers and a handful concerning foreign Churches in England.

Roman Catholics found themselves subjected to discriminatory laws for a very long period after the fall of James II, in addition to which they were fined for non-attendance at Anglican services and for attending Catholic ones. These measures drove Catholics underground, but their persecution had begun much earlier than the end of the seventeenth century, since, apart from during the reigns of Mary and James II, they had been second-class citizens since the time of the Dissolution of the Monasteries. Nevertheless, records were kept, and these have been collected by the Catholic Record Society. Another source of help is the Catholic Family History Society.

If you suspect that you have Huguenot forebears, contact the Huguenot Society of London, care of the Huguenot Library, which is located in University College, London. There is also a series of state papers concerning the Huguenots in the National Archives. Huguenots – French protestants – came over in waves, often via Germany and Holland, in the years following the St Bartholomew's Day massacre of 1572, and again after the revocation of the Edict of Nantes by Louis XIV in 1685, by which protection accorded to Huguenots since 1598 was removed. Huguenots followed Calvin's teaching and the name derives from the Swiss German *Eidgenosse* or, literally, oath-companion. Many anglicised their names, and were fully assimilated into English society. Be aware that traditions in your family about Huguenot ancestry may be myths, and that if you do have French ancestry, it may stem from refugees from the French Revolution. The Huguenots brought great intellectual and mercantile expertise to England, and enriched our culture.

Migration and mobility

Most of us probably have some foreign blood. The British Empire brought a vast number of foreign countries and cultures together, and attracted many people from them to the Mother Country, as Great Britain became known. At the same time many Britons left for lives overseas, in what were then the colonies of Canada, Australia, India (it may be that you have ancestors associated with the East India Company), and parts of Africa. Earlier still we had established colonies in what was to become the USA, the first of these being Virginia, named in honour of Queen Elizabeth I, the 'Virgin Queen', founded by Sir Walter Raleigh in 1584. The most famous early colonists to America were the Pilgrim Fathers, who sailed there on the *Mayflower* to escape religious intolerance at home, in 1620.

Some of these migrations were voluntary, others enforced. Nearer home, Irish immigrants came in droves to England to find better work. They were not always welcome, even though before Eire achieved independence they were British subjects.

At the same time, there was a certain amount of mobility within the country itself. People moved to find better work, because they were evicted, or to avoid outbreaks of plague. Broad economic and social changes also played their part: the Black Death of 1348, part of a worldwide pandemic which reduced the population of Britain by one third, led to population shifts. Many villages were deserted, much farmland lay neglected, and surviving workers could claim high wages. A century later there was a shift from town to country as the emergent textile industry sought cheaper labour. The Civil War caused great social disruption, and members of the conflicting armies found themselves moving around the country far more than they would have done in peacetime or in normal circumstances. And the Industrial Revolution saw huge migrations from the countryside to the burgeoning cities, where there was work aplenty, and relatively well-paid, but where conditions were cruel, and where competition for jobs gave the factory bosses the upper hand. In the Middle Ages craftsmen moved from place to place and apprentices could and did make great journeys to attach themselves to the right master.

Within the Church, before the Reformation probably the most powerful single such organisation on earth, clerics travelled from abbey to abbey all over the known world. Banking, an ancient practice emanating in its modern form from northern Italy, was already international in its scope by the fourteenth century. In mainland Europe, artists of standing, though classed as artisans until the Renaissance, moved from country to country to work, usually for Church patrons. The great carved statues and altarpieces of men like Veit Stoss and Tilman Riemenschneider can be seen in churches right across modern Germany, Poland and Central Europe, for example. Other professions whose members might be expected to travel include medicine and teaching. Merchants, pedlars and strolling players are others.

Census returns can be of considerable help when attempting to trace moving targets as far back as 1841, but earlier than that, unless they left some kind of impression behind them, it becomes harder. Poor Law records and parish registers are good initial sources of information.

Among the most mobile members of society and somewhat on the fringes of it are the gypsies and modern 'travellers'. If your interests lie in the direction of gypsies, the Gypsy Lore Society (which publishes a *Journal*) may be of help.

The National Archives hold records of emigrants under Colonial Office, Treasury, Board of Trade and Home Office rubrics. Britons went to Africa and India principally as administrators and colonists, and the same is true of emigrants, whether temporary or permanent, to the United States before 1776; though a proportion of those sent to America were convicts, men, women and children sentenced to transportation. Voluntary emigration to the States continued long after independence, especially from Ireland. The young country needed to populate itself and welcomed those with any kind of expertise. About six and a half million people emigrated there between 1837 and 1920, some traceable through passenger lists in the National Archives. In the wake of the potato famine of the mid-nineteenth century, and the brutal treatment of the Irish by the English during that time, a flood of Irish emigrants sailed west.

The Caribbean colonies saw their fair share of indentured servants, virtual slaves tied to plantation owners for a fixed term which could be as long as seven years, during which time they could expect to be treated very poorly.

Australia's penal colonies grew up once America had gained its independence from us. Captain James Cook's voyage of discovery in 1770 was a very timely one. But there was a fair number of voluntary emigrants seeking better lives and attracted by the climate and the vast tracts of farmland available, and emigration to Australia continued well into the second half of the 20th century and, under stricter rules of admission, continues today. Some emigration was, however, less than fair or kind. Between the late 19th century and the 1960s, various charities, with the best intentions no doubt, ran schemes to aid the emigration of children who were either orphans or for various reasons either had no family or were separated from them. The separations may have been temporary, but the children were sent abroad nevertheless, and families' consent was not sought. The Child Migrants Trust was set up in 1987 in an attempt to reunite families. The children, most of whom had no idea what they were in for, were placed with adoptive families who unfortunately often treated them as unpaid labour.

Britain has very old Chinese, Italian and Jewish communities, and Africans have lived here since at least the seventeenth century. Subsidy Rolls and Port Records are useful sources for tracing foreign ancestors who may have settled here. The Port Records go back a long way – in the case of Particulars of Customs Accounts back to 1272. These were superseded from 1565 to 1799 by Port Books, but all contain detailed notes of ships, their masters, their cargo, who was travelling on them and what their rights of domicile, or national status, were.

The end of the Second World War saw another wave of emigrants. Expatriate Poles who had fled the Germans, served in the RAF, and now did not want to return to a communist homeland, stayed to found families here (along with their Government in Exile); a not insignificant number of Italian and German prisoners-of-war married and settled; Jewish refugees from all over Europe found homes here; and a few years later the first waves of Caribbean immigrants arrived to help augment the depleted workforce. One of the earliest groups to arrive from Jamaica came on the famous SS *Empire Windrush*, and their names can be found in passenger lists held in the National Archives. Since the war, the number of immigrants from former colonies and members of the British Commonwealth, such as India and Pakistan, has steadily increased, and immigration across the board is now subject to restriction.

Property records

Beyond and often before parish records lie manorial and other landholding records. Most of us have to do with 'land' even if only as the owner or renter of a small flat somewhere, and 'land' always has paperwork attached, which can go back centuries. Such records can help us make the link between properties and people.

One helpful central resource from which to start is the Manorial Documents Register, to which reference has already been made. It's a compilation of manors, organised by county, and can be consulted at the National Archives. The documents deal not only with how given tracts of land or farms were parcelled out, and leased, let or held by some other arrangement with the manor's lord, but with day-to-day transactions and petty infractions of the law. In the early days, manors were at the core of the administrative system, and their Courts Leet or Courts Baron would deal with local complaints, and with matters such as boundaries in disrepair, straying cattle, and so on.

Reading records of these proceedings isn't easy, for they are hand-written and until towards the middle of the eighteenth century very frequently in Latin; but the form they take is consistent, and as attendance was compulsory at the courts, the lists of those present can yield valuable information to the family historian. Once again, there are specialist

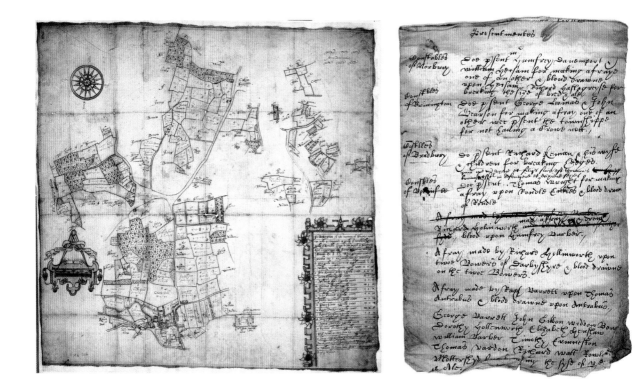

ABOVE

The Manorial Documents
Register can be viewed at
the National Archives.

ABOVE RIGHT

They contain maps and
also day-to-day accounts of
petty infractions of the law.

publications to guide and assist you. Be aware that manorial holdings and local parishes may overlap geographically, but not share the same exact boundaries, and that there may be many manors in a parish, or vice versa, depending on size.

Another way of tracing ancestors through property is through taxation. Income tax is a relatively recent invention – December 1798 – but taxes were levied on land and property before then in a variety of ways, the records of which, though they can be dry, can also yield interesting results.

The hearth tax was imposed in various forms towards the end of the seventeenth century and provides a wealth of names as parishes were obliged to make lists of those persons liable to pay it (it was, broadly speaking, based on the number of hearths in any given household). Lists were also provided of the names of those too poor to attract the tax. Unfortunately for the family historian, it was almost as short-lived as the equally unpopular community charge of the 1980s, but for a brief period it provides a reliable record of who was where when and what their status was. Similarly the window tax, which replaced the hearth tax, yields useful lists of names, and evidence of it can still be seen in the bricked-up windows of older houses – the fewer you had, the less you paid. Records of these taxes and of land taxes are available in the National Archives and in some county record offices.

Ancestors in the Armed Forces

I don't intend to go into too much detail about specialised occupations, but a word seems appropriate on the armed forces, since researchers who have military ancestors may well find they can follow very specific paths to trace them. There was no regular standing army

Before the introduction of Income Tax in 1798, revenue was raised in a variety of ways such as window tax.

until Cromwell's New Model Army during the Commonwealth. After the Restoration in 1660, from the remains of this highly trained and professional body came the first regiments. The very first two were the regiments of the Horse Guards, later called the Life Guards and the Royal Horse Guards, known collectively as the Household Cavalry, and designed to act as a bodyguard for the monarch. There were also two regiments of foot guards, which later became the Grenadier Guards and the Coldstream Guards. More and more regiments were formed in the course of the next century or so, and later they were joined by specialist units known as Corps – they include the Royal Engineers, the Pay Corps, the Royal Army Medical Corps, and so on.

The modern Royal Navy dates back to Henry VIII, but for a long time it was only loosely constructed and run by officers who often had little or no maritime experience, with men under them who hated being there anyway, many of them having been press-ganged into service, or were there only to escape a worse fate at the hands of the law. The Royal Marines, who began life as the Duke of York and Albany's Maritime Regiment of Foot in 1664, was first raised to provide a disciplined fighting force on board, and for a time ships were viewed as little more than troop-carriers. The state of the navy improved under Oliver Cromwell, who used it to establish a British presence in the Caribbean. As the Duke of York, James II proved himself an able naval administrator, and under him, through the work of such administrative geniuses as Samuel Pepys, the navy was trimmed into shape, though it didn't become the sleek fighting force that it was under Nelson for another seventy-odd years, and it was known for the harshness of its conditions and the cruelty of its punishments.

The Royal Air Force, is, of course, of very recent date, created from various air corps in 1918.

Records exist in the National Archives for all the armed services, though the archives of their museums – the National Army Museum, the Royal Naval Museum, and the Royal Air

Force Museum – are an important resource. You may also wish to consult the archives of the National Maritime Museum and the Imperial War Museum. You will find it easier if your ancestor was an officer, and/or if he or she was decorated.

Heraldry

One final area to touch on in discussing research into your early ancestors is heraldry. This is a highly specialised discipline, and it may well be that you won't feel it's relevant to your search. However, it's possible that one of your ancestors was granted a coat of arms, and if so – if you've found a coat-of-arms on a bookplate, or unearthed a signet ring with a crest – following it through can be well worth while, since a crest is a kind of illustrated or coded genealogy, giving details of marriages, of legitimacy, of allegiance, and of trade. The Messerschmitt coat of arms features, among other things, a very ordinary-looking knife: Messerschmitt means, literally, 'knife-smith'; the surname in English would be Cutler. Similar clues and visual puns exist on many armorial bearings.

You don't have to be aristocratic or military to have a coat of arms. In the past they've been awarded to merchants and landowners, more recently in return for significant public service. You can apply for a coat of arms yourself, but that's a long and pricey process and won't guarantee success. But Sir Elton John has one, featuring piano keys and CDs, together with a punning motto. Hard to say whether that's really neat, or really naff.

Researching heraldry is a job requiring patience and time, since you effectively have to learn a specialised technical language largely based on Old High French. Then there are definite and complicated rules to be followed, and conventions to be observed. But it's a fascinating if oblique way of approaching history, and in terms of family history can lead to surprisingly gratifying rewards. The institutions to contact in the first instance are the College of Arms and the Institute of Heraldic and Genealogical Studies (for details, see Part Three). You could also get in touch with the Heraldry Society, which publishes two journals, *The Heraldry Gazette* and *The Coat of Arms*. There are several useful books available too – try to

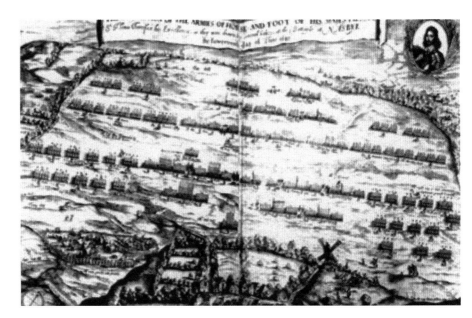

Look for coats of arms on book plates.

go for one with colour illustrations because even if it's more expensive it'll be easier to follow when you're learning what 'gules' is and what's 'or', while at the same time juggling with descriptions like 'Barry of six or and az., an inescutcheon arg.; on a chief gold, gyroned of the second, two pallets of the same' – and so on, not to mention pied greyhounds proper, and knowing the difference between shields and crests, and what a blazon is.

We hope you now have at least an indication of the way forward

The meaning of elements of a coat of arms can be researched at the College of Arms in Queen Victoria Street, London.

W hen the long-running sci-fi series *Doctor Who* was brought back to our screens after an absence of some years, the producers chose the talented Scottish actor David Tennant to become the latest embodiment of the Time Lord. David now wants to travel back through history to trace his Scottish ancestry and across the Irish Sea to Londonderry. He uncovered some surprises along the way.

David was born in Bathgate, a post-industrial town between Glasgow and Edinburgh, in 1971. His father is a minister in the Church of Scotland. (David's real surname is McDonald, but when he was starting out as an actor another performer was already known by that name. He settled instead for the stage name Tennant because he saw Pet Shop Boys' Neil Tennant's name in an article in *Smash Hits* and thought it sounded good.)

He began his historical investigations by focusing on his father's side of the family, but unfortunately he quickly learned that the paper trail on his father's family goes cold relatively early on, and it would take a lot of research to get back to the time of the clans, as David had hoped. So he turned his attention to his maternal grandfather, Archie McLeod, whose forebears originally hailed from the Isle of Mull, where they lived as small tenant farmers until they were driven off their land and into the cities during the Highland Clearances of the early 19th century. David's mother Helen remembered that, when she was born, Archie worked as an engineer's machinist at John Brown's shipyard on Clydebank. But she also remembered that Archie had earlier been a professional footballer.

Taking up the shipyard cue first, David discovered that Archie had worked there for about twenty years from 1938. At the time he joined John Brown's it was the largest shipyard in the UK. Today it is no more, but shipbuilding expert Ian Johnston was able to fill David in on what it must have been like when the yards were in full swing. The shop floors would have been smelly, smoky and noisy. There was no protective clothing in those days, and men like Archie, on £3–4 a week, had to provide their own gloves, vital in the winter months when icicles hung from the roof and a spanner could freeze onto your hand. Archie would have set off by tram from his tenement building in Couper Street, Glasgow, at 6.30 in the morning in order to reach work by 7.30. It was important not to be late, for if you were you'd find yourself locked out until lunchtime and you'd lose half a day's pay. The men worked a ten-hour day, and during that time they were only allowed half an hour for lunch and seven minutes for toilet breaks.

David learned from Ian what Archie's job involved. An engineer's machinist was a semi-skilled position, using machine tools to cut, bend and smooth metalwork. It was a job that required patience and a steady hand and eyes. The machines were steam-driven and made an enormous noise. They were also dangerous, and there were very few health and safety precautions. Deafness was a common side-effect of the work, and accidents were frequent. During the Second World War the Clydeside shipyards were also a regular target for German bombing raids, and there were many casualties.

This all seemed a long way from how David had imagined his grandfather. To find out more about Archie's footballing career, David went to see Uncle John, who told

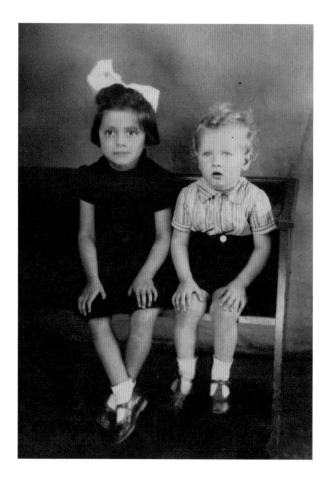

David's mother, Helen, and her brother, John.

him that, yes, all the stories were true! After being capped for the Scottish Juniors, Archie was signed by Derry City Football Club. David followed the trail to Londonderry, where Archie had arrived as a 24-year-old in 1932. He hadn't met his Irish relatives before, so he hoped that they could they fill him in on Archie's time in Derry

David has two much older cousins in Derry – actually first cousins once removed – called Billy and Barry. They are Catholics: their mother, David's great-aunt Maisie, broke with family tradition and married a Catholic. Billy and Barry are also life-long supporters of Derry City FC and have been season-ticket holders for forty years. Not only were they able to tell David plenty about Archie, who was a famous and popular footballer in his day, but they took him to a match where he met men whose fathers and grandfathers had cheered Archie on.

In the days when Archie was playing, 12,000 people used to flock to the matches; it's only 4,000 nowadays. He's still a celebrity in the town – he is still the highest goal-scorer in Derry City history – but his career, though brilliant, didn't last long. During a match in 1938 he sustained serious injuries which ended his career. In those days footballers were paid nothing like the sums they are paid now, and there was no insurance, so he had to find other work. Hence the return to Glasgow and the shipyards.

But during his heyday Archie had married a local beauty queen called Nellie Blair, and David followed her trail next. He made contact with two other cousins – Protestants this time, but also first cousins once removed – called Billy and Betty. From them he found out that the Blairs were a prominent Protestant family, and that Nellie's father William, grandfather James and great-uncle Robert all played roles in the political battles that surrounded Irish independence and Northern Ireland's secession from the Republic.

Billy and Betty couldn't remember much about William Blair (David's great-grandfather), except that he never spoke about his experiences during the First World War. They showed David an Orange Order sash which had belonged to their father, David's great-uncle Jim. They remembered that William had a connection with the Hamilton Marching Band, and his father James appeared to have been quite a big wheel in the local Orange Lodge.

To find out more, David paid a visit to the Apprentice Boys' Memorial Hall, high up on the Siege Walls of Londonderry near to the Protestant Cathedral of St Columb and looking down on the Catholic district of Bogside. There he met Orange Lodge member William Temple, and under his guidance searched the membership records of the lodge for information on his Northern Irish Protestant forebears. They quickly established that not only were James and his brother Robert deeply involved with the lodge, but that Robert (David's great-great-uncle) had been its Grand Master.

The location of the Memorial Hall and the Protestant cathedral were and are of great significance for Protestant Orangemen like James and Robert. It was within the Siege Walls that the cry of 'No surrender!' was first heard, as William III of Orange's Protestant garrison successfully defended Londonderry against the Catholic army of King James II in 1689. The siting of two massive Protestant buildings above the

Archie McLeod, David's grandfather, the highest goal-scorer in the history of Derry City Football Club.

... MEN LIKE ARCHIE ... HAD TO PROVIDE THEIR OWN GLOVES, VITAL IN THE WINTER MONTHS WHEN ICICLES HUNG FROM THE ROOF AND A SPANNER COULD FREEZE ONTO YOUR HAND.

David at the Derry City ground.

Catholic Bogside district was a political act as much as a religious one.

The siege mentality of the Ulster Protestants continued even after the Battle of the Boyne in 1690 when James II's Franco-Irish army was routed. Secret societies were founded and the sectarian violence began that has continued into our own times. The Orange Order was established in 1795, and soon attracted enormous support. But during the nineteenth century the movement for Irish emancipation from English rule – the mainly Catholic Home Rule movement – also gathered strength, culminating in 1914 in the passage through the Westminster Parliament of the Home Rule Bill. In 1912, many Protestants, including David's great grandfather William and his great-great grandfather James, signed the Ulster Covenant againt Home Rule. Implementation of home rule was interrupted by the outbreak of the Great War, however. Many Unionists, who remained determined to keep Northern Ireland out of an independent, Catholic-dominated Irish republic, saw the war as a means of demonstrating their loyalty to King and Country and volunteered for the British army. This led David to consider the role of his great-grandfather, William, who joined up as a member of the Hamilton Marching Band.

David's grandmother, Nelly McLeod, and 1-year-old Mary.

The band's historian Billy Cairns told David that the band would not only have led the Orange Day parades, but would have played concerts for the local community. A newspaper article from 1915 reveals that the whole band signed up for the war and became the battalion band for the 10th Inniskilling Fusiliers, who saw serious action on the Somme. The article further mentioned that William Blair was a member of the attached Medical Corps. Band members would automatically have been seconded to work as stretcher-bearers on the battlefield.

The years immediately after the Great War saw William's father James on the local Londonderry council, sometimes stormily asserting the right of Northern Ireland to remain separate from the Republic. In the end this was achieved, but it did little to assuage the sectarian tensions that also affected David's family. Maisie and her Catholic husband were not ostracised by her Protestant relatives, but the tensions have politicised David's cousin Barry, who has been involved in civil rights work and cross-community relations.

At the end of David's visit to Londonderry, Barry took him back to Derry City FC, where Archie McLeod used to play, to watch Protestant and Catholic youngsters play football; living embodiments of the principles espoused in 1998's Good Friday Agreement, signed in the hope of bringing thirty years of sectarian blood-shed to an end.

CHAPTER THREE

Recent Times

THE PERIOD OF BRITISH HISTORY WE ARE CONCENTRATING ON IN THIS BOOK IS FROM THE MID-SIXTEENTH TO THE EARLY NINETEENTH CENTURY; BUT A BRIEF CANTER THROUGH THE VICTORIAN ERA AND UP TO OUR OWN TIMES IS HELPFUL FOR THE SAKE OF COMPLETENESS. YOU WILL FIND MORE DETAIL IN THE SIBLING VOLUMES TO THIS, LISTED IN THE BIBLIOGRAPHY. THE FIRST FOUR GEORGES PASSED APPARENTLY UNLAMENTED INTO HISTORY. AS WALTER SAVAGE LANDOR (1775–1864) WROTE WASPISHLY:

An early photograph of Victoria and Albert in 1854.

I sing the Georges four,
For Providence could stand no more.
Some say that far the worst
Of all was George the First.
But yet by some 'tis reckoned
That worse still was George the Second.
And what mortal ever heard
Any good of George the Third?
When George the Fourth from earth descended,
Thank God the line of Georges ended.

They were followed by William IV, an amiable chap who came to the throne in middle-age after a career in the Navy. His successor was our other great queen, Victoria, though she is great by virtue of the period she presided over, rather than for any particular deeds of her own.

Victoria and Albert

In 1837, the first year of General Registration, Queen Victoria came to the throne. She was eighteen, and not directly in line, but the last of the true Hanoverians, her uncle William IV, had outlived his two legitimate daughters and died without an heir. William himself was a younger brother of George IV, and Victoria, who was born in Kensington Palace, lost her father, the Duke of Kent, when she was still a baby, and her upbringing was left in the care of her mother, Princess Victoria of Saxe-Coburg, and her mother's brother, Leopold of Saxe-Coburg.

The German connection was reinforced by Victoria's marriage to her cousin Albert, almost exactly the same age as she, in 1840. Albert never endeared himself to the British: he was not included in official prayers for the Royal Family, he was given no titles despite the fact that he became a British citizen, and it wasn't until 1857 that he was granted the official appellation of Prince Consort. Albert was a stern father to his numerous children, and in himself showed a tendency to punctiliousness, studiousness and humourlessness. He would have loved to become involved in politics, but found himself quietly but firmly cold-

The Prince Albert Memorial by George Gilbert Scott was designed in 1862–3.

shouldered. Nevertheless, his ideas, which tended to be good on the whole, did influence political thinking to an extent. Unfortunately he saw Germany's future as firmly at the centre of the world stage, and never really took to his adopted land, perhaps because he remained at heart a provincial princeling from the pretty little town of Coburg. But it can't be denied that he managed to become positively involved in the machinery of Britain despite the fact that he had no officially recognised function in it.

So, Albert's influence was not all bad, though he has been, perhaps a little unfairly, been credited with introducing to the English the *sang-froid*, and inability to express any warm emotions adequately, for which they remain famous. Englishmen also stopped wearing colourful clothes, and took to the grey, black and white which dominated English male sartorial style between the 1850s and the 1950s. Albert also introduced the Christmas tree to England from his native Germany. Before, we'd made do with Yule logs, holly and mistletoe.

The Prince Consort was, above all, an intelligent and active man whose heart was fundamentally in the right place. He became positively involved in social and industrial reform, and he was an enthusiastic promoter of the arts and sciences. In many ways, he was the ideal person to preside over a period which was to see an enormous expansion of the British Empire, in a century which would see the country reach its peak as a world power. During Victoria's reign the Empire doubled in size: New Zealand joined it in 1840, Canada became a Dominion in 1867, and Australia a Commonwealth in 1900. Expansion stretched as far as Burma (Myanmar), islands in the Pacific and elsewhere far overseas, Egypt and South Africa. The Victoria Cross, the highest military decoration, was introduced during the Crimean War (1853–1856), which was one of the very few conflicts in which we participated in the century between 1815 (the end of the Napoleonic Wars with the final crushing of the French dictator at Waterloo) and 1914 (when we had to fight Victoria's grandson, the dreadful Kaiser Wilhelm II, another megalomaniac with plans for world domination).

Perhaps Albert's greatest single contribution to our cultural history was the Great Exhibition of 1851, and its consequences. It was visited by six million people, and made a profit of £186,000. This money was used to buy thirty acres of land in Kensington, and on them were built the Victoria and Albert Museum, the Science Museum, the Imperial College of Science and Technology, the Royal College of Music and the Albert Hall. Gilbert Scott's totally Victorian memorial to him on the edge of Kensington Gardens now appropriately presides over a great legacy.

Victoria, from the first, doted on him. His influence over her, and, through her, the state, was as profound as it was benign. When he died of typhoid fever at Windsor just before Christmas in 1861, aged only 42, he left her inconsolable, and she mourned him for rest of her life, which was to last another forty years. You only have to look at portraits of her done before and after his death to see the effect it had. For a time, the nation itself seemed to go into mourning, and the gloom which emanated from the Royal palaces cast its shadow over

Charles Dickens at his writing desk.

the land. By luck, Victoria's reign saw a succession of able, intellectually acute and vigorous prime ministers, from Melbourne to Salisbury, with perhaps the greatest, Gladstone and Disraeli, alternating with each other – the first was a Liberal, the second a Conservative in the real sense of the word – in the middle of it. The Queen (Empress of India as well from 1877), however, was and remained a Conservative at heart all her life, and made no secret of it, though by now constitutional monarchy was firmly in place.

Apart from geographical, material and commercial expansion, the arts flourished too, throwing up a significant movement in painting, that of the Pre-Raphaelites, and, in literature, the writer who stands next to Shakespeare, and whose works the most modest home library is still likely to contain – even if we'd rather watch him on TV these days – Charles Dickens. A roll-call of eminent Victorians would fill pages and pages – Lord Tennyson, Florence Nightingale, David Livingstone, Elizabeth Gaskell, Cardinal Manning, Thomas and Matthew Arnold, Cardinal Newman, General Gordon, Elizabeth Barrett Browning, General Napier, Lewis Carroll, Edward Lear, the Brontë sisters, Isambard Kingdom Brunel, Oscar Wilde, George Stephenson, Robert Louis Stevenson, Sir Edwin Landseer, Christina Rossetti, Gilbert Scott, Gilbert and Sullivan are just a few at random who spring to mind, and there are many, many more who readers may feel are more important than those on this arbitrary list. The nineteenth century, whatever its many faults, as a whole is one of the three most brilliant periods in our history, the others being the great ages of Elizabeth I and Charles II. Here I have mentioned only a handful of those people who fell within Victoria's long reign. Before it, under George IV and William IV, there was a splendid flowering in the sciences, the arts and in literature – but I won't start another list!

Victoria herself was not without her faults. Her unswerving conservatism, bourgeois imagination and preference for all things German at least resulted in a fun-loving heir who much preferred France (Edward VII), but who sadly didn't last long, becoming King at an advanced age and by then already well-indulged in the habits of his great-uncle, George IV.

She was, however, imbued with a strong sense of duty, and on the occasion of her Golden Jubilee in 1887 condescended to appear before her people again, after many years in seclusion at one or other of her many palaces, or on the Riviera. But taking her cue from Albert, she was never inactive or negligent of her responsibility, and involved herself in the business of governing the country (helped by a particular fondness for Disraeli) at a time of great social and political reform. Her reign saw the passing of the Mines Act (1842), which forbade the employment of women and children underground; a series of factory acts which led to the establishment of a ten-hour working day; the Education Act (1870); the Public Health Act and the Artisans' Dwellings Acts of 1875; Trade Union Acts in 1871 and 1876; and Reform Acts in 1867 and 1884, which enabled a greater section of the populace to vote.

She was the first monarch of the realm to pay an official visit to France since Henry VI in 1431, a mark of how long we two neighbours had been bickering, and her extended family and progeny meant that she was related to many of the royal families of Europe. Tsar Nicolas II was a grandson-in-law, and Victoria was related to the royal families of Belgium, Denmark, Greece, Norway, Romania and Sweden as well.

When she died in January 1901, Victoria completed the third-longest recorded reign of any monarch, after Franz Josef of Austria, who ruled from 1848 to 1916, and the indomitable Louis XIV, who notched up an astonishing 72 years as King of France. He took the throne soon after the beginning of the English Civil War, and died a year after the accession of our King George I!

THE NINETEENTH CENTURY, WHATEVER ITS MANY FAULTS, AS A WHOLE IS ONE OF THE THREE MOST BRILLIANT PERIODS IN OUR HISTORY, THE OTHERS BEING THE GREAT AGES OF ELIZABETH I AND CHARLES II.

Victorian society

Despite the bullishness of Victorian Britain, with the dramatic expansion of its overseas power and its material success, life in the early and middle years of the nineteenth century for ordinary people remained bad, and in some urban areas became worse. Workers had few rights, and labour was shamelessly exploited. There was no sense of a welfare state, and the age saw some appalling official behaviour, such as English policy in Ireland during the potato famine in the 1840s. The large industrial towns of the North and the Midlands were homes to vast slums where life expectancy was low and where often several families were crowded into a single room to live.

Their fate was chronicled by important social observers, whose work can help us at least indirectly in tracking the fate of our humbler ancestors. Among them are writers you may wish to consult. Henry Mayhew, a journalist and novelist, compiled a sociological study, *London Labour and the London Poor*, between 1851 and 1862, which comprises a series of interviews and reported interviews, giving a compelling picture of what life was like for members of what we would call the 'underclass'.

Here's part of Mayhew's record of an interview with two 'orphan flower girls' (aged 15 and 11):

Henry Mayhew was an advocate of social reform, and one of the founders of the satirical magazine *Punch*.

My brother can write, and I pray to God that he'll do well with it. I buy my flowers at Covent Garden; sometimes, but very seldom, at Farringdon. I pay 1s. (5p) for a dozen bunches, whatever flowers are in. Out of every two bunches I can make three, at 1d. a piece. Sometimes one or two over in the dozen, but not as many as I would like. We make the bunches up ourselves. We get the rush to tie them with for nothing. We put their own leaves round these violets [she produced a bunch]. The paper for a dozen costs a penny; sometimes only a halfpenny. The two of us doesn't make less than 6d. a day, unless it's very ill luck. But religion teaches us that God will support us, and if we make less, we say nothing. We do better on oranges in March and April, I think it is, than of flowers. Oranges keep better than flowers, you see, sir. We make 1s. a day and 9d. a day, on oranges, the two of us. I wish they was in all the year.

These girls were better off than most people in their class.

Another early sociologist you may want to consult is Charles Booth (1840–1916), who was born into a wealthy Liverpool ship-owning family, and moved to London in the mid-1880s. Alarmed by the state of the destitute in England, he organised and funded one of the most exhaustive social surveys of London life ever undertaken. He was also an early advocate of social welfare and pensions, things we take for granted, but which were barely known 150 years ago. Life was only grand if you belonged to the middle class and above. You only have to read another Victorian man of conscience, Charles Dickens, to find that out. Booth's findings run to seventeen volumes, published between 1889 and 1903, under the title *Life and Labour of the People in London*.

Perhaps the most famous observers of Victorian social inequality were two German immigrants, Friedrich Engels (1820–95) and Karl Marx (1818–83). Engels worked in the textile industry in Manchester for twenty years before moving to London. This experience produced his *Condition of the Working Class in England*, in which he describes what life was like for the factory worker of his day: 'The interior of Bradford is as dirty and uncomfortable as Leeds ... Heaps of dirt and refuse disfigure the lanes, alleys and courts. The houses are dilapidated and dirty and are not fit for human habitation ... The workers' houses at the bottom of the valley are packed between high factory buildings and are among the worst-built and filthiest in the whole city.'

Average life expectancy in the inner-city slums built on the back of Victorian capitalist expansion varied between 15 and 22 years. Small wonder that Marx, who had arrived in England in 1849 and was to remain here for the rest of his life, collaborated with Engels two years earlier in Brussels on *The Communist Manifesto*. Charles Booth would have sympathised with their point of view. Forty years after its publication, he found that 30 per cent or more of the population of London lived on the verges of the poverty line, or below it.

Edwardian England

With the twentieth century we are on more familiar ground: all of you who read this book were born in it; some of us will have lived through the Second World War as children or young adults; and all of us will be aware of the history of this country at least in outline since about 1950. So I will skim the first half of the twentieth century before we go back much further in time, in Part Two.

Victoria was succeeded by her son, Edward VII. He was in his sixtieth year when he ascended the throne, but had never played any active role in the affairs of state because Victoria had continued the Hanoverian tradition, started by George I, of treating the heir

THEIR FATE WAS CHRONICLED BY IMPORTANT SOCIAL OBSERVERS, WHOSE WORK CAN HELP US AT LEAST INDIRECTLY IN TRACKING THE FATE OF OUR HUMBLER ANCESTORS.

The philanthropist, Charles Booth, whose work was a founding text of British sociology.

apparent with mistrust. Nevertheless he did deputise for his mother in some minor functions during the reclusive years of her widowhood.

Edward was an intelligent, humorous and able man who had a keen interest in foreign affairs, and whose wide travels throughout Europe, North America, Russia and Palestine led to the creation of a wealth of foreign contacts, which he used as King so ably as to earn himself the sobriquet of 'Peacemaker' within two years of his accession. The Boer War in South Africa had ended in 1902; but Europe, with the territorial ambitions of Kaiser Wilhelm II, Edward's nephew, already on the rise, looked unstable. This situation led Edward, a Francophile partly in reaction to his parents' outlook, to sign the Entente Cordiale with the country which had always traditionally been our enemy, in 1904.

The last seventeen years or so of Victoria's reign had been pretty moribund in terms of political change in England, since governments had largely (and none too successfully) been preoccupied with the state of affairs in Ireland, still part of Great Britain until finally seceding in 1922. This was about to change; 1902 saw an Education Act providing for state-funded secondary education, and it was followed by a series of measures to protect the interests of the young. Old-age pensions were introduced in 1908, and Labour Exchanges (now Job Centres) appeared in 1909. The basis of a National Insurance scheme and the funding for it were organised in the same year.

Edward had all the aplomb of his Hanoverian ancestors, but he was far more sophisticated and mondain than any of them. Above all, and for all his faults (most of them harmless), he was affable and popular. He enjoyed the benefits of his birth and purse to the full. A great gambler, bon viveur and womaniser, he owned a racing yacht, the *Britannia*, and became the first monarch to own a Derby winner, sparking off the keen interest in equestrianism that

Edward VII, who reigned from 1901 to 1910, has the distinction of holding the post of heir apparent for the longest period in English history.

persists in the Royal Family to this day. He was also a keen hunter, both at home and abroad, of big game – a less attractive trait, perhaps. His fondness for food soon showed in his figure and he gained the nickname 'Tum-tum', though woe betide anyone who used it in his presence. He could have a nasty temper, and was prone to holding grudges.

His wife was Alexandra, a daughter of the King of Denmark, and they had six children, of whom the second son, surviving the first, succeeded him in 1910. Many would argue that it is a pity he could not have reigned longer, but whether he would have been able to curb the militaristic ambitions of his nephew is an open question.

Short though his reign was, the Edwardian era, as it's now known, ushered in by 'the naughty Nineties' and prefigured by the notoriety of such flamboyant London figures as Oscar Wilde, is remembered as one during which the country took a deep breath, shook off some of the more sombre Victorian hypocrisies and let the sun come out again. It was a time when social life, for those who could enjoy it, became livelier and more relaxed, when clothes and the decorative arts, as well as the *style de vie*, became grander, more magnificent and more ornate. Even modest suburban villas were decorated with swags of floral plasterwork, and their marble fireplaces seemed to have come from more august surroundings.

It was also a kind of mini-Golden Age, a period of transition not only between the nineteenth century and the twentieth, but between our times and many centuries, which now were to come to seem particularly remote, as the truly modern and technological age brought, over the next hundred years, changes unimaginable to our ancestors, as well as wars, disasters and atrocities on a scale hitherto undreamed of. The Edwardians seem to be bathed in the sunshine of a glorious English autumnal afternoon, and only towards the end was there any hint of the storm that was gathering.

George V and World War I

George V, as the second son, had never expected to ascend the throne. He was 45 when he did so, having spent his life until the death of his elder brother in 1892 in the Royal Navy – a career which had attracted one or two of his predecessors and would beckon the present Duke of York. An irascible man devoted to his stamp collection, and a superb marksman, he hadn't got on with his father and he wouldn't get on with his sons – another stubbornly surviving tradition from the first four Georges. He was married to the uncharismatic German, Princess Mary of Teck, whom older readers will remember from newsreels of the early 1950s. By the twentieth century, we start to have cinematic records of our history. Mary of Teck's great-grandfather was George III, so her grainy presence on the balcony of Buckingham Palace provides us with a curious bridge stretching back to the eighteenth century.

George's twenty-five-year reign covered a rocky period. The difficulties began immediately as the House of Lords, with a large majority of Tory peers, had rejected the 1909 Liberal government's 'People's Budget'. This action by the Lords was unprecedented and the Liberals, furious, were seeking to restrict the powers of the Lords by Act of Parliament, something which has only recently been fully achieved – some would say, over-achieved. The situation led to a constitutional crisis and two general elections in 1910 – something else that was without precedent. George, not himself a natural Liberal, was however obliged to create enough Liberal peers to balance power, and the Parliament Bill of 1911 reduced the power of veto of the Lords, as well as the maximum period between parliaments – from seven to five years.

IT WAS NOT A TOTAL
WAR, LIKE THE
SECOND WORLD
WAR, IN THAT
CIVILIANS WERE TO A
LARGE EXTENT NOT
SUBJECT TO ITS
PREDATIONS

The first blow to the technological pride and confidence of the nation, seen by some as symbolic, came with the sinking of the *Titanic* with great loss of life on account of a botched rescue, in April 1912. This tragedy was, however, soon overshadowed by a far greater one – the First World War of 1914–1918.

It was not a total war, like the Second World War, in that civilians were to a large extent not subject to its predations. Cultural life continued to flourish in the great cities of Europe, and as far as the sciences were concerned, the British Astronomer Royal, Sir Frank Dyson, with a splendid disregard for the war that happened to stand between them, contacted Albert Einstein, whose General Theory of Relativity had been published in 1915, with the suggestion that an eclipse of the sun due on 29 March 1919 'would provide an excellent chance for such proof [of the theory], since the darkened sun would pass through a particularly bright group of stars, the Hyades'. The light rays from the stars could be measured as they moved close to the sun at the moment of eclipse.

For the fighting men it was a disaster – there was no conscription until 1916, but men went to war to protect their country, and also because there was tremendous peer-pressure to do so. What had been seen as a very short war in prospect dragged out to a wretched slogging match in northern France and Belgium, during which the lines scarcely moved at all, and during which twice as many men died as in the later conflict. It was followed by a lethal influenza epidemic in 1919.

George, while not actually leading his men into battle, made several visits to the Front and was badly injured when his horse fell and rolled on him. He never fully recovered and the pain he endured did nothing to improve his temper. But he had achieved a closer contact with his people than any monarch had done since Charles II.

He was 53 when the war ended but he was not to be granted a peaceful middle-age. The Irish problem had come to a bloody head with the Easter Rising of 1916, but at least an independent parliament was founded in Dublin two years later. Discussions between London and Irish leaders at last produced a settlement whereby Northern Ireland, with its Protestant majority, was partitioned off and attached to the United Kingdom.

The inter-war years

At about the same time, in 1918, women enjoyed a partial victory in their struggle, begun in the United Kingdom in the nineteenth century and taken up by other countries, to have the right to vote. Principal among the agitators were the women of the Pankhurst family, and an organisation, the Women's Social and Political Union, which Emmeline Pankhurst had helped found in Manchester in 1903. The movement itself went back to the 1850s at least, but although women were allowed to vote at local elections from 1869, it wasn't until 1918 that they were allowed to vote for MPs, but still not before they had reached the age of 30. It would be another ten years before British women enjoyed the same rights as the men. Women in the USA achieved full suffrage in 1920; but Belgian women had to wait until 1948. The Suffragette Movement, as it was popularly known, attracted great attention by virtue of its forms of protest, such as women chaining themselves to railings and going on hunger strikes; but there were also bomb attacks – in 1914 Emmeline Pankhurst was serving three years in jail for her part in a plot to blow up the prime minister's house in Walton – and Emily Davison died from the injuries she sustained when she threw herself in front of the king's horse at the 1913 Derby. The fight was hard-won.

George V was the first monarch of the House of Windsor, he changed the name of the royal house – formerly Saxe-Coburg-Gotha – during World War I.

Considerable industrial unrest had followed the war, and culminated in the General Strike of 1926, in which the transport trade unions struck in sympathy with the miners. It lasted ten days in May and spread to involve two million people. Newspaper production was halted, but the BBC (then the British Broadcasting Company) had been formed in 1922, and the nascent radio news services had a baptism of fire. There was still no let-up. The world went over an economic precipice in 1929 after the Wall Street Crash and the crisis lasted a good two years. Unemployment spiralled and the failing finances of the nation induced the king to persuade the party leaders to form a coalition government, which they did in 1931.

Meanwhile, Britain's relations with its colonies and dominions were shifting. After 1914 such countries as Australia, Canada, New Zealand and South Africa expressed the view that they should have some say in how the general foreign policy of the Empire should be handled. Thousands of troops from the Dominions had fought and died in the war, and Australian and New Zealand forces had sustained particularly heavy losses at Gallipoli. The independence of the Dominions from direct British rule was ratified by the Statute of Westminster of 1931, which established what we now call the Commonwealth, but Britain retained control of the Colonies and of India. India gained its independence, and Pakistan was created, when the British ceded rule in 1947. The transition was bloodily achieved, and caused enormous social upheaval, but it was done. African and Pacific and other island colonies were still arriving at independence through the 1960s and 1970s.

George V was an extremely conscientious monarch who maintained good relations with his parliaments and prime ministers, and who managed to engage with his people to a remarkable degree. He had an instinctive talent for public relations, which led him to invite the

THE WHOLE
BUSINESS ECLIPSED
AS A TALKING POINT
THE OTHER ISSUES
OF THE DAY, WHICH
INCLUDED
UNEMPLOYMENT
RUNNING AT TWO
MILLION, THE BERLIN
OLYMPICS AND THE
INCREASINGLY
AGGRESSIVE
ATTITUDE OF THE
GERMAN
CHANCELLOR,

public to share the private griefs and joys of his own family, opening it up and humanising it in a way no other Hanoverians had. He managed entirely to expunge his German connections and became in many ways more British than the British. He was the first king to attend a Cup Final; he was seen at the Derby as well as at Ascot; he instigated the Royal Christmas broadcasts; he went to Royal Command Variety Shows; and he presided over the British Empire Exhibition of 1924 in celebration of the British Empire. The much-loved stadium built for that event was the home of major football and other sporting events for decades afterwards, and has only recently been pulled down to make way for more modern facilities.

But his job took a heavy toll on him, and he died at Sandringham of bronchial pneumonia just before midnight on 20 January 1936, in his 71st year.

George was followed by his eldest son, Edward; but Edward VIII reigned for a scant eleven months – he was never actually crowned – before famously abdicating to marry Mrs Wallis Simpson, an American divorcee. He spun out the rest of his life in relative obscurity as the Duke of Windsor, and is best known as the subject of a rash of plays and TV series in the 1980s. Edward's desire to marry a woman who was a commoner wasn't a problem – English kings had married commoners before, and so had Edward's younger brother. But Mrs Simpson was a divorcee twice over and both her ex-husbands were alive. In fact, Henry II had married a divorcee – Eleanor of Aquitaine – back in the twelfth century; but Edward was no international and absolute ruler like Henry; the idea was unpopular, and there could have been serious constitutional repercussions.

The whole business, while it was going on, i.e. for most of 1936, eclipsed as a talking point the other issues of the day, which included unemployment running at two million, the Berlin Olympics and the increasingly aggressive attitude of the German Chancellor, the Spanish Civil War, and the battles in the East End of London between socialists and Oswald Mosley's Blackshirts, a political splinter group sympathetic to the ideas of Hitler.

Edward is also the monarch with the shortest-but-one reign, the shortest being that of Edward V, the older of the Princes in the Tower, who reigned for two months before he and his brother were murdered, possibly by their uncle, Richard III, or perhaps, a few years later, by Richard's successor, Henry VII, the first Tudor, a man with a very slender claim to the throne, which might have been compromised by the continued existence of the Plantagenet line.

Edward's successor was his younger brother Albert, who, however, ruled as George VI. This George was, as his father had been, second-in-line and had no training for the throne. Like his father he had followed the navy as his career, and had seen active service at the Battle of Jutland. He had, however, made a grand tour of what had been the British Empire in the 1920s, and been present at the opening of the new Australian parliament buildings in May 1927. He also inherited his father's interest in and involvement with his people, though he lacked social confidence. This was on account of a dreadful stammer which he sought, doggedly and ultimately successfully, to overcome.

He was only the fourth English king to ascend the throne while his predecessor was still alive – the others being Henry IV, Edward IV, Richard III and William III – and he did so when the morale of the country was low. There was not much sign of economic recovery, and there was every sign that another major war, well within living memory of the last, was in the offing. Between his accession and the war, he made various state visits abroad, and was the first British monarch to set foot in the USA, where his welcome was 'remarkably cordial'.

When the war came the king, a decent, shy chain-smoker who somehow lacked the

George VI with his wife, Lady Elizabeth Bowes-Lyon, when they were Duke and Duchess of York; George was, like his father, a second son who had never expected to take the throne.

presence either of his father or elder brother, rose to the occasion. Supported by his wife, Elizabeth Bowes-Lyon, familiar to us in her great age as Queen Elizabeth the Queen Mother, he refused to leave London, even during the worst air-raids, visited the Fronts in Italy, France and North Africa; and, following his father's example, did his best physically to associate with his people. When the war was over, and the next five years of Labour rule saw the nationalisation of the railways, the coal industry, gas, electricity, iron and steel, as well as the introduction of a national health service and educational reforms, he found himself presiding over what was in effect a social revolution, the beneficial effects of which were not reversed until the 1980s.

George had never been strong physically, and the extreme demands his relatively short reign placed on him took their toll. He died in 1952, in only his fifty-seventh year. With his death, and the close of the first half of the twentieth century, which had already seen enormous social and technological change, we enter our own era, and bring this part of the book to a close

Julia Sawalha's first leading television role was in the teen drama *Press Gang*. Since then she's starred in the BBC's dramatisation of *Pride and Prejudice* and in the *Horatio Hornblower* series; but she's probably best known for the part of Saffy in *Absolutely Fabulous*. Fortunately, when she investigated her real family history she discovered that it was not quite as dysfunctional as Saffy's, though it was certainly fascinating.

Julia's roots are Huguenot (French Protestant) on her mother's side and Jordanian on her father's. She'd never talked to her mother about her family history before becoming involved with *Who Do You Think You Are?*, but once she'd started she quickly got on the Huguenot trail, seeking the help of specialist researcher Michael Gandy, who gets about five calls a week from people who think they may be descended from Huguenots.

As Michael explained, plenty of people who settled in Britain with French surnames were not Huguenots. 'Huguenot' was the name given to French Protestants who adopted the Calvinistic form of reformed Christianity. The new religion, which in France also represented a movement of political opposition to the crown, won widespread support during the early years of the Reformation in the central and southern parts of the country from all classes – nobles, workers and artisans – despite the austerity of Calvinistic teachings; most of the north, including Paris, remained loyal to the Old Faith.

King François I and King Henri II attempted to suppress the Calvinist heresy, but despite a massacre of Huguenot nobles in Paris on St Batholomew's Day 1572 the movement was not wiped out. Indeed not long afterwards the Protestants' leader was crowned King of France as Henri IV, though only after converting (nominally) to Catholicism. Henri proclaimed the Edict of Nantes in 1598, granting freedom of religious expression to the Huguenots and freeing them from persecution and social discrimination. And so things remained for almost a century, during which, despite some setbacks, the Huguenots grew in power as a political faction. However, in 1685 Louis XIV, partly influenced by second wife, Mme de Maintenon, herself born a Huguenot but a Catholic convert, and partly fearful of the Huguenots' power, revoked the Edict of Nantes. A large proportion of France's skilled workforce fled to Holland, Brandenburg and Britain.

Armed with her great-grandmother's full name, Gladys Ellen Dubock, and her date of birth, Julia set off for the Family Records Centre in London.

She quickly located the birth certificate of Gladys, the first Dubock in the family tree. From this she was able to trace the marriage certificate of her great-great-grandparents James Dubock and Eliza Jane Lusby. This led her to James's birth certificate and the names of his parents William Dubock and Rosanna Bridgeman.

From James' birth certificate, Julia was able to locate the marriage certificate of William and Rose (Rosanna) and finally uncovered her first Huguenot clue. The profession of William's father, another William Dubock, was recorded as weaver. This was backed up by his son William's birth certificate. It also provided the name of his mother, Elizabeth Walker.

Julia searched the online 1881 census returns and found William Snr and his family. Surprisingly, this time he was not recorded as a weaver, but as a grocer and

ABOVE
Julia's great-grandmother,
Gladys Ellen Dubock.

TOP
Julia's maternal
grandmother, Gladys
Kathleen Bridges.

OPPOSITE
Baby Julia with father
Nadim and Julia Snr.

cheesemonger. All clues to William's Huguenot roots seemed to have disappeared.

Finally Julia made a breakthrough. In the 1861 census, William (spelt William Dabock) was recorded as a silk weaver. The same was true of the 1851 census, where his wife Elizabeth was also recorded as a silk weaver.

Weaving was a well-known Huguenot trade, so the signs were hopeful. The earlier William also lived in the Huguenot heartland of Spitalfields in East London.

Mike Gandy's researches on Julia's behalf had traced a further three generations of her mother's family, all weavers and all living in the same area, back to a Peter Du Bock, born around 1744. This was an exciting breakthrough. Spitalfields historian Mike Berlin took Julia on a tour of the district where her ancestors lived and worked – which in Peter Du Bock's time would have been at the very centre of a thriving community. Many Huguenots settled there as it was conveniently placed for trade just outside the City of London. They were so proud of their culture and so protective of it that they did not assimilate, and in the 18th century Englishmen and women about to embark on the Grand Tour of continental Europe would come here to brush up on their French. Many Huguenots owned songbirds and decorated their homes with flower boxes and tubs. Many of their houses remain, and one has been restored to its original state by Dennis Severs, who runs it as a kind of living museum; wandering through its rooms, stairways and passages one experiences a re-creation of how life was lived by the Huguenots of the period. Their prosperity also allowed them to establish several churches.

However, the community eventually fell on hard times. During the first quarter of the 19th century, two-thirds of the weavers became unemployed, and the area declined. Julia's great-great-grandfather William, like many of his colleagues, had to find another trade; some worked on the railways, others on the docks. The saddest cases ended up in the workhouse. William didn't suffer that fate, though the street where he lived, Old Nichol Street, became a slum. (Interestingly, Barbara Windsor's maternal great-grandmother lived on the same street.)

During those difficult days Julia's ancestors relied on help from a number of Friendly Societies created for the purpose. Their archives might contain information relevant to Julia's search, for she still had no conclusive proof – though all the other evidence pointed to it – that her maternal ancestors were indeed Huguenots. Records held at the French Church in Soho Square prompted her to visit the French Hospital, which provided shelter to destitute weavers and their families in the East End. It still exists, but has relocated to Rochester in Kent. There Julia at last found the proof she needed, for the hospital was and remains open exclusively to Huguenots and their descendants. There they were – several Dubocks and Dubocs are listed as residents during the late 18th and the early 19th centuries.

This information led Julia and her mother to Normandy, to the little town of Luneray, near the Côte d'Alabâtre on the Norman coast. Julia's mother was a little disappointed – she'd hoped the family might have come from the south! But they learned from records there that their ancestor Daniel Duboc had fled, along with many other Huguenots, when they were once again subjected to intimidation and persecution after 1685.

The story of Julia's father's ancestors is very different, though it is also about a family forced to move from one place to another. Julia's father Nadim's family were of Bedouin stock and settled in the Jordanian town of Madaba. It appeared that her grandmother, also Julia, had an arranged and not altogether happy marriage, but she was a woman of very strong character who ran her own business and didn't show the requisite respect for tribal culture. Julia found her fierce independence intriguing.

Julia looked forward to travelling to Jordan for this part of her research; although she had only ever spent a few weeks there on various family holidays, she felt a strong affinity for the country. She had grown up listening to her father's stories. What would lie behind them?

Both her paternal grandparents are now dead, and when they were alive she could not speak to them when her family visited them at the Amman hotel her grandmother ran, as they had no language in common. Now was her chance to find out more about them.

In Madaba, Julia met a cousin, Shahib Sawalha, who explained that all Sawalhas will tell you they come from Madaba, even if they weren't born there, as it's the tribal as well as the family seat. He told her that her grandmother had always been a forceful personality, and that her grandfather Joachim had been quiet and conservative. Grandmother Julia had a keen business sense, knew the value of money, resented not having had a better education, and rather than weave a carpet would go out and buy one!

The family is Christian (Jordan's population is about 4 per cent Christian today, the rest mainly Muslim), but it is also Bedouin, the Bedouins being among the earliest settlers in what is now the modern Hashemite Kingdom of Jordan, a tribal people with strong traditions and standards of behaviour of their own; in their ethical system women are strictly subordinate. Julia's tribe is the Roman Catholic Uzayzate, originally

HER PATERNAL FAMILY HAD BEEN SUBJECT TO AN ALMOST MEDIEVAL SOCIAL CODE UNTIL QUITE RECENTLY, YET WITHIN A FEW GENERATIONS IT HAD PRODUCED ... A MODERN BUSINESSWOMAN

from Karak, at the southern end of the Dead Sea. They moved from there to Madaba in the 1880s, and Julia wanted to find out why.

From local expert Dr Geraldine Chatelard, Julia learned that the Sawalhas were one of the largest families in the Christian Uzayate tribe. A complicated system of alliances and treaties bound the various tribes and families living around Karak together. This was enforced by a tribal code of honour, treaty and negotiation, which ensured the tribes could live together in peace and security.

However, in 1876, an Uzayzat warrior wounded a man from one of the tribe's main allies. Protected by a three-day grace period provided by the tribal code, the entire tribe had to leave Karak, until a compensation deal could be struck with the injured man's family. Had the Uzayzat remained behind, any of their men could have been open to revenge attacks by the injured man's tribe.

But without their old allies' protection, the tribe were vulnerable. Soon after the move, an Uzayzat girl was kidnapped by a man of another rival tribe. Honour-bound to retaliate, but without the support they needed to bring pressure on their assailants and force a bloodless settlement, the Uzayzat attacked the man's tribe and killed a number of his kinsmen. Trouble escalated and soon inter-tribal fighting had broken out across Karak. The Uzayzat were forced to flee forever and re-settle in Madaba.

Julia's grandmother, Julia Marar, married into the Sawalha family in the 1920s. At this time the village of Madaba was without electricity or running water. There are no records relating to her grandmother's early years, so no birth, death or marriage certificates were available to Julia during her search. She had to rely on oral histories and the memories of her relatives and family friends to piece the story of her grandmother's life together.

Julia learnt that her grandmother was a clever and entrepreneurial businesswoman from a very early age. Supported by her husband Joachim, she established a sewing workshop and made traditional Bedouin clothes. A self-taught seamstress, she soon employed a number of other local girls and caused a stir in the village with her blunt, businesslike outlook on life. Many believed that Julia was not behaving in the way a Bedouin wife should, failing to show her husband the proper respect and turning her back on traditional beliefs and upbringing. Despite this pressure, her husband Joachim continued to support her, even passing over some of his land to help pay for her business enterprises. Julia continued to break from the traditional bounds of her early years. She moved her family to the capital of Jordan, Amann, and opened a string of new businesses. After opening her hotel in the 1960s, Julia became the first female member of the Jordanian hoteliers', association, an incredible achievement in a country where traditionally a woman's role had been to cook, clean and leave business matters to the men.

So Julia learned that her paternal family had been subject to an almost medieval social code until quite recently, yet within a few generations it had produced, in her grandmother Julia, a modern businesswoman who was brave enough to successfully challenge tribal traditions and etiquette.

PART TWO

THEIR LIFE & TIMES

Age of Modernity

(from the middle of the eighteenth century to the beginning of the nineteenth)

GEORGE III WAS 22 WHEN HE CAME TO THE THRONE LATE IN 1760. HIS GRANDFATHER GEORGE I WOULD TURN OUT TO BE THE LAST BRITISH MONARCH TO LEAD TROOPS INTO BATTLE, ALMOST A MEDIEVAL CONCEPT; BUT THE CLOSING YEARS OF HIS FATHER GEORGE II'S REIGN HAD ALSO SEEN THE OPENING OF THE BRITISH MUSEUM (1753), A TEMPLE OF RATIONALISM AND ERUDITION, BASED ON A PRIVATE COLLECTION BUILT UP BY THE MILLIONAIRE PROPERTY DEVELOPER, PHYSICIAN AND SCHOLAR SIR HANS SLOANE, AND BEQUEATHED BY HIM TO THE NATION.

ABOVE

Sir Hans Sloane, 1660–1753.

FAR RIGHT

George III, during whose reign Great Britain and Ireland were joined to form the United Kingdom.

Sloane typifies the age. He had built up a vast collection of samples of animal and insect species, as well as a herbarium of 800 species gathered when he was physician to the governor of Jamaica (the alcoholic ex-buccaneer Henry Morgan) in the late 1680s. Of Scottish-Irish ancestry, he lived to be 93, and in his time was physician to George II, and president of the Royal Society and the Royal College of Physicians. His own best work was a *Natural History of Jamaica*; but as well as his animal specimens he left behind collections of coins, pictures and prints, as well as a library of 50,000 books and 3560 manuscripts. He purchased the Manor of Chelsea in 1712 and about ten years later presented the Chelsea Physick Garden (a herbarium) to the Society of Apothecaries. His name, of course, lives on not only in the great institution of the British Museum, but in Sloane Square, Sloane Street, Hans Crescent and so on, in London SW3.

Sloane is a good example of what one might call the New Curiosity. Already by the end of the seventeenth century a vogue for travel literature had begun, and Sloane, though he was probably the prince of collectors of 'oddities', was by no means alone. Without film or television to record fauna and flora, elements of the real thing had to be collected, dried, stuffed, pressed between the leaves of books, preserved in alcohol and brought home, to give an impression of what the original had been like. Artefacts of every kind were collected and shipped to England. Freaks were also eagerly sought, and often, to supply demand, faked. And we began to be increasingly familiar with fellow human beings from the distant countries beyond the seas which our ships were opening up. We were familiar with Africans and Arabs, but now even more exotic races came into our consciousness. We shouldn't, however, forget that the famous Native American princess Pocahontas came here early in the *seventeenth* century, and that the explorer William Dampier brought back the tattooed Filipino Prince Jeoly at the end of it. The slave trade was a disgrace, and did not end, so lucrative was it, until William Wilberforce achieved abolition of slavery in the British colonies early in the 19th century.

George III

George, unlike his grandfather and great-grandfather, was born in England and, though, like them, was also Elector of Hanover, he was by culture and education English, and lived here, liked it, spoke English at least as well as German, and indeed was in many ways the model of the slightly stuffy English gentleman. The third of the Hanoverians differed from his forebears in one other respect, a result of the first. He wanted to be involved in governing the country. Like all the Hanoverians, he had a very stubborn streak. (Whether he got on with his father or not is a moot point, since Prince Frederick died when George was 13; he certainly grew to dislike his own firstborn son, and the feeling was mutual.) His education was managed by his mother, Augusta of Saxe-Coburg, and the Earl of Bute, whose relationship with Augusta may have been more than a little close. Certainly his influence over George was strong, and early in the reign he was prime minister for a short time.

The thing is, though, that George III really wanted to rule the country himself, and wasn't unintelligent, so he was convinced he could do it and that he knew best. Bute was the obvious choice, a mentor and a crony, but he was deeply unpopular and not very strong – and the popular verdict on him was that he was unfit for office because (a) he was Scottish; (b) he was the 'king's friend'; and (c) he was honest.

For the first decade of his reign George experimented with other prime ministers but he found them all too independent and intractable. By 1770, however, he had formed his own 'party', the 'King's Friends' – George was canny enough to know that he couldn't knock parliament around as Charles I had attempted to – and in that year found that Lord North was the ideal compliant PM, in that they thought along the same lines and could work together. North, formally a Tory, remained in power until 1782. Meanwhile, George and a variety of prime ministers embarked on a disastrous policy of taxing the Colonies (partly to pay for the Seven Years War), which finally cost us America, whose thirteen states rebelled, and after a nasty and unduly prolonged war seceded from us to become the United States, which a century later turned into a world power.

George's reign was one of the longest of any of our monarchs – nearly 60 years. But in 1780 his mind gave way – some people believe that he was suffering from a rare genetic metabolic disease (now recognised as a group of diseases) called porphyria. Put *very* simply, it is a recurring chronic condition which in the 18th century would have had all the appearance of madness. It's important to remember that medical science was among the least advanced areas of knowledge, even by 1800, and that any profound exploration of the psyche did not take place until towards the end of the 19th century. Towards the end of his life, poor King George was also afflicted with blindness.

George was still able to rule in the intervals of lucidity which remained to him between 1780 and 1811, when his son definitively took over the reins in the period preceding his own kingship – that period famously known to us as the Regency, which has given its name among other things to styles of architecture, dress, taste and painting, as well as to Regent Street in London, built by John Nash, and Regent's Park. The Prince Regent was most fortunate in his ministers, notably the famous William Pitt the Younger, son of the Earl of Chatham, who as William Pitt the Elder had controlled British policy for much of the first part of the eighteenth century.

George III lingered on for another nine years after 1811, dying at the end of January 1820, when his son, by then in his fifty-eighth year, formally succeeded him as George IV, our last really glamorous monarch.

George III reprimanding William Pitt the Elder over trade wars; Pitt was to resign in 1761.

Social activities

The period saw the beginnings of some uneasy (on the part of men) consciousness of women's rights, though it would be a long time before these began to be realised. Women, however, did participate in some areas of sporting activity, such as hunting to hounds. Sport in those days mainly consisted of hunting, shooting and fishing in the countryside, though falconry still existed, and there were various ball games – precursors of croquet and golf. The great painter William Hogarth and the mystical poet William Blake, both city men, deplored the cruelty to animals which was still involved in many sporting activities, from cock-fighting and hare-coursing for the lower classes, to stag- and fox-hunting for the better-off. Blake wrote cogently:

A Robin Red breast in a Cage
Puts all Heaven in a Rage.
A dove house fill'd with doves and Pigeons
Shudders Hell thro' all its regions.
A dog starv'd at his Master's Gate
Predicts the ruin of the State.
A Horse misus'd upon the Road
Calls to Heaven for Human blood.
Each outcry of the hunted Hare
A fibre from the Brain does tear.
A skylark wounded in the wing,
A Cherubim does cease to sing.
The Game Cock clip'd and armed for fight
Does the Rising Sun affright.
Every Wolf's and Lion's howl
Raises from Hell a Human Soul.

Among other amusements not involving animals and generally urban-based, there were freak-shows (often faked) and fights, both between men and between women. Fights were very popular and could be most bloody. Bare-knuckle contests were no-holds-barred and would last until one or other opponent was beaten unconscious or even killed. A visiting Frenchman wrote an account of a fight between two women in the mid-eighteenth-century: 'Both ... were very scantily clothed, and wore little bodices and very short petticoats of white linen ... Their weapons were a sort of two-handed sword, three or three and a half feet in length; the guard was covered, and the blade was about three inches wide and not sharp – only about half a foot of it was, and that cut like a razor. The spectators made numerous bets, and some peers that were there some very large wagers ... '

The fight was conducted with great severity; there were two male umpires armed with poles to separate the combatants if it got too rough, and one woman was cut three times, in each case the cut being sewn up there and then or covered with a plaster, the woman herself being given a tumbler of gin to fortify her. And similar bouts between men were even bloodier. There were even fights between groups of men and women.

Horse-racing had been popular since Charles II's time at least, but jockeys would whip their mounts and each other mercilessly to win. In a world that was still brutal and inured to death and physical suffering, there was little concept of sparing people or animals pain.

There were gentler activities. Charles II was no mean sailor and introduced yacht racing on the Thames. The word *yacht* is originally Dutch, and Holland, where Charles had spent some of his exile, had excellent boat-builders (and still has). There were also rowing races with skiffs. On land, people raced carriages and ran against each other on foot. There was quite a refined form of wrestling – in the proper Greek manner – and there had been since at least Henry VIII's time Royal (or, as we call it, 'Real') Tennis.

The royal cock pit in 1809.

An early cricket game at the Artillery Ground in London in 1743, London and England games were played here from as early as 1725.

There was a kind of football: 'A score of rascals appears in the street kicking a leather ball filled with air ... They will break panes of glass and smash the windows of coaches ... and almost knock you down without the slightest compunction; on the contrary, they will roar with laughter ...'

Cricket, a calmer business altogether, was also making an appearance: 'They go into a large open field and knock a ball about with a piece of wood ... ' At the time, the wicket had only two stumps and no bails, and pads were unheard of. The ball was bowled fast along the ground and the bat was a bit like a hockey stick. But it was a start, and it became a national game organised by counties well before 1750. In 1814 the Marylebone Cricket Club moved to a permanent ground in St John's Wood leased by one Thomas Lord.

Something else our ancestors loved, in those pre-television days, was gaming and gambling, card games and any number of board games, the latter reaching their peak in the Victorian age. Towards the end of the nineteenth century, croquet had a brief but intense vogue, and an important club was set up for it at Wimbledon. But then, in 1874, a new game was introduced to the market in a smart boxed set. It was accompanied by a tiny pamphlet of only eight pages, published by Harrison and Sons of 59 Pall Mall (while the rules of croquet read like the constitution of a small country). The game in the box was called *Sphairistike* (from the Greek), and it was the invention of a youngish military man, Major Walter Clopton Wingfield. It was easy to play, gave you lots of exercise and required only half the size of a croquet lawn. We know it as Lawn Tennis. A new age had begun. At Wimbledon today there is only one, three-quarter-size croquet lawn.

Political unrest

George III was not a very wise man, and he was mistaken in his ambition to try to reverse the process of constitutional monarchy. It has to be said of him too that most of the setbacks, some very serious, experienced by the country during his reign, must be laid at his door and that of the weaker advisers he selected. But he seems to have been quite a popular figure as a private individual, a man who had the common touch, and was indeed down-to-earth, earning himself the nickname Farmer George for the model farms he created on the Windsor estate. He was a neurotic man, but also a good musician, and he loved furniture and garden design. For hobbies, he enjoyed button- and watch-making. He was an active patron of the arts and sciences which continued to flourish throughout the reign, and his collection of books formed the basis for the British Library.

Personally apparently amiable, thought not overburdened with intelligence, he loved his wife and most of his fifteen children (attitudes to the young were growing milder among the middle and upper classes); of whom two sons, George, Prince of Wales, and his younger brother William, succeeded him. That many of the latter years of his long life were spent in the shadows of mental distress and blindness is a source of regret, and it has to be said that, though he might have ruled more wisely, the break with the American colony was something that would have happened anyway, sooner or later. They were a long distance away and growing apart from us both in terms of social and spiritual organisation.

But there were other problems to deal with in the arena of politics at home and abroad before matters were to come to a head with America. When George came to the throne, the so-called Seven Years War was just over halfway through. This had been sparked by Franco-British colonial rivalry both in the eastern and western hemispheres, but it also involved our aiding Prussia, which found itself virtually encircled by enemies. This time the battle-lines were not drawn up along Protestant–Catholic lines. We were allied to Hanover and Prussia. Against us were ranked France, Austria, Russia, Sweden, Saxony and – later – Spain. Without going into a long discussion of the complexities, the result left us rather better off (we gained Canada; the French Post control of the main Indian markets), and we were undisputed masters of the seas. But, considering the position of advantage we were in when the war came to an end in 1763, the terms hammered out by our negotiator, the Duke of Bedford, at Paris, might be called generous by some, supine by others. Bedford feared Britain would be seen as becoming too powerful, which in turn would threaten lasting peace.

He therefore allowed the French fleet to remain untouched, and restored the islands of St Pierre and Miquelon in the gulf of the St Lawrence River to them, together with rights to the Newfoundland fishing industry, worth one million pounds a year *then*. And we returned several Caribbean islands taken in the war, valuable both for produce (Guadeloupe had a huge sugar industry) and as strategic naval bases (France still owns Martinique). Meanwhile we gave Havana and Manila back to Spain.

At the same time we negotiated nothing to protect the interests of our allies, the Prussians, who felt betrayed by us. The loss of America overshadows these other setbacks, and there's little doubt that we behaved foolishly in maintaining our hard-won dominance in the second half of the eighteenth century.

This, on top of unpopular new taxes, served to increase the unpopularity of the government. Bute resigned and was replaced by the Whig, Lord Grenville; but, confusingly, George III simply refused to accept the fact. Pitt the Elder raged from the sidelines and his protégé John Wilkes, the Whig MP for Aylesbury, railed at Bute and the king in his magazine, *The North Briton*. In issue Number 45, of April 1763, he attacked the government so rigorously that he was arrested and taken to the Tower, but this act was in breach of parliamentary privilege. He was released, and became the darling of the hour. The popular cry went up, 'Wilkes and Liberty'. It was a dangerous moment.

TOP

John Wilkes, the journalist, politician and champion of liberty.

ABOVE

Dr Samuel Johnson (1709–1784) – poet, writer, wit, critic and journalist – was contracted to write his dictionary for the princely sum of £1,575.

But Wilkes, for all his political forcefulness, was also a rake and a roué, and a member of the notorious Hell-Fire Club. Soon afterwards, he was forced to flee abroad when he part-published a long poem, *Essay on Woman* (so called because it spoofed Alexander Pope's *Essay on Man* of thirty years earlier), to avoid imprisonment for libel and obscenity. Wilkes's poem can still be obtained, in rare and expensive editions, but they are reconstructions of the original. Perhaps the most famous (and perceptive) couplet it contains is: 'Life can little else supply, But a few good fucks, and then we die.'

Wilkes returned to England in 1768 and became an MP again. He is remembered now as an early champion of freedom of speech and parliamentary democracy. Among other things in his *North Briton* article he had pointed out that 'The prerogative of the Crown is to exert the Constitutional Powers entrusted to it in a way not of blind favour and partiality, but of wisdom and judgment. This is the spirit of our Constitution. The people too have their prerogative, and I hope the fine words of Dryden will be engraven on our hearts: "Freedom is the English Subject's Prerogative."'

Wilkes had particularly singled out George III's favour towards what Wilkes called the Scottish Faction, and it was perhaps his nationalism (specifically towards England) that irritated the literary giant of the later eighteenth century, Dr Samuel Johnson. When Johnson, a Tory, famously remarked that 'patriotism is the last refuge of a scoundrel', there's little doubt of whom he was thinking. Interestingly, the 54-year-old Johnson was to meet the 23-year-old James Boswell, his future biographer and lifelong friend, in a London bookshop a month after Wilkes published his broadside. Boswell, of course, was a Scot.

Johnson had published his masterpiece, the *Dictionary*, on 15 April 1755. It marked the end of nine years' labour and was the first-ever book of its kind in English to focus on words in everyday use. Its influence on the standardisation of our language is incalculable, since it remained the authority for 150 years. Today, it is simply a superb read, and also an interesting eye-opener as to how the meanings of some words have changed. A urinator, for example, is 'A diver; one who searches under water'. And here too we find an array of delightful lost words: 'A fribbler: one who professes rapture for the woman, and dreads her consent.' Most famous, though, is Johnson's definition of a lexicographer: 'A writer of dictionaries, a harmless drudge, that busies himself with tracing the original, and detailing the signification of words.' (Johnson was rewarded with a pension from King George.)

The book, peppered with usage examples from literature, arrived at a good time, because the literary arts were having a new lease of life. As well as the development of the newspaper and the periodical (John Walter's *The Daily Universal Register* first appeared on 1 January 1785; in 1788 it changed its name to *The Times*. W. S. Bourne's *Observer* followed in 1791), the novel was developing fast under the pens of such men as Henry Fielding and Tobias Smollett; and in the theatre, Oliver Goldsmith and Richard Sheridan – both Irish – were the rising stars. There was also a new interest in history, and the particular fascination with classical times resulted in Edward Gibbon's massive *Decline and Fall of the Roman Empire*, whose sixteen volumes appeared between 1772 and 1788.

The arts, inventions and society

In December 1768, under George III's charter, the Royal Academy of Arts was founded. There were to be 40 academicians representing all branches of the fine arts, the purpose of the institution to be educational and to hold annual exhibitions. It was first housed in rooms

The Great Pagoda
in Kew Gardens
was erected in
1762.

in Somerset House (it's been in Burlington House since 1869) and its first president was the 45-year-old Joshua Reynolds, already a famous portrait-painter, whom George knighted in 1769. Reynolds was one of the leaders of London society. He founded the literary club in 1764 of which Johnson, the actor-manager David Garrick, James Boswell, Oliver Goldsmith and the statesman and philosopher Edmund Burke were all members; and he wrote a series of essays on art, including a study of his contemporary, the portraitist and landscapist Thomas Gainsborough. The third major artist of this period, William Stubbs, specialised in animals, particularly horses. His painting of the stud stallion Whistlejacket is so realistic that Whistlejacket himself, when he saw it, is said to have attacked it. To protect the painting Stubbs had to beat him off with his palette and mahlstick! Finally, it would be wrong not at least to mention the portraitist George Romney, whose lighter touch makes him more accessible to us than Reynolds; and the master of the heroic history painting, Benjamin West.

In architecture, the Palladian style was giving way to neo-Classicism and especially striking were the eclectic designs of Robert Adam. At roughly the same time William Chambers, who had visited China, designed the Pagoda for Kew Gardens. And Classicism influenced the potter Josiah Wedgwood and the sculptor John Flaxman.

THE SPINNING JENNY
WAS LOOKED ON
WITH DELIGHT BY THE
BOSSES, BUT NOT
RECEIVED WELL BY
HARGREAVES'S
FELLOW-WEAVERS,
WHO RIGHTLY SAW
THEIR LIVELIHOODS
THREATENED

But this was not just a great age for the arts: in the late 1760s two British inventions paved the way for the Industrial Revolution. James Hargreaves, a weaver and carpenter from Blackburn, invented a water-driven textile spinning machine which he named after his wife, Jenny. The spinning jenny was looked on with delight by the bosses, but not received well by Hargreaves's fellow-weavers, who rightly saw their livelihoods threatened. A few years later his machines were smashed, but it was like trying to hold back the tide. The machine was later taken up and improved by another northerner, Richard Arkwright. The other significant invention of this time was even more revolutionary: James Watt's steam engine.

In society in general, the family as a unit had gradually become less formal and more affectionate. There was now greater freedom for children, and spouses regarded each other – to an extent – as equals. People were becoming more aware of themselves as individuals, perhaps partly as result of a more flexible society in which men (and, slowly, women) of talent could assert themselves in careers. Women actors and musicians were the first of their sex to do so, but actors, even by David Garrick's day, tended to be regarded as not quite respectable. Men had a much wider choice of career, and it's interesting that successful civil servants like Samuel Pepys as early as the mid-seventeenth century should express their own sense of importance by way of keeping a diary. Novels began to probe psychology. As children came to be regarded as precious, more effort was made – again, slowly – to try to improve their health and welfare. Cheaper paper production and faster printing methods, together with greater literacy – again, chiefly among the urban middle classes, but after all it was increasingly those people who had an influence and a say in what direction the country took, rather than the illiterate poor – meant that more and more books became more easily available.

Men were not about to relinquish their position of dominance, however, and this may still have been due to a genuine belief that women's minds were fundamentally different from theirs. Even as intelligent a man as Jean-Jacques Rousseau, writing in 1762, could still argue that women were less clever and physically weaker than men, and therefore dependent and born to obey. (This notwithstanding that women had at least tried to give themselves a voice as early as the time of the Civil War, and had for centuries been left to manage estates and take responsibility for major decisions.)

It would become increasingly hard to maintain this stance, particularly as several individual women were making it plain by their own writing and opinions that they were patently not in the least intellectually weaker or more dependent than men; and as early as 1706, as parliament was taking more and more executive power from the monarch, the religious writer Mary Astell, the daughter of a Newcastle merchant, was asking some awkward questions: 'If absolute sovereignty be not necessary in a state, how comes it to be so in a family? Or if in a family, why not in a state? ... Is it not then partial in men to the last degree to contend for and practise that arbitrary dominion in their families, which they abhor and exclaim against in the state? ... If all men are born free, how is it that all women are born slaves?'

Mary Astell also had a lot to say on the subject of women being deprived of a decent education, and she was not a lone voice. Nevertheless, Rousseau's stance was commonly held by both men and women for many decades yet, and even alert feminine intellects such as Jane Austen's couldn't quite make the leap of accepting and believing that there was no essential intellectual difference between men and women. Austen's heroines are intelligent and independent, as was their creator; but unlike Jane, in the end they can't get along

Jean-Jacques Rousseau (1712–1778), the writer, philosopher and the 'Man of Nature'.

CHAPTER 4

without men. Mary Wollstonecraft, a fiery proto-feminist who published a *Vindication of the Rights of Man* in support of Tom Paine's work, and followed it with a *Vindication of the Rights of Woman* in 1792, still wrote that women, while sharing with men the responsibilities of active citizenship, should also 'be intent to manage her family, educate her children, and assist her neighbours'. But Mary Wollstonecraft did make great strides and had the support of her husband, the equally freethinking William Godwin. Their daughter, incidentally, was Mary Shelley, second wife of the poet. Mary wrote the short novel *Frankenstein* in 1818 at the age of 21. (As time passed, some men began to cotton on to the fact that an educated wife was more interesting than an uneducated one.)

Family values

At least marriage and sex could be enjoyed without guilt and repression, and children could be treated as sources of pleasure and reward, not *de facto* rebellious demons who needed to be kept in check every waking hour. Privileged children were beginning to be cosseted, as a result of a reversal in thinking. No longer was it believed that children were born in a state of Original Sin – now, broadly speaking, people thought children could be moulded, and should be allowed to express themselves. Aphra Behn had pointed out in her novella *Oroonoko* as early as 1688 that all things made by God start out good, but can be spoiled by man's meddling. By 1744, Molly Hervey was pointing out the benefits to children of education.

Greater affection and less formality between parents and children could, however, lead to super-indulgence: Charles James Fox, an influential if maverick politician of the later 18th century, and also an immoderate bon viveur and drinker, was, as an infant, allowed by his father Lord Holland to paddle and bathe in a huge bowl of cream he'd spotted on his parents' dining table. Admiral Graves and his wife never had their children's hair cut, never allowed them to be contradicted, and permitted them to run amok round the house, to the disquiet of visitors. On a wider level, interest was growing in the welfare of less advantaged children. Although during the first half of the century the population had only grown by about one million (to 7.5 million for England and Wales), in the second half, as notions of hygiene developed and medical science improved, it grew by three million. Scotland went from one million to three over the century, and gradually a drift to the cities started as industrialisation made work available in them. This would lead to new problems for the poor in the next century. And as the population increased, so did life expectancy – from about thirty to about forty over the century.

Children, however, were still at great risk. Jonas Hanway, a much-travelled man, who, once home, attacked tea-drinking (to Dr Johnson's anger), and also became the first Englishman to carry an umbrella (much derided), was, more seriously, a philanthropist with a special concern for poor children. In a pamphlet published in 1766 he pointed out that 47 per cent of them died before reaching two years of age, as a result of poor nursing, and argued for an Act of Parliament to send waifs to the countryside to be nursed, away from city pollution and corruption.

Many children, instead of being nourished with care by the fostering hand or breast of a wholesome country nurse, are thrust into the impure air of a workhouse, into the hands of some careless, worthless young female, or decrepit old woman. It is hard to say how many lives these cities have lost, or how many they yet lose annually by the poverty, filth and vice of parents, which no public institutions in this land of freedom can save ... We ought no

The early feminist, Mary Wollstonecraft (1759–1797).

IT IS NO
COINCIDENCE
THAT THE FORK, THE
HANDKERCHIEF AND
THE NIGHT-DRESS
ARRIVED MORE OR
LESS TOGETHER AND
SPREAD SLOWLY
TOGETHER IN THE
LATE SEVENTEENTH
AND EARLY
EIGHTEENTH
CENTURIES.

more to suffer a child to die for want of the common necessaries of life, though he is born to labour, than one who is the heir to a dukedom. One thousand or 1200 children have annually perished under the direction of parish officers ... not that they ordered them to be killed, but that they did not order such means to be used as are necessary to keep them alive.

Never shall I forget the evidence given at Guildhall, upon occasion of a master of a workhouse of a large parish, who was challenged for forcing a child from the breast of its mother, and sending it to the Foundling Hospital. He alleged this in his defence, 'We send all our children to the Foundling Hospital; we have not saved one alive for fourteen years.'

The increasing value of personal relationships – and it's interesting to note that friendship and love as we understand the terms are very modern concepts – together with a greater desire for personal privacy, went hand-in-hand, as the century wore on, and medicine finally made a little progress, with a desire for greater personal cleanliness. As Lawrence Stone points out in his splendid *The Family, Sex and Marriage in England, 1500–1800*, 'It is no coincidence that the fork, the handkerchief and the night-dress arrived more or less together and spread slowly together in the late seventeenth and early eighteenth centuries.'

But despite improvements and the beginnings of protest it would still be a long time before women acquired something that even approached equality, and most continued to find themselves treated as chattels. This was the norm for many ordinary people. It should also not be forgotten that, on marriage, all the woman's property went into her husband's hands. If for any reason they separated later, the children would stay with him unless he did not want them. And still on the statute books in the eighteenth century was a law providing that a man convicted of murdering his wife would be hanged; but a woman convicted of murdering her husband would be burned at the stake. A woman suffered this fate in London as late as 1725, though the punishment fell increasingly into disuse.

Professor Stone recounts the story of an arranged marriage in the 1740s. Mr Grosvenor went to visit his prospective bride (the daughter of a wealthy friend of his) for the first time in the company of his lawyer, Mr Elers. But Mr Grosvenor when he saw her found her not to his taste, and as he didn't actually need the £800 a year she was bringing with her (and over which he would have complete control), he suggested that Mr Elers might like to marry her himself. This was agreed to by Elers and the girl's father and so everything was rearranged.

Many marriages were arranged to comply with financial considerations, though marriage for love and even against sense was by no means unknown at every level of society. As early as the mid-seventeenth century Samuel Pepys, intensely aware of the value of money and socially ambitious, nevertheless married his French wife, who brought no advantages with her, for love, and remained devoted to her all her short life. As the eighteenth century progressed, more and more people (who could afford it, but even a few who could not) put happiness before material gain. These marriages weren't always happier, but they naturally tended to be, since the choice of partner was made on the basis of affection and having interests in common, and such marriages also tended to reveal a greater equality of responsibility in the decision-making within the family. As early as 1714 George Mordaunt put this inscription on the tomb of his wife: 'With unavailing tears he mourns her end. Losing his double comfort, wife and friend.' And here the word 'friend' is used in the sense we would understand, not in the old sense of 'one who could be useful to me'.

Husbands and wives started to call each other by their first names, and to use terms of endearment. It must have come as a great relief, and it lasted until the suffocating days of

OPPOSITE TOP
Lord North – George's Prime Minister during the American Revolution.

OPPOSITE BOTTOM
Joseph Wright's 'Experiment with an Air Pump' shows a popular 'parlour trick' of the age, where the air is evacuated from the jar causing the bird to faint; the middle and higher classes were very interested in scientific experiments.

Victorian England. But for now, kissing and familiarity even in public were open enough to raise the eyebrows of visiting Frenchmen, and in the mid-eighteenth century sexual freedom and even licentiousness matched that of the 1960s and 1970s. John Cleland's famous *Memoirs of a Woman of Pleasure* was published in two parts, in 1748 and 1749, was a roaring success, and eclipsed his serious work (he also wrote other novels and plays, and three volumes of philological studies): 'Standing then between Harriet's legs, which were supported by her two companions at their widest extension, with one hand he gently disclosed the lips of that luscious mouth of nature, whilst with the other he stoop'd his mighty machine to its lure, from the height of his stiff stand-up towards his belly; the lips, kept open by his fingers, received its broad shelving head of coral hue ...' *Fanny Hill*, as the book is better known today, made his publisher, Ralph Griffiths, £10,000, a vast sum by the standards of the time. Poor Cleland, who'd sold him the rights outright, was paid 20 guineas (£21).

Colonial issues

George III quickly lost his fight to retain Bute as his prime minister, and the solid but unimaginative Grenville took the reins. He had the best interests of the country at heart, but he lacked imagination, as did George; and this set them on a disastrous course involving the taxation of their colonies, whose inhabitants had no right to vote in Britain. The American colonists in particular took a very dim view of this. It was a slow burn, and it was interrupted by a changing group of prime ministers with conflicting ideas until the Tory Lord North, George's ideal man after Bute, took over in 1770.

AUSTRALIA BECAME
AN IMPORTANT PART
OF THE EMPIRE THAT
BRITAIN WAS
BUILDING, AND
ALTHOUGH FOR ITS
EARLY DAYS IT IS BEST
KNOWN AS A PENAL
COLONY, NOT ONLY
CONVICTS WENT
THERE

These were interesting times. The once amicable and profitable trade with America had dropped away alarmingly, as relationships soured. It was no accident that Captain James Cook was sent to the southern hemisphere in the *Endeavour*, in 1768, ostensibly to observe a transit of the planet Venus, in fact under secret orders to discover if possible and map Australia, reports of which already existed from much earlier landfalls there by, among others, the Dutchman Abel Tasman and our own William Dampier. Cook was also charged with making contact with any locals, establishing trade links, and claiming the territory for the Crown. We also needed to scout for tall trees suitable for ships' masts, which hitherto had been supplied by Virginia. Cook's expedition was well-manned and well-supplied, and had the advantage of the use of John Harrison's recently-invented chronometer, the exceptionally accurate time-measuring machine which for the first time enabled navigators to determine the lines of longitude. Harrison had worked on the problem for most of his life. In achieving his invention only a few years before Cook's famous voyages, Harrison himself displayed perfect timing.

Australia became an important part of the empire that Britain was building, and although for its early days it is best known as a penal colony, not only convicts went there. Many working-class people took up the challenge of emmigration to escape crowded, unhealthy conditions and lack of employment at home.

While Lord North ran the government at home and Cook sailed the seven seas, the 1760s and 1770s saw the political economist Adam Smith publish his seminal *Wealth of Nations*, Joseph Priestley isolate and identify oxygen (celebrated in a famous chiaroscuro work by Joseph Wright of Derby, *Experiment with the Air Pump*, now in the National Gallery), Sarah Siddons make her debut at Drury Lane with David Garrick, and the first Derby run at Epsom in 1780. (The *very* first English classic race, the St Leger, founded by Lieutenant-Colonel Anthony St Leger, later Governor of St Lucia, was first run on 24 September 1776.) Dominating everything, however, was the war with the American Colony and our loss of it – the War of Independence.

Boston Tea Party

Most of the taxes imposed on the colonies had been repealed, but one tax did remain: 3d. per pound (lb. not £; approx. = 0.5kg) on tea. This may or may not have been a face-saver, though the East India Company which delivered the tea was by now nearly bankrupt, and the government had to bail it out. Whatever the reason, the American separatists saw the tea tax as a good excuse to push their argument for secession from the Mother Country. There were protests. In 1770 little boys in Boston threw snowballs persistently at British troops, who started shooting. The most famous incident, however, still long before conflict opened formally in 1775, was the Boston Tea Party of December 1773, when a group of Americans boarded three East Indiamen and threw their cargoes of tea into the harbour. For the separatists, who called themselves Patriots, this was a great coup; but it infuriated Britain, and though there were those on both sides of the Atlantic who urged moderation and a political solution, it was really too late for that. The war lasted from 1775 until 1783, and ended in a victory for the Americans, who had already declared their independence in 1776, and for their French allies. It was a bold experiment; no one had tried the idea of a state without a monarch before. But the French would take note, and very soon follow suit.

The Treaty of Paris in 1783 brought an end to the war. It states that: 'His Britannic

The Bostonians, dressed as Native Americans, throw the crates into the sea.

'Two pairs of portraits – presented to all the unbiased electors of Great Britain', featuring Pitt the Younger, the Prime Minister, and Whig leader, Charles James Fox.

Majesty acknowledges the said United States, viz. New Hampshire, Massachusetts Bay, Rhode Island and Providence Plantations, Connecticut, New York, New Jersey, Pennsylvania, Delaware, Maryland, Virginia, North Carolina, South Carolina, and Georgia, to be free, sovereign and independent states ... '

But the real end had come two years earlier, with the defeat of the British at Yorktown in 1781. Lord North is said to have taken the news very badly, exclaiming, 'It is all over.' Not long afterwards, he resigned, and was followed by three prime ministers in quick succession before the 24-year-old William Pitt the Younger (second son of William Pitt the Elder) took over the reins of power in 1783, and established a Tory 'dynasty' which was to last, except for one brief Whig interruption, until 1828.

George III had begged Pitt to take over and restore order. The king had himself considered abdication after the American debacle, but his control over both his mind and his country had begun to give way by 1780, a year in which London was rocked for a time by violent anti-Catholic riots fomented by a half-crazy aristocrat, Lord George Gordon.

Pitt the Younger and the Napoleonic Wars

The general British mood after the loss of America was one of anger. Though young, Pitt the Younger was already an experienced and skilful politician, but he would need all his talent to guide the country back to stability. The Irish peasantry were still living in a state of abject subservience. More and more people were concerned at the corrupt and narrow condition of the electoral system in Britain, and American independence, though many thought it justified, was a serious (if temporary) blow to British pockets and self-esteem.

Luckily the king and his prime minister got on well, and the sovereign retained, or at least quickly regained, his popularity (he was known as Good King George), since most were inclined to blame fumbling politicians for the loss of the Colony. Pitt was young, fresh and decisive – a perfect new broom.

Britain's greatest naval hero, Vice-Admiral Horatio Nelson.

But the way was far from smooth. In 1788, George fell dangerously ill. Spies in France reported an imminent and mighty upheaval. The Prince of Wales was looked upon as frivolous and shallow. But George didn't die; and he recovered his senses to a great degree. While the following year the French Bourbon monarchy collapsed effectively for ever, the Hanoverians remained firmly in place. There was no need, with a constitutional monarchy and a strong government, to have another revolution. In 1789, the Marylebone Cricket Club celebrated its second birthday; and the Prince of Wales's faction, under Pitt's great rival Charles James Fox, had been deprived of their opportunity to topple the Tories.

But Fox wasn't out of the race by any means. While it's fair to say that upheaval in France was due largely to the Bourbons stubbornly hanging on to central power and refusing to move with the times politically, the French democrats, the new intellectual aristocracy, were greatly admired. Fox sang their praises, and there was enough support among British radicals for the Jacobin movement for the French to think for a moment that they could after all export their republican ideas north of the English Channel. (Don't confuse Jacobins with Jacobites, the supporters of James II in exile and his heirs. Jacobins were hardline democrats of this period who derived their name from the Dominican convent in Paris where they originally held meetings: 'Jacobin' is an old French word for a Dominican.)

Britain tried to remain neutral. But the French were on a roll, and full of proselytising zeal. Early in 1793 they annexed the Austrian Netherlands (later Belgium), and immediately afterwards declared war on the Dutch and on us. Wearily Pitt accepted that we were once again at war with our old enemy.

We had the Dutch and the Prussians as allies, but their support, for the moment, was weak. Meanwhile the French under Robespierre were fielding a brilliant young lieutenant of artillery who was proving himself a soldier of genius, a stubborn little Corsican called

Napoleon Bonaparte. Our navy had fallen into a sad condition of neglect, so much so that when the fleets at Spithead and the Nore were required to set sail in 1797, they refused on grounds of poor pay and conditions. The sailors weren't wrong: their plight was appalling and now they were expected to fight for a country that had treated them shabbily. There was probably not a little sympathy among the seamen for the new French ideals anyway.

Pitt simply wanted to maintain the status quo – he didn't care what the French did within their own borders; but as time passed and Napoleon became stronger and more ambitious, finally eclipsing and succeeding the early revolutionaries, it became clear that the army he had created could sweep all before it. It was new, it was self-confident, and it was fighting, as it were, for itself, not some monarch or aristocratic oligarchy. Meanwhile the Bank of England was strapped for cash, and the nation as a whole was unwilling to stump up to pay for yet another European war which didn't seem to pose an immediate threat to us.

Luckily Pitt had an instinct for the navy, and this was sharpened by news that Spain had got wind of our weakness. He managed to solve the problem of pay and to improve conditions enough to get the fleets of the Nore and Spithead operational within a month, and they then sailed and successfully defeated a threatening enemy fleet at Camperdown. Meanwhile, Pitt's naval advisers had presented him with an officer who had an impressive record of service, Horatio Nelson. He was 40, a commodore, and had lost an eye and an arm in action. He was small in stature and physically not very fit, but he was a brilliant sailor, and Pitt knew that if Napoleon couldn't be beaten on land, at least not yet, he could be defeated at sea. Nelson had already done so on several occasions, and his action against the French off the Egyptian coast at Aboukir Bay on 1 August 1798 confirmed our superiority. We began to feel more confident. And on 3 December, frustrated by trying to persuade people to pay for the war by other means, Pitt introduced income tax. Pitt wanted 10 per cent from everyone earning more than sixty pounds a year.

The war would drag on and on. Napoleon had himself crowned Emperor at the age of 35 in 1804, and planned an invasion of England, but his scheme was wrecked by Nelson's comprehensive defeat of the combined French and Spanish fleets off Cape Trafalgar on 21 October 1805, at which engagement Nelson died. To maintain his power Napoleon extended his campaigns in Spain and Portugal, which were rebelling against his yoke, and then embarked in 1812 on his disastrous campaign in Russia, where his army was defeated and all but totally destroyed by General Kutuzov, aided by his allies, 'General Patience and General Winter'.

It was the beginning of the end for Napoleon. He was exiled to Elba in 1814, and though he escaped back to France, where he rallied an army, he was defeated by the Duke of Wellington and Marshal Gebhardt Blücher at Waterloo (in modern Belgium) on 18 June 1815. He was then sent to the remote South Atlantic island of St Helena where he died six years later.

George III's declining mental and physical health had meant increasing autonomy for Pitt, but the strain of the work, plus a propensity to allay it with drink, broke his health in the end and he died in 1806, in his forty-seventh year. Five years later George's mental collapse became complete; he was blind, and unfit to rule. He spent his last eleven years of life in seclusion, when his son George succeeded him. But George had been ruling as Regent since 1811, so the transfer of power was an academic one.

PITT SIMPLY WANTED TO MAINTAIN THE STATUS QUO – HE DIDN'T CARE WHAT THE FRENCH DID WITHIN THEIR OWN BORDERS; BUT AS TIME PASSED AND NAPOLEON BECAME STRONGER AND MORE AMBITIOUS, FINALLY ECLIPSING AND SUCCEEDING THE EARLY REVOLUTIONARIES, IT BECAME CLEAR THAT THE ARMY HE HAD CREATED COULD SWEEP ALL BEFORE IT

The Regency years

Jane Austen is one of the greatest novelists in our language. Yet if you read her novels, you will find no references to the Napoleonic wars or to the Industrial Revolution; to the great migrations to towns that were to bring such untold misery to so many; no note made of the exploitation of workers once the need for a large workforce was reduced by the introduction of machines that could do the work of ten and did not need to eat or sleep; of the smashing of those machines by the desperate, and the smashing of the desperate by the forces of order, and of the consequent growth of something quite new: an organised labour movement. (Attempts to curb the formation of trade unions were met with popular resistance across the board; when the Tolpuddle Martyrs were sentenced to transportation to Australia in 1834 for modestly trying to do so, there was such an outcry that their sentence was commuted and they were home two years later.) But Jane Austen stuck sensibly to the world she knew and described it with the sharp sense of satire and the pellucid eye for character which have ensured her reputation.

Many see the Regency as a genteel period when the arts once again flourished, but became more refined. And so it was. George was artistically sensitive, an admirer of Jane Austen, a set of whose books he kept in each of his palaces. The first knighthood he conferred was on the Scottish writer, Walter Scott. He donated his father's library to the nation to form the basis for the present British Library, and he was influential in the foundation of the National Gallery. The Duke of Wellington, who was his last prime minister, said of him: 'He was the most extraordinary compound of talent, wit, buffoonery, obstinacy and good feeling, in short, a medley of the most opposite qualities, with a great preponderance of good, that I ever saw in any character in my life.' George patronised the painters of his day, encouraged younger ones like John Constable, and showed an interest in Constable's close contemporary J. M. W. Turner, perhaps the greatest English painter ever to have lived.

George started to build Buckingham Palace. He was also President of the Royal Society, and gave knighthoods to the chief astronomer of the day, William Herschel (another German immigrant), and the chemist Humphry Davy, famous as the inventor of the miners' safety lamp, so his patronage ran the gamut of another burgeoning period for the arts and sciences. But there is a danger of not being aware of any other world when you are in the company of such people as 'Beau' Brummell, and he was George's close companion for a long time.

George Brummell had a great influence over the Prince Regent, particularly at Bath and Brighton, the fashionable spots where he held court. The son of Lord North's private secretary, he'd been to Eton and (briefly) Oxford, but his main interest was style – in dress, in manners and in his way of living. In this he embodied, to a great exent, those aspects of the Regency which most of us know best: the lovely furniture, the high bodices, the dresses inspired by Greek antiquity, the smart, fast little carriages, the balls, the champagne and John Nash's Brighton Pavilion, that bizarre and yet somehow likeable folly inspired by the fashion for the Orient, which took 27 years to build, and virtually ruined George IV.

Brummell followed in the footsteps of the other famous dandy, 'Beau' Nash (not to be confused with the architect John Nash), who'd helped form Bath into the fashionable neo-Classical spa it became. But Richard Nash was an innovator, at work in the early part of the century, and there was more substance to him. Brummell embodied perhaps the worst of the Regency's froth, and, true to type, he ran through his £30,000 inheritance, got above

ABOVE
Jane Austen, the most famous novelist of her era, wrote social satires rather than the typical works of that Romantic period.

OPPOSITE TOP
J.M.W. Turner's 'Lincoln from the Holmes'.

OPPOSITE BOTTOM
George 'Beau' Brummell, the epitomy of British 'dandyism'and the famous clothes-horse and wit.

himself, quarrelled with the new king in 1813, fled to France, and expired mad and impoverished in Caen in 1840, aged 62.

The future George IV was, as we've seen, an intelligent man, but, in the end, far more pleasure-loving than he was interested in the country or the affairs of state. Unfortunately, for all his surface sophistication, he reduced the court to a stuffy little circle of snobs, where manners and appearance mattered far more than intellect. He was a committed epicure, and from being a handsome young man quickly grew into a gross, bibulous middle-aged one, the butt of savage satirical cartoons by James Gillray and Thomas Rowlandson, whose drawings accurately and bitterly reflect some of the less pleasant aspects of the political and sensual life of the age.

George hated his wife, Caroline of Braunschweig, to whom he'd been married in 1795, a political marriage George agreed to if parliament would discharge his debts, then running at £650,000. Caroline was plainish, noisy and provincial. George was in love with a Catholic widow, Maria Anne Fitzherbert, six years his senior, whom he'd had to give up for the marriage, and he hated his wife for that for the rest of her life.

Though they had a daughter, she died in childbirth, and the child was itself stillborn, so there was no direct heir. Had this not happened, we might not have had the monarchy we have now, and there would have been no King William IV and certainly no Queen Victoria.

George and Caroline soon parted. He banished her to Blackheath, where she lived in solitude, the object of much sympathy. However, she had lovers of her own, and her indiscretions came to the attentions of George, who had her investigated for mothering an illegitimate child, splendid grounds for divorce; but nothing could be proven. He banished her

IT WOULD TAKE FIVE
MORE BILLS BETWEEN
1867 AND 1969,
TO EXTEND THE
FRANCHISE TO ALL
MEN AND WOMEN
OVER THE AGE OF 18

from the court in 1814 and she returned to the Continent, but she retained her title – Princess of Wales – and the love of the people, who detested his treatment of the woman he openly called 'the vilest wretch this world was ever cursed with'.

When he came to the throne in 1820 he offered her £50,000 to renounce her title and stay in Braunschweig; she took the money, but she still wanted to return as queen. George tried to bully parliament into granting him a divorce, but they were unshaken, and he wasn't a strong enough man to handle them. The whole thing became increasingly sordid, but Caroline returned to England to a rapturous popular reception.

Perhaps by now she'd overplayed her hand, or underestimated George's Hanoverian stubbornness and ruthlessness. He was due to be crowned at Westminster Abbey on 21 July 1821. Caroline appeared at the doors of the abbey, quite prepared to gatecrash, but the doors were slammed in her face. This humiliation was too much; and she had lost the support of the one man in government who was on her side, George Canning, who hadn't abandoned her, but who had resigned. And that was the end of whatever cause she was hoping to pursue. As the novelist Sir Walter Scott (incidentally a great admirer of Jane Austen) wrote, it was 'a fire of straw, burnt to the very embers'.

On 7 August, still in London, Caroline died. She was 53. The reason for her death is unclear to this day.

George himself, worn out by excess, died on 26 June 1830, not really mourned by anyone. He is said to have retained a picture of Mrs Fitzherbert to the last. A postscript to his reign: Construction of the Liverpool and Manchester Railway had begun in 1826, under the direction of the Scottish engineer and inventor of the steam locomotive, George Stephenson. Now, on Wednesday 15 September 1830, the line was to be inaugurated and a number of notables were there, some on board the train. But alas, the maiden railway journey was marked and marred by the first railway accident. William Huskisson MP was inadvertently knocked down and killed by Stephenson's glamorous and amazing invention,

'The Sultan' by
Thomas Rowlandson
– one of a series of
caricatures depicting
the sexual practices
of the English
aristocracy.

Rocket, as, underestimating its speed, he could not get out of its way in time. But poor Huskisson's demise couldn't cloud the excitement: from now on, travel was going to be a very different experience, and places far apart would be connected in the same number of hours as they formerly had been by days.

William IV

William IV was the next king, and with him this chapter ends. He was the third son of George III and had spent eleven years in the navy, hence his sobriquet, the 'Sailor Prince', when he ascended the throne aged 65. A diffident man – he didn't really even want a coronation – he was popular with the public. He was also a family man. From 1790 to 1811 he lived with the actress Dorothy Jordan, and had ten children by her. With his wife, Princess Adelaide of Saxe-Meiningen, whom he married in 1818, he had two daughters, who sadly did not live to succeed him. The great question of his reign concerned parliamentary reform, which George IV had rejected; William, though cautious, was more biddable, and inclined towards the Whig Party.

A Reform Bill of 1831 was repeatedly rejected by the Lords. William was persuaded to create enough Whig peers to see it through, which he was reluctant to do; but he did use his influence with the Lords to see the Bill passed the following year. It didn't go very far, but it did extend the right to vote to members of the property-owning middle class. It would take five more Bills, between 1867 and 1969, to extend the franchise to all men and women over the age of 18.

The reign also saw some changes, not necessarily huge improvements, to provisions for the poor (but the new measures included the creation of the dubious workhouse system); and, as we've mentioned, slavery was abolished in the British colonies (in 1833).

William's six years on the throne, though, were generally quiet ones for Britain. After the great domestic and foreign upheavals of the late 18th century, this prelude to the Victorian era was one of autumnal calm.

ABOVE LEFT
An engraving depicting the bribery of Caroline of Brunswick by George IV.

ABOVE
William IV, painted in front of Windsor Castle.

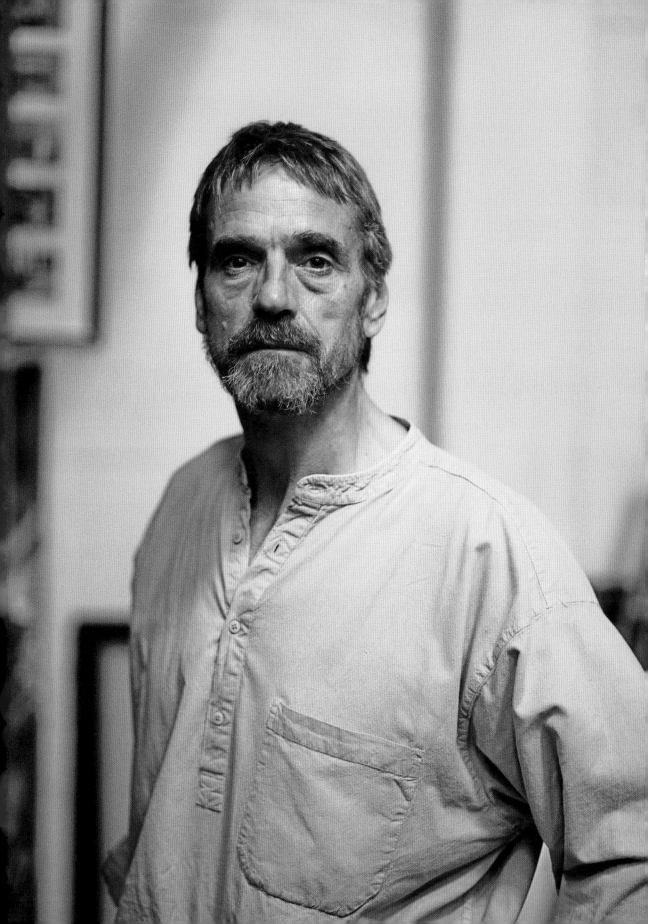

Jeremy Irons was born in the autumn of 1948 at Cowes on the Isle of Wight to Paul and Barbara Irons (née Sharpe). Brought up in St Helens, riding and sailing, the family moved to Hertfordshire when he was 13 and he continued his education in Dorset at Kings School Sherborne, where his strengths developed in music, sports and English literature. Not until his final year did he act in a play – an engrossing experience – upon which he lays the blame for failing his A-Levels. After a year working in South London as a busker and social worker he began his training at the Bristol Old Vic School. Once in the market he built a career playing the classics before coming to London and working both in the West End and television. His work in both *Brideshead Revisited* and *The French Lieutenant's Woman*, which he made simultaneously, brought him international recognition. He went on to win an Oscar, a Tony, and has become one of out most distinguished film and stage actors. In 1978 he married the Irish actress Sinead Cusack who introduced him to her country. He felt a strong affinity with Ireland and they eventually took over a cottage and some acres by a river in West Cork.

Surprised by his affinity for the Irish and with Ireland he has wondered whether there existed some connection by blood. Knowing a little of his English forebears, who his father had warned him were, on his side, "boringly middle class and of little interest", he was curious to know the source of his theatrical, not to say anarchic, streak.

Some years ago Jeremy had received a letter from Susan Nollett, a second cousin which said that one of Jeremy's ancestors, Thomas Irons, his great-great-grandfather, had ridden into Westminster on a donkey to present a petition to government on behalf of the Chartists. Thomas was arrested and sent to Newgate gaol. Jeremy wants to find out if this is true or an apocryphal story.

At Susan's house Jeremy is shown the 1840 marriage certificate of Thomas and Catharine Brown which reveals that Thomas was a police constable living in Pimlico. Susan also gives Jeremy an original sketch of Thomas Irons drawn by a fellow inmate whilst Thomas was in Newgate gaol.

Jeremy knew Sir Robert Peel had founded England's first police force in 1829, but to find out more he visited the Metropolitan Police Archives. He learned that the "Peelers", as they were known, were widely disliked by all classes. Employment requirements were to be younger than 35, at least 5'7" and prepared to work 12-hour beats, seven days a week, with one week off a year.

The weekly wage of 15 shillings was certainly better than a labourer was paid. The uniform was heavy worsted serge, and pounding the beat must have been thirsty work. London water was not to be trusted, beer being a safer alternative.

After six years with the Met – longer than most – and after 37 warnings, Thomas was sighted leaving a pub, after absenting himself from his beat for half an hour, and dismissed from the Force.

Family lore spoke of him as a Chartist. To find out more about that political movement Jeremy visited Malcolm Chase, a leading Chartist historian. The Chartist movement started in 1838 with the aim of presenting a charter to Parliament demanding amongst other things, the right of every adult male to vote. At this date only those

FRUSTRATED BY PARLIAMENT'S LACK OF RESPONSE THE CHARTISTS NOW PLANNED CONCERTED ARSON ATTACKS UP AND DOWN THE COUNTRY.

ABOVE
Jeremy with dog, Speed.

OPPOSITE
Jeremy's great-grandparents, William and Katherine Sharpe, in a family group.

men owning property over a certain value had that privilege. By 1848 three separate petitions had been presented to Parliament to no avail. A huge rally was planned for Kennington Common as a prelude to a march on Westminster. This was the year of the second French Revolution, Europe was seething with political unrest, and the threat of this rally unnerved the establishment. The aging Duke of Wellington, hero of the battle of Waterloo, was put in charge. Bridges over the Thames were closed, and Queen Victoria was bustled off to the safety of the Isle of Wight. The rally went off peacefully, only the leaders were allowed to deliver the petition to Parliament who took little notice, and from that day on meetings of more than six persons were outlawed. Frustrated by Parliament's lack of response the Chartists now planned concerted arson attacks up and down the country. The night before, covert meetings took place in all the major cities, but in London an informer, Thomas Powell, alerted the police. They raided the Orange Tree Tavern in Orange Street and arrested the Chartist leaders. Three hundred police also raided an upstairs room over the Angel Tavern in Webber Street, SE1.

They arrested the fourteen men present, searched their homes and found a small arsenal of weaponry. The men were locked up in Newgate Gaol. One of those fourteen was Thomas Irons.

Jeremy was shown the print of a portrait of one of the Chartist leaders William Cuffey, drawn by an Irishman named Dowling also being held in Newgate. Clearly the drawing of Thomas Irons was by the same artist. Both men were portrayed, not as revolutionaries, but as decent working men, no doubt in an attempt to counter government propaganda as their trial approached. At the trial over half of those arrested were sentenced to transportation to Australia. Thomas, who had no weaponry about his house or person, and who explained his presence as just having dropped in to have a drink with friends, escaped their fate and was sentenced to 18 months in the Horsemonger Lane Prison in Surrey.

Malcolm Chase unearthed copies of the Chartist paper *The Northern Star*, which listed the small weekly grants raised by public collection that supported the prisoner's families throughout their sentences. Mrs Irons with her large family was given more than most. Her fifth child George was born while her husband was in gaol. Upon his release Thomas appears to have trained as an engineer, for he is next found working as such in a cabinet-making factory powered by steam engines in East London. But for Thomas, who as young man had left his native Dundee to make his life in London, neither this city nor his family of seven seemed to satisfy him. He took a job as a ship's engineer on a steam ship, and it is thought in his mid-50s contracted yellow fever and died far far from home at anchor off Rio de Janeiro.

Having identified a wonderlust but as yet no Irish blood among his Irons forebears, Jeremy turned to his mother's side, the Sharpes. Pip Sharpe, his second cousin and

TOP
Katherine Rutton, née Sharpe.

ABOVE
Henry Loftie Rutton, Jeremy's great-great-grandfather.

ABOVE RIGHT
Jeremy with Maggie Bird at The Metropolitan Police Archives.

OPPOSITE
Catherine McCreight and family.

keeper of the maternal family archive, was able to trace the family back to their great-grandparents William and Katherine.

William appears to have been living in Dublin when he married Katherine Rutton, a woman of great artistic skill, as a painter, wood carver and sculptor of miniature portraits out of bread dough. William, who inherited a modest fortune, appears to have been more of a bon-viveur than a businessman, and it seems it was Katherine's artistic talent that kept them afloat. To find out more, Jeremy set out on the ferry for Dublin.

Helped by genealogist Nicola Morris he discovered that Katherine's father, Henry Loftie Rutton, though born in Ashford, Kent, had married in Ireland a wife who had died in childbirth. His second marriage to the daughter of a wealthy Irish landowner William McCreight, also named Catherine, this time with a 'C', led to the birth of three daughters, of which only one, his beloved Katherine, survived. Pip Sharpe had leant Jeremy a manuscript book containing poems written by Henry to his daughter and by her to him, which showed their deep love for each other.

Linen weaving had long been a staple cottage industry in both Ireland and Scotland. But industrialization turned it into a more lucrative venture as large mills

were built wherever there was water power. The McCreights had settled in Northern Ireland at the end of the 17th Century. William McCreight became a wealthy landowner in Gilford, County Down. His son-in-law Henry also seems to have been a successful property developer. From Griffiths Valuation Index, a survey or land occupation in Ireland, Jeremy learned of the existence in Gilford of a line of workers, cottages called Rutton Row, named after Henry Loftie Rutton. A visit to the town showed that the cottages had been demolished in 1974.

His disappointment was countered by a letter from Nicola Morris saying she had traced a marriage certificate between David McCreight, Jeremy's great-great-great-great-grandfather and yet another Catherine, this one from Cork in southern Ireland. David and his two brothers had worked as superintendents at the linen mill in Innishannon, before managing the linen mill a few miles north at Blarney. The flax for the mill in Innishannon was bought from Clonakilty and Skibbereen.

So when Jeremy takes his boat upriver to buy his groceries in Skibbereen, he passes the site of the mill from which, over 250 years before, his ancestor David McCreight would have ordered the flax to weave into linen in his mill in Innishannon.

It would seem Jeremy had found the Irish connection he was looking for.

CHAPTER FIVE

Age of Growth

(from the early to the mid-eighteenth century)

WILLIAM AND MARY DIED WITHOUT ISSUE, SO MARY'S SISTER ANNE SUCCEEDED THEM. A DULL, INSIPID
WOMAN, WHAT WE WOULD CALL SUBURBAN TODAY, HER MAIN INTERESTS WERE HORSES AND BLOODSPORTS.
SHE WAS MARRIED TO PRINCE GEORGE OF DENMARK (A NONENTITY OF WHOM CHARLES II HAD COLDLY
REMARKED, 'I'VE TRIED HIM DRUNK, AND I'VE TRIED HIM SOBER, AND THERE IS NOTHING IN HIM.'), AND BY HIM
HAD 17 CHILDREN, MOST OF WHOM DID NOT SURVIVE INFANCY, AND ALL OF WHOM WERE DEAD WHEN SHE
ASCENDED THE THRONE IN 1702, AGED 37. SHE HADN'T GOT ON WITH HER SISTER MARY IN THE LATTER YEARS
OF MARY'S LIFE, AND APPARENTLY WILLIAM HAD LITTLE TIME FOR HER. PERHAPS BECAUSE OF THAT SHE LEANT
HEAVILY ON JOHN CHURCHILL, BY NOW EARL OF MARLBOROUGH, AND HIS BEAUTIFUL BUT BOSSY WIFE SARAH.

Earl of Marlborough

William II, Prince of
Orange, and his wife, Mary
– daughter of Charles I.

The Marlboroughs had come a long way from the impoverished minor aristocrats he was
descended from. She'd been a maid-in-waiting to Anne Hyde (James II's first wife) when
she was Duchess of York. He, already in middle life, was on the threshold of the greatest
phase of his career, and before his undeserved fall, he was to be given the Palace of
Blenheim, named after one of his great victories, designed by Sir John Vanbrugh at a vast
cost to which the nation contributed £500,000. Later on, the greatest English landscape gar-
dener since the Tradescants, Lancelot 'Capability' Brown, would lay out some of the gardens
on the 2500-acre estate in the form of the battle-lines of Marlborough's most celebrated
engagements. But all this was in the future.

The childless Carlos II of Spain died on 1 November 1700, bequeathing his throne to
Louis XIV's grandson, Philippe d'Anjou; but this was contested by the Austrian Emperor,
who claimed it for his son, the Archduke Karl. As a consequence of this, war broke out
between the two countries, being fought in the Netherlands and in northern Italy. William
III of England had foreseen what was coming up and in the last months of his life expended
his considerable diplomatic skills in setting up a Grand Alliance against France, whose
ambitions he correctly perceived needed curbing if the general balance of power in Europe
were to be maintained. The War of the Spanish Succession lasted twelve years, from 1702 to
1714, and was fought between France, with Spain and Bavaria as her allies, against Britain,
Holland, Prussia, Austria, Denmark and Portugal.

War against France was declared formally on 4 May 1702, and Marlborough, at the head
of a combined British and Dutch army, sailed for the Spanish Netherlands. There followed
a long continental campaign in which Marlborough distinguished himself greatly, winning
a series of significant battles whose names are widely remembered still – Blenheim,
Ramillies, Oudenarde and Malplaquet. Unfortunately for him, however, his success, rising

power and his influence over the queen earned him the envy of the then dominant Tory Party at home, who wished to hasten a compromise peace deal, which would undo every advantage Marlborough had gained in the field. At the same time, the tide of the war turned, his stock fell, and his wife began to lose her influence with the queen who was tiring of her hectoring manner. Marlborough was recalled to face trumped-up charges of taking backhanders from army contractors (in fact he was brilliant at logistics and his army was one of the best-equipped ever), which were disproved, but he still couldn't escape the disgrace his enemies had planned for him. Under George I he was entirely rehabilitated and greatly mourned at his death in 1722.

Under the Treaty of Utrecht, 1713, and other subsequent arrangements, it was decided that Philippe should get Spain, but that the same monarch should rule over France and Spain together. Austria acquired the Spanish Netherlands and Spanish possessions in Italy. Britain gained French territories in the New World, including Newfoundland, with its lucrative fisheries, as well as Gibraltar and Menorca. The power of France was effectively broken. In 1715, almost symbolically, Louis XIV died. By the end of the century, there would no longer be a monarchy in France.

THERE FOLLOWED A LONG CONTINENTAL CAMPAIGN IN WHICH MARLBOROUGH DISTINGUISHED HIMSELF GREATLY, WINNING A SERIES OF SIGNIFICANT BATTLES WHOSE NAMES ARE WIDELY REMEMBERED STILL – BLENHEIM, RAMILLIES, OUDENARDE AND MALPLAQUE

Jacobite unrest

While the war was being fought, an important change in the nation's domestic arrangements took place. In 1707, Scotland was formally united with England and Wales as 'one united kingdom by the name of Great Britain'. This was essentially a ploy to bring the Scots under one roof and to diminish the risk of any likelihood of their raising a standard in support of James II's followers – the Jacobites. In fact James II's son, known to us as The Old Pretender and to the French as the Chevalier de St Georges, tried unsuccessfully to land in Scotland in 1708. The French had proclaimed him James III of England and James VIII of Scotland on his father's death. He fought on the side of the French in the War of the Spanish Succession, and made a successful landing in Scotland in 1715, but nothing came of it. Still only 27, he retired to Rome, where he died in 1766.

The Jacobites continued to cause problems, however. The Young Pretender, James II's elder grandson, was born in Rome in 1720. Known to us familiarly as 'Bonny Prince Charlie', he managed to land in Eriskay in July 1745 and had much better success than his father. The clans rallied to his standard, which was just as well since he'd arrived with only seven men, and he took Edinburgh in September, establishing a court at Holyrood. In the same month he started south, marching on London, with a force of about 6500 men, taking Carlisle and getting as far as Derby. His success was partly due to the fact that the best part of the British Army was then engaged in fighting on the Continent in another European war – that of the Austrian Succession this time; but the Duke of Cumberland, George II's third son, a brilliant but ruthless young soldier, was dispatched with a force to meet the Scots, who retreated back north of the border, and were utterly crushed at the Battle of Culloden, in April 1746 – an action so bloody that it earned the 26-year-old Cumberland the nickname 'Butcher', though he also had a flower named after him. In England it's called Sweet William; in Scotland, Stinking Billy.

Bonny Prince Charlie himself managed to escape – 'over the sea to Skye' – and made his way back to France, but, like his father, spent his latter years in Italy, dying in Rome in 1788. There is one legacy of his time. The Jacobites had taken up a version of a jingoistic song,

John Churchill, Duke of Marlborough, who was gifted the Palace of Blenheim for his victories – which remains in the Churchill family today.

written by an unknown hand but now, in autumn 1745, taken up by the Hanoverians and set to music by Thomas Arne, one of our great composers, the son of an upholsterer. Here are the opening words. The music will be familiar: 'God save our noble King, God save great George our King, God save the King ... '

London under Queen Anne

Queen Anne was a natural Tory – don't confuse these people too much with modern Conservatives – but with one or two notable exceptions, her most interesting and prominent subjects were Whigs. And though this faintly tragic, faintly comic woman (who became so immensely fat in later life that she could no longer ride a horse when hunting, but had to go after the deer in Windsor Forest in a specially designed narrow carriage with high wheels – a sort of early-eighteenth-century 4x4) presided during her twelve-year reign over a country all the time at war abroad, and at home the scene of vigorous political rivalry, she could also boast that it was a place of extraordinary artistic, financial and intellectual activity. Anne's placidity (except when hunting) and the nation's vigour brought about another shift towards the weakening executive power of the monarchy.

London, as always, was the focal point. It had a population of some 700,000, though that figure was falling, who were crammed into far narrower confines than the overblown city of today. There were draymen and costermongers and shopkeepers and pickpockets and dockers, porters, labourers, beggars, bankers, actors, court officials and administrators, crooks and whores and watermen. Forget privacy or hygiene, by and large. Most of the poorer inhabitants were crammed into tenements in the 'liberties' – slums outside the City walls, especially around Fleet Street. The better-off artisans, mainly engaged in high quality cabinet-making, picture-framing and upholstery, could do better, but it was a cheek-by-jowl existence for everyone. You'd always be able to hear your neighbours, and everyone would know everyone else's business.

Anne, who had gout and anyway preferred Bath and Windsor, hated the capital. One can hardly blame her. It was a miserable place to get about in, it was filthy, the streets were still unpaved (it'd be a century before John MacAdam brought decent 'macadamised' surfaces to the roads of Bristol). The Palace of Whitehall had burnt to the ground in a fire in 1698, only the Banqueting House designed by Inigo Jones surviving. But the place was fantastically alive, a great centre of finance and trade. Despite the costs of the wars, Britain was becoming more and more prosperous. Although the combined population of England, Wales and Scotland was about a third that of France, Britain was richer. The success of the East India Company was partly the cause, but international trade in general was strong.

It was also hugely fashionable; people were self-conscious, questioning, sharp. There were dozens of coffee-houses, tea was drunk by those who could afford it, and now there was another fashionable non-alcoholic drink – chocolate, taken at breakfast or mid-morning, very strong. The shops that served the drinks began to attract their own particular clientèles: Whigs went to the St James's; Tories frequented the Cocoa Tree; Truby's was for the clergy. Poshest of all was White's; but the financiers of the City went to Edward Lloyd's. Cafés like these were evolving into clubs. The last would turn into a great financial institution.

FAR RIGHT
Queen Anne, whose reign was renowned for the decreasing influence of the Crown on political issues.

CHAPTER 5

An engraving of the Thames from 1760, with Christopher Wren's St Paul's Cathedral dominating the townscape.

A period of creative minds

This hotbed of vitality was of course fuelled by the great creative spirits of the Restoration, who lived on actively well into the eighteenth century. Sir John Vanbrugh lived from 1664 to 1726; Sir Christopher Wren from 1632 to 1723. But new men were coming onto the scene (still British society was too male-dominated to allow for many women to come to prominence – they were much better off in France – but, as the 18th century progressed, more and more would emerge, of such interest and character that one can only regret what might have been had women been permitted better education and freedom of expression centuries earlier).

Some of the most prominent Whigs – Marlborough, Robert Walpole (who would be the first politician actually known as 'prime minister' – the term was originally a derogatory one), Vanbrugh, the playwright William Congreve and the writers and early journalists (a new profession) Joseph Addison and Richard Steele formed the Kit-Cat Club, to discuss political ideas and the affairs of the day. The club, named after Christopher Cat who ran the inn where it first met, lasted until 1720, and its members had their portraits painted on small canvases, to fit into their later clubroom, by Godfrey Kneller, German-born and one of the up-and-coming great portraitists of the age. A much more contentious and important painter would soon be studying at the Academy of Painting, the first to be established in England, which Kneller became governor of in 1711. His name was William Hogarth.

Addison and Steele wrote essays and plays, Steele producing the first real periodicals, *The Tatler*, which ran from 1709 to 1711, and *The Spectator*. Another proto-journalist of the period was the polymath Daniel Defoe, best-known as a novelist and the writer of *Robinson Crusoe* and *Moll Flanders*; but he also produced a very valuable survey of early 18th-century England, of great use to the family historian, called *A Tour Thro' The Whole Island Of Great Britain*. In literature in general there was a turning away from the slightly overblown mannerism of the Restoration, towards harder-hitting, more direct language which reflected the increasingly Classical taste of the age. Two giants of this period are Jonathan Swift (1667–1745), whose *Gulliver's Travels* remains entrenched in the national psyche, and Alexander Pope (1688–1744), a precocious genius whose blend of satire and sensitivity places him among the best half-dozen poets of our literature. Pope's verse and imagery display conceits which may strike us as artificial (Swift's prose is far more down-to-earth), but the lightness of touch introduces a completely different world from that of the poets of the 17th century. (Pope was very small, not more than 1.5m. tall. His waspishness earned him a lot of enemies, so when he went out he carried a brace of pistols, and bought himself a Great Dane, called Bounce. Whenever he could, he went about escorted by his great friend John Gay, a massive Irish playwright.)

The two men, Swift and Pope, despite the age difference, were great friends, united in their disapproval of hypocritical and morally heinous society. *Gulliver's Travels* (inspired in part by the memoirs of the famous 17th-century pirate and explorer William Dampier) is seen today more or less as a popular children's book, especially the 'Voyage to Lilliput', which is the only one of the four most of us know. In fact it is a savage satire. But in his affection for Pope and his other close friends, Swift could be witty and tender. Of Pope's work he generously wrote:

When he can in one couplet fix
More sense than I can do in six,
It gives me such a jealous fit,
I cry, Pox take him, and his Wit!

And it was of course Swift who also wrote, in a letter to Pope of 29 September 1725, that 'I have ever hated all nations, professions and communities, and all my love is towards individuals ... But principally I hate and detest that animal called man; although I heartily love John, Peter, Thomas, and so forth ... '

The first half of the eighteenth century was an age when reason and materialism were highly valued. St Paul's was completed by 1710. The middle class increased and established itself as a power to be reckoned with. Trade flourished. In architecture, William Kent designed Horse Guards in Whitehall in the Palladian style which would become popular. It was an age of culture and confidence, as well as a certain amount of hypocrisy. Defoe divided society into the great, the rich, the 'middle-sort', a comfortable working class and the poor, who were many and who suffered. Cities like Bristol and Liverpool were growing as a result of the slave trade. Defoe could see nothing wrong with the use of child labour.

For all the emphasis on rationalism and increasing intellectual awareness and curiosity, this was a poor age for the great institutions. The universities were in decline, priests could hold livings they never visited, schools were neglected, and parliamentary boroughs and town councils could be run in the most corrupt manner without fearing challenge.

European influence

But if formal education was in a decline – and there were still only two universities in the entire land – another form of tutelage was becoming fashionable, at least for the great and the good, in the form of the Grand Tour, which young men (mainly) would take with a tutor for about eighteen months, visiting the recently rediscovered (in terms of interest) antiquities of Italy and other parts of Continental Europe. The young man might pick up a little of the Italian language, and a dose of clap from a whore in Naples perhaps; and would certainly come back with some antiquities of his own, real or fake, and a sense of Renaissance and Classical architecture which he had not had before. The Palladian style

DANIEL DEFOE PRODUCED A VERY VALUABLE SURVEY OF EARLY EIGHTEENTH-CENTURY ENGLAND, OF GREAT USE TO THE FAMILY HISTORIAN, CALLED A TOUR THRO" THE WHOLE ISLAND OF GREAT BRITAIN

became profoundly popular and many great men had their houses built in it. William Kent, one of the best architects of the movement, built Chiswick House for the Duke of Burlington; Robert Walpole had his great house, Houghton Hall, built in the high Palladian style. John Wood and his son would redesign fashionable and expensive Bath in neo-Classical style, making that city one of the most beautiful in England.

The period also saw the advent of master cabinet-makers whose work can still be found and owned today if you have the money to pay for such valuable antiques. Otherwise go to the Victoria and Albert Museum, or to any large stately home near you, where there will almost certainly be some of their work on display. The designs inspired by Classicism and the parents of a thousand imitations (they each published books of their designs), were by three great craftsmen in particular: Thomas Chippendale (1718–1779), George Hepplewhite (d. 1786) and, my favourite, Thomas Sheraton (1751–1806).

Building wasn't all plain sailing, however, and cowboy builders are nothing new. Poor Henry Purefoy of Buckinghamshire planned a new servants' hall in the late 1730s. His first stonemason was useless, so he was replaced; but the second was no better: 'This is the third day you have been from my work,' Purefoy reproached him in September 1738. 'I think you are a very unworthy man to neglect it so this fine weather.' Finally some of the masonry was finished, but then Purefoy had a nightmare getting carpenters to lay floors. Then he ordered a marble fireplace from London, had to wait three months for it, and when it arrived it was the wrong size, partly broken and with bits missing. It took four months to get that sorted out, by which time Purefoy found that a black marble slab destined for another room wasn't marble at all, but fake. It took four months more to sort that out, and the saga was still going on in 1741, when records of it cease.

Chiswick House, designed by the Duke of Burlington himself (he was known as the 'architect earl') and William Kent, was inspired by the Villa Capra near Vicenza.

Foreign artists were attracted here by English patrons. Canaletto painted some agreeable cityscapes of London for sale to local patrons; and Georg Friedrich Händel, that most English of composers, arrived from his native town of Halle (via, Hanover, where else?) at the age of 26 in 1711. Handel (as he became) stayed, and his music is still used prominently in ceremonies of state to this day. At the time, he wasn't popular with everyone. Thomas Hearne, the Oxford don and antiquary, dismissed him and his orchestra at the time as 'a lowsy crewe of foreign fidlers'. (But Hearne also dismissed Vanbrugh as 'a blockhead'.)

Of all the arts, drama fared least well in this period. It had enjoyed two golden eras in the last century or so, but, despite the best efforts of brilliantly successful actor-managers like David Garrick (a man of Huguenot stock, by the way, and one of those irritating people to whom nothing but good ever happened), nothing of any real worth reached the stage during the reigns of the first two Georges, with one or two notable exceptions, such as John Gay's *The Beggar's Opera*. The next two major playwrights, Oliver Goldsmith (c. 1730–1774) and Richard Sheridan (1751–1816), would make themselves felt later in the century. Poetry, too, was in something of a trough, apart from Thomas Gray (whose *Elegy written in a Country Churchyard* and *On a Favourite Cat, Drowned in a Tub of Gold Fishes* most of us remember from school; and maybe James Thomson (*Sophonisba* and *The Seasons*). But a great age of poetic expression would come at the end of the eighteenth and beginning of the nineteenth centuries, with Byron, Keats, and Shelley, Blake and the Lakeland Poets.

This was, however, the time when the novel began to appear in a recognisably modern form. Printing had become cheaper and easier, books were more readily available, the middle classes were literate and many of the women who belonged to it had leisure to spend reading. Most novels deal with contemporary issues and themes, and among the great writers of the eighteenth century can be counted Fielding, Richardson, Laurence Sterne (whose extraordinary *Tristram Shandy* in some ways prefigures *Ulysses*) and Tobias Smollett. Fielding and Smollett are essential reading for the family historian wishing to capture the true flavour of these times – and the English they use is robust and accessible.

The first half of the eighteenth century also had its dark side. Conditions for the poor had not improved despite a gradual increase in prosperity, which indeed was very evident at the top end of society. Great houses were being built, and fortunes made and spent, but infant mortality was still running at 20 per cent in the first year of life.

Even the concept of how babies came about wasn't understood. No one knew about ovulation; there were theories that children were produced when semen fertilised menstrual blood. It was even regarded as possible for women to give birth to creatures other than human babies – dogs, cats or rabbits, for example. So we should not make the mistake of thinking that, just because it spawned a phenomenal number of extraordinarily gifted people – Bishops Butler and Berkeley, Clive of India, the Wesley brothers, Captain Cook, Dr Johnson, James Watt, James Boswell, Edmund Burke – the list goes on and on – the 18th century, and our ancestors' beliefs with it, in general did not remain remote from our own age and our own thinking.

With Queen Anne's death in 1714 the Stuart dynasty finally came to an end. Her successor was a great-grandson of James I. His mother, Sophia, was a daughter of James I's only daughter, Elizabeth of Bohemia. Sophia had married the Elector of Hanover (Hanover being one of the many more-or-less small kingdoms Germany was made up of at the time) and was herself a Protestant. Her son, George, became the first Hanoverian King of England as George I on 1 August 1714.

THE YOUNG MAN WOULD CERTAINLY COME BACK WITH SOME ANTIQUITIES OF HIS OWN, REAL OR FAKE, AND A SENSE OF RENAISSANCE AND CLASSICAL ARCHITECTURE WHICH HE HAD NOT HAD BEFORE

George I was perceived by the general public as 'too German', and dispised for his failure to speak the language and his succession of German mistresses.

George knew full well that he had been given the throne in order to preclude any Catholic succession. He was 54 years old in 1714, he didn't speak English (and never learned it), he didn't like Britain or the British, and he spent most of his time at home in Hanover anyway. He didn't even bring his family over, though he did import two mistresses. He'd placed his wife under house arrest after twelve years of marriage in 1694, as he suspected her of adultery. She remained confined until her death in 1726. His two children were George – the future George II – and Sophia. The two Georges, father and son, cordially disliked one another. In himself, George was what his contemporary Lady Mary Wortley Montagu (a delightful and much-travelled woman whose letters have survived) described with her usual candour as 'an honest blockhead'.

Clothing and cleanliness

Lady Mary is also interesting on the ever-present subject of hygiene and her attitude, though to be fair she might have been teasing a rude interlocutor, shows how little regard our forebears had for it, for she once said to someone who'd remarked that her hands were not as clean as they might be, 'If you call that dirty, you should see my feet!'

Our ancestors were not very interested in keeping clean. They didn't shave their body hair, and they seldom washed or cleaned their teeth. They wouldn't have been as sensitive to human odours as we are, since everyone to a greater or lesser extent, stank. If anything, stink would be covered up with scents, and dirt with make-up, which was another source of disease, since medical knowledge was in the doldrums, and the same preparations were being used as had been two or three hundred years earlier. Men and women used a base compounded of white lead; rouge might be derived from red leather, and lip-colour from carmine or from coloured ground plaster-of-Paris. False eyebrows of mouse-skin were sometimes stuck on, and patches of diverse colours in various shapes, made of silk, velvet or paper, stuck to the face, often to cover small pox scars.

Clothes were handmade and expensive – few had many, and they were seldom if ever washed. Everyone, great and small, had lice – Pepys' maid combed them out of his hair regularly, and he lived in an era when men shaved their heads and wore wigs in order to keep the lice down. But we must remember that to our ancestors such things were facts of life and they were unconscious of them, as they were to the way they must have smelt – just as we are of the constant drone of traffic, the glare of electric light day and night (who in a city of any size ever experiences true silence or darkness, who of us sees the night sky in its true glory?) and the smell of car exhaust. And as for dirt, who in a big city doesn't have to change his shirt daily (something James Boswell, Johnson's friend and biographer, was already choosing to do in London towards the end of the eighteenth century)?

Charles II let his spaniels pup on his bed, and at least once on a Royal progress his courtiers defecated all over the house they were staying in. The diarist Samuel Pepys once at his house involuntarily surprised a visiting duchess crouched over a chamber-pot under a table in the dining-room: no one was embarrassed. The bidet had been introduced in France in about 1700 (the words means 'old nag' in French as you have to straddle the thing as you would a horse), but was condemned here as being immoral – if the genital area was clean, it would be attractive. There was a fear of water that was rational, since water was pretty impure; and public baths had for a long time been associated with sexual dalliance and brothels, but that only partly explains why, for example, men did tend to keep their

Lady Mary Montagu
(1689–1762).

genitalia clean, but women didn't. Again the reason may be found in prudery: private parts were associated with sex and therefore immorality: properly brought-up people weren't even supposed to look at their own pudenda! Yet at the same time, though they wore chemises and petticoats, women didn't wear knickers, and the modern brassiere was quite unknown. In his *Diary*, Samuel Pepys and his cronies more than once have a good laugh as some unfortunate woman falls in a ditch or from a coach, and exposes her privates.

Underwear on the whole didn't come in until the invention of the spinning jenny made cotton faster and cheaper to produce. Early mass-produced underwear featured the Union Suit – combined long-johns (good for warmth in those uncentrally heated days) with an undoable flap at the bottom back. Knickers for women appeared in the mid-nineteenth century when the crinoline became fashionable, for reasons of modesty and warmth.

Poor men might still wear a loincloth, but for most this had long been replaced by a loose pair of leggings called braies, which the wearer stepped into and then tied round the waist and calves, like breeches. Knee-breeches in fine fabrics followed, as did the codpiece, which was separate and could be untied, enabling a man to urinate without removing his trousers. Henry VIII started a fashion for padding the codpiece, which with time became more and more outrageous until the end of the sixteenth century.

As for toilet cleanliness, toilet paper was invented by the Chinese, in 1391. The Imperial Bureau of Supplies began producing 720,000 sheets a year for the emperor's use, each sheet measuring about 60cm by 100cm. Earlier, the Romans used a sponge on a stick which they

Portrait of George II by Isaac Wood, 1738.

moistened in salt water, or wool soaked in rosewater if you were posh. Muslims and Buddhists today, deeming toilet paper unhygienic, also use water. In the Middle Ages, hanks of sheep's wool came in handy, as well as grass, leaves, or balls of hay. Sailors might use an old rope's end. There was also something called a gompf stick – a kind of scraper kept in the privy. Later still, old newspaper or leaves from discarded books were recycled, though in the countryside the old methods remained, and shitting in a river or stream was very common. In modern Nepal you see this practised, but the countryside there is strewn with toilet paper, which at altitude and in the dry cold does not decompose, left by the thousands of trekking tourists.

To return to George I; it has to be said that he was probably a pretty unpleasant piece of work, but he had two unconscious virtues: he wasn't interested in power and he wasn't interested in religion. This attitude helped maintain the tolerance established under William III, since George was blessed with intelligent advisers.

Robert Walpole and the East India Company

One side-effect of George I's total lack of interest in his new realm was that power passed from the throne into the hands of politicians. The first Cabinet government occurred in his reign, and his chief minister, Robert Walpole, not only became the first prime minister, but also established Whig rule, which was to last for half a century. Walpole was a Norfolk squire who spent a fortune on wine and lived so liberally that he weighed about 140kg. Like most of his contemporaries he used his position to line his pockets, but was essentially a good and intelligent man. His chance of real self-advancement came in 1720. It was a period when people had begun to speculate enthusiastically with their money, and in 1710 the Tory government of the day granted a charter to a company trading mainly in slaves to Spanish South America, arranging with it to take over part of the national debt, which, as a result of various wars had spiralled to 50 million pounds. The South Sea Company, designed to stand behind the Tories as a counterbalance to the Bank of England and the East India Company, which were controlled by the Whigs, had secured to it, under government guarantee, actual or anticipated commercial rights, in anticipation of which it took over nine million of the national debt. Various speculative financial schemes were floated, and by 1719 the company was proposing to take over the whole massive debt and advance £7,500,000 to the government. The apparent success of the company started a kind of gold rush, with speculators and investors of every class and pocket thronging to get in on the act. Shares valued at £100 in January had gone up to £1100 by July; but people had been investing in a house built on sand. Many of the complicated sections which made up the company were fraudulently conceived, and as these were exposed so they, and the money, melted away. By the autumn prices had fallen back to £150. Many were ruined, but Walpole, who'd always warned against the venture, now moved in to clear up the mess. He re-established the company on a sure footing, sorted out the complexity of the debt, gained the gratitude of the nation and assured himself of power for the next 21 years, during which he managed George I and, for much of his reign, George II. George II could at least speak some English; Walpole had to communicate with his father in Latin, the only language they had in common. But the first two Georges as people were, frankly, a pain. They hated each other, they hated England and they thought everything, from carriages to cookery, was better back home in Hanover.

A nation of alcoholics

Meanwhile, there was nothing to be smug about. Poor hygiene and disease – small pox had replaced bubonic plague but was no less virulent – meant that the population was actually declining. There were perhaps 50,000 prostitutes operating in London, and though men were beginning to use sheaths made of sheep's gut or fish-skin (tied on with a red ribbon) to protect themselves, pox (as gonorrhoea was popularly called) was common. One suggested remedy was a diet of spiders spread on brown bread.

Dental health was grim too. Though the Chinese had invented the toothbrush in 1498, using boar- or horse-hair, it didn't catch on here until much later, and although the French were using them by the seventeenth century, they weren't commercially produced here until the master brushmaker William Addis did so in about 1780. Toothpaste (of a sort) arrived in the 1820s. Meanwhile, people washed their mouths with vinegar or chewed

Scenes of drunkeness and debauchery in 'Beer Street', by William Hogarth in 1751. It is coupled with a similar engraving called 'Gin Lane'.

aniseed, mint or cloves. Toothpicks were also in use and if all else failed bad breath could be concealed or wafted away by the use of a fan. If the worst came to the worst and you had to have a tooth taken out, there were professional dentists, but barbers and wigmakers did the job too, as did blacksmiths and pharmacists, farriers and cobblers, wielding pliers or special claw-like contraptions to twist a tooth free.

This whole situation wasn't helped by the arrival in about 1720 of gin. Cheap to produce, this was to be the opiate and the bane of – principally – the London poor for the next thirty years. Beer might have some slight nutritional value; gin had none, and you could get drunker on it quicker. It spread like wildfire. By 1735 there were 7000 gin-shops in Middlesex alone. During 1743, when the population of London was about 625,000, eight million gallons of gin were consumed in the capital alone. The government, fearful of riots, put off efforts to control it, though one or two measures were timidly passed. But a time came when one in every eight Londoners was dying of drink.

It provided oblivion from your woes at 1d. a quart (i.e. more or less 0.5p a litre), and was

Thomas Coram established the Foundling Hospital in Lambs Conduit Fields, Bloomsbury, London in 1741.

CHAPTER 5

in truth like opium was later to poor Chinese. Horrible stories of its effects have come down to us: of an intoxicated nurse, mistaking a baby for a log, and putting it on a fire; of a mother, redeeming her infant from a poorhouse where it had been provided with new clothes, killing it and selling the garment to buy gin.

William Hogarth, perhaps the greatest British artist of his day, concentrated on satire and social realism in his work. His famous series *The Rake's Progress*, *The Harlot's Progress* and *Marriage à la Mode* are all well known, but his most powerful didactic engraving is *Gin Lane*, executed in 1751, which shows an identifiable London district, then a sink of poverty and iniquity, St Giles in central London. In the distance a statue of George II can be seen on the bizarre pyramidal steeple of the church of St George's, Bloomsbury – a building by Wren's talented pupil Nicholas Hawksmoor, which still survives. King George presides over a terrible scene of abandoned drunkenness and death. Designed to be reproduced as a cheap print, there's no doubt of the practical application Hogarth meant this appalling scene to have: to those who could read, a set of verses underneath hammers the message home:

Gin, cursed Fiend, with Fury fraught
Makes human Race a Prey.
It enters by a deadly Draught,
And steals our Life away.

Hogarth may have produced the picture at the behest of his friend and admirer Henry Fielding, the novelist (best known for *Tom Jones*) and magistrate. Fielding had long campaigned for legislation to counter the evils of gin, which culminated in the Gin Act of 1751, which taxed the drink out of the reach of the poor, who had to return to beer, which was believed to be wholesome, and in praise of which Hogarth produced a pendant piece, *Beer Street*. It shows a selection of staunch and healthy Britons, most of the men pot-bellied but vigorous, grasping tankards; and the verses are of a very different character:

Beer, happy Produce of our Isle
Can sinewy Strength impart.
And wearied with Fatigue and Toil,
Can chear each manly Heart.

Child neglect

The artist's concern for the plight of his fellow-Londoners is further borne out by his close association with Thomas Coram, a retired sea-captain who in 1741 established a home for abandoned or orphaned children – the Foundling Hospital. The treatment of children by the desperate poor, in a society completely inured to death, could be appalling. As Christopher Hibbert reports in his study, *The English*:

In many of the wretched overcrowded homes of the poor the arrival of yet another baby was a disaster. Elder brothers and sisters might be put out as servants or to some kind of other child labour from the age of seven or even six, but even so it often proved beyond the means or the wit of parents to feed a further child. Unwanted babies were left out in the streets to die or were strangled and thrown onto dung-heaps or into open drains.

BEER MIGHT HAVE SOME SLIGHT NUTRITIONAL VALUE; GIN HAD NONE, AND YOU COULD GET DRUNKER ON IT QUICKER. IT SPREAD LIKE WILDFIRE. BY 1735 THERE WERE 7000 GINSHOPS IN MIDDLESEX ALONE

Henry Fielding, the English novelist and dramatist, best-known for his novel, *Tom Jones*.

Those that survived were an irksome charge on the parish and were put out to parish nurses, notorious as gin drinkers, who were known to maim or disfigure them so that when they were old enough to go out begging they might by exciting more pity be more successful.

Babies unlucky enough to be too sickly to be worth even this ghastly investment were often given enough gin to kill them.

Coram's Hospital was much admired, but Coram ran it on his own, and it ruined him. Luckily he had friends who clubbed together to get up a pension for him, but it was often only the initiative of individual philanthropists like Coram that brought any relief to the poor. When the government tried to open the Hospital to the entire country a few years later, it was swamped and the experiment ended in disaster.

Coram was not alone. Henry Fielding, who wrote the life of a real-life villain of his day, *Jonathan Wild*, and knew the London underworld well, undertook with his brother, also a magistrate, to form the Bow Street Runners, named after the court in Bow Street where John Fielding presided. The Runners, who were formed originally as writ-servers, developed into a kind of proto-police force; but there was no actual national police force in Britain until 1829.

Social mobility

Then as now, though, London and every large city existed on a number of levels, and those on one often had no contact with and sometimes little awareness of those on another. There were signs, however, of increasing social mobility in the aspiring middle class, and by making money even hitherto humble tradesmen could move upwards. Some, like Samuel Pepys, could afford their own carriage. Some even applied for coats-of-arms for that finishing touch.

Daniel Defoe (1660–1731) was the son of a butcher called Foe. Daniel embroidered his surname to make it classier, and began his own career in hosiery. Then he managed a brickworks which he part-owned, dealt in textiles and became a member of the Butchers' Company. He took part in the Monmouth rebellion against James II, and became a friend of William III, for whom he acted as a spy. He travelled widely abroad, and in England as well, leaving a terrific account of what he saw, perhaps particularly interesting for his take on provincial England, which doesn't get a huge amount of historical press, though you will find local historians and historical societies helpful away from London, and there's quite a lot of local and privately printed literature available to the amateur genealogist in this respect.

All this about Defoe, admittedly an exceptional man, is to show what someone of humble origins could now become if he set his mind to it. There were no shackles to bind him to a place or a master if he chose not to be so bound. Of course, for the majority that remained true, and Defoe took risks most of us would baulk at. He was put in the pillory three times for seditious publications, and the pillory could be a serious punishment – people didn't just throw rotten tomatoes, but bricks and chunks of broken glass, and those in the pillory often died there. Defoe was lucky – on one occasion the sympathetic mob pelted him with flowers – but he wasn't afraid of sticking his neck out. All the time he was writing – this had become a popular form of communication with the rise of literacy – even though Hogarth's admonishment about the evils of gin was pictorial there were still words to back it up – and so indefatigable was he that he bought from Alexander Selkirk, the sailor who was the model for Robinson Crusoe, all the man's notes and papers, and from them, when he was himself in his late fifties, created the first of a whole series of popular novels he was to write between then and his death. (*À propos* literacy, you wouldn't believe the number of pirates, privateers and buccaneers who kept journals and published their memoirs.)

But other men were making a different kind of progress. Industry of one kind and another had existed for centuries, but not on any scale. Now the first murmurings of the Industrial Revolution could be heard. They were pretty modest at first – in 1701 the splendidly named Berkshireman Jethro Tull invented the wheeled seed-drill. But from now on wheat and barley would be grown in rows, and less seed would be wasted than it had been when strewn by the sower. It pointed to what was going to be a profound transformation of the way we live.

George I died in Germany, on the way back to his beloved Hanover, in June 1727, and his son, who happened to be in Richmond (the one near London) at the time, succeeded him. George Augustus made the usual formal statement of love and duty, etc., but he would not be much of an improvement on his father and he would last a long time – 33 years. One redeeming feature was his wife, the intelligent and sympathetic Caroline of Anspach, another German, but one of sophisticated and cosmopolitan outlook. Unfortunately, she died in 1737. George had been devoted to her, but, like all the Hanoverians, he detested his son and the feeling was mutual. Frederick, Prince of Wales, however, predeceased his father in 1751. The succession would be through his son, another George.

But that's a long way in the future. Walpole was still in power, maintaining peace with Britain's neighbours, and getting on well with Caroline, which was good, since George II didn't like him much himself. His vice-chamberlain for ten years, John Hervey, looked back on him less than fondly:

No English or even French cook could dress [prepare] a dinner; no confectioner set out a dessert; no English player could act; no English coachman could drive or English jockey ride, nor were any English horses fit to be ridden; no Englishman knew how to come into a room, nor any English woman how to dress herself ... nor any man or woman in England whose conversation was to be borne – the one as he said, talking of nothing but their dull politics, and the other nothing but their ugly clothes. Whereas at Hanover, all these things were to be found in the utmost perfection.

Daniel Defoe, one of the founders of the 'English novel'.

Walpole falls out of favour

Time passed, and the people began to tire of Walpole – they were already as fed up with George as he was with them – and by the late 1730s things began to falter. There was a serious falling-out between Prince Frederick and his parents; Queen Caroline died, taking her sensible counsel with her; and a young Whig called William Pitt began to be prominent. Pitt and his associates were loud in their criticism of Walpole, who had sensibly tried to avoid the expense and, as he saw it, futility of engaging in any more wars. He wanted to preserve and crystallise the British economy and political system. But unavoidable problems were brewing in the form of Spain, which was beginning to rally, and to assert its long-held belief that the British should not be allowed to trade in its American domains. Spanish ships stopped and searched British merchantmen. This was already regarded as an affront by the British, who hadn't had much time for the Spanish since Elizabeth's day, but then, in 1731, one Captain Robert Jenkins allegedly had one of his ears cut off by a Spanish coastguard. God knows why it took him so long, but he produced the ear (some people believed he'd actually lost it in a brawl), preserved in a bottle, before parliament in 1738, claiming restitution. He couched his appeal for justice in very purple terms: his brig, the *Rebecca*, had been accosted by the Spanish off Havana on its way back home, and, in an altercation, the commander of the coastguards had cut the ear off, declaring that he'd have done the same thing even if Jenkins had been the King of England. It almost sounds like a put-up job.

Whatever else, it was the opportunity Pitt and his belligerent 'Young Patriots' had been looking for, and it spelled the beginning of the end for Walpole, though to be fair even he must have been able to see the inevitability of being sucked into fresh combat. Europe was still very volatile. Austria, France and Spain were already at each other's throats. British merchants clamoured for their right to the lucrative South Sea trade to be protected or asserted by force of arms; the economic arguments would not be gainsaid, let alone those of simple *amour-propre*. And the British were spoiling for a fight.

The War of Jenkins' Ear, a name as foolish as the conflict, broke out on 19 October 1739. Walpole, watching the jubilant populace of London, remarked drily, 'They are ringing their bells now, but soon they will be wringing their hands.' Certainly the fight was inconclusive, though it's memorable for two reasons, the introduction of 'grog' to seamen by Admiral Vernon, who wore a naval cloak of coarse wool known as grogham and therefore bore the nickname 'Old Grogham'; and the appearance in 1740 of a song which was probably written by the poet James Thomson for a masque about Alfred the Great:

When Britain first, at heaven's command,
Arose from out the azure main,
This was the charter of the land,
And guardian angels sang this strain:
Rule, Britannia!
Britannia, rule the waves!
Britons never will be Slaves.

The key is that the angels weren't making a *statement* that Britannia rules the waves anyway, as we sometimes mis-sing the words today, but were *commanding* us to do so. And so of course we did, later in the century, and for some time to come.

Country life

And although history was being made in the capital, we must not forget that 80 per cent of the population still lived and worked on the land. Country squires governed still, in their generally fair, but deeply provincial way. Henry Fielding's portraits in *Tom Jones* of Squire Western and Mr Allworthy, the first a drunken boor but a good country sportsman and not a bad sort at all, the second a more rational and sophisticated manager of his estates, are good examples of the types that could be found. Life in the country was probably pleasanter for poor workers than it was in the towns. Christopher Hibbert comments that:

Horace Walpole referred to the East Anglian variety [of such men] as 'mountains of roast beef'. They spoke in the same thick dialects as their tenants whose prejudices they shared. They were patriotic and stubbornly xenophobic, particularly disliking the French. They also disliked nabobs whose fortunes inflated the cost of country life and the great lords who were intent on buying them out ... They heartily agreed with one of their number, William Cattel of Yorkshire, who violently opposed a proposal for a national census in the 1750s, a 'presumptuous' and 'abandoned' proposal which, if put into effect, would provide dangerous information for enemies abroad as well as enemies at home, 'placemen [government lackeys] and tax-masters'. The proposal in short was 'totally subversive of the last remains of English liberty' in the pursuit of which William Thornton, rather than provide an account of the number and circumstances of his family, would order his servants to give any interfering official of the government 'the discipline of the horse pond'.

But again there was a downside. The rich minority was buying up more and more land, and enclosure was on the increase. The ordinary smallholding yeoman's fortunes began to decline again. Communication around the country remained poor, as despite the introduction of turnpikes to help drum up some money to pay for road maintenance, people refused to pay, and even beat up the wretches who maintained the tollbooths (Pitt himself was guilty of passing a pike without paying), and so cross-country journeys remained nightmarish and long, and weren't helped by the number of highwaymen, courteous and non-violent as many of them genuinely were, who'd nevertheless relieve you of your valuables (and of course there were highwaymen who *weren't* romantic gentlemen-of-the-road types or demobbed army officers on their uppers, who would cheerfully break your limbs and rape your women into the bargain). After all, if caught they were going to be hanged anyway.

Among the rural criminal class you could also find poachers and smugglers. Hunting was a way of life for the English country gentleman, and has remained so to this day for a parcel of them, though most of us would probably agree with Oscar Wilde when he described a fox-hunt as 'the unspeakable in full pursuit of the uneatable', or Dr Johnson's description of angling as 'a stick and a string, with a worm on one end and a fool on the other'. Indeed, sports *per se* were defined as Hunting, Shooting and Fishing. Anything else, and anything whose play involved the use of a ball, was a Game. Meanwhile, shooting had largely supplanted falconry, and fox-hunting was gradually replacing deer-hunting. Deer, indeed, were bred as ornaments to parks, not as a prey animal any more.

But well-stocked streams, rivers and parks encouraged poorer folk to help themselves. They braved mantraps, spring-guns and legbreakers – as well as the death sentence – to supply themselves and city-folk with cut-price game.

THEY HEARTILY AGREED WITH ONE OF THEIR NUMBER, WILLIAM CATTEL OF YORKSHIRE, WHO VIOLENTLY OPPOSED A PROPOSAL FOR A NATIONAL CENSUS IN THE 1750S, A 'PRESUMPTUOUS' AND 'ABANDONED' PROPOSAL WHICH, IF PUT INTO EFFECT, WOULD PROVIDE DANGEROUS INFORMATION FOR ENEMIES ABROAD AS WELL AS ENEMIES AT HOME, 'PLACEMEN [GOVERNMENT LACKEYS] AND TAX-MASTERS''

Highwaymen terrorized public highways during the 17th and 18th centuries.

Smugglers were tough men, often laid-off seamen (as were pirates) who brought lace, brandy and wine, tobacco, tea and gin (good Dutch stuff this time) across from France and Holland without the knowledge of the Revenue. Though they were known to be brutal to excisemen who crossed them, many were rather like the cigarette-and-booze traffickers of today, though more romantically portrayed, at least. Ordinary people profited from their labours, and few minded their activities. The author of *The Rights of Man*, Tom Paine (1737–1809), was sacked from a post as an exciseman for winking at goods brought in. But the exploits of smugglers were often celebrated in popular songs:

Said the Captain to the Crew
We have skipt the Revenue
I can see the Lights of Dover on the Lee.
Tip the Signal to the Swan,
And anchor broadside on;
And out with the Kegs of *eau de vie.*

The little War of Jenkins' Ear brought about Walpole's fall. He was 66 in 1742 and had been at the helm for over two decades. But he showed no sign of tiring, and he went with great reluctance, accepting an earldom as a sweetener and going home to Houghton, where he died three years later. Maybe the nation was tired of him. George would certainly miss him; he'd carried the king, been his manager and kept him financially sound for the entire reign so far. But even the king couldn't save him.

Political manoeuvrings foreign expansion

PITT'S BELLIGERENCY
WAS PAYING OFF,
INCREASING BRITISH
INTERNATIONAL
POWER WITH EVERY
STEP HE TOOK

Now there was some jockeying for position among the British *nomenklatura*. There were maybe 1200 people of real wealth and influence in the country and they wanted to hang on in there. Walpole himself had lined his pockets to the extent that he could afford to spend £1500 a year on wine (and he avoided paying excise on it) and a good £365 a year on candles for Houghton alone; and he'd made sure that his son, Horace, the builder of the fantastic, mad little gothic Strawberry Hill, where he amassed a fabulous art collection, had a couple of fat sinecures to coast him through, as well.

Pitt, a copy-book political opportunist, tucked himself under the aegis of the Prince of Wales. Though he didn't become prime minister (the complexities of this phase of British politics are too great to go into here), he was *éminence grise* for decades, becoming secretary of state in 1756, but premier in all but name. His aggressive foreign policy earned him popular support, and he reasserted British naval supremacy, and he did it by the only means possible – war.

In the meantime, in the early 1750s, British expansion was evident in a new area – India. We had owned Mumbai since Charles II's time, and our coastal trade there was energetic. Now, with the gradual decline of Dutch and Portuguese interests, we began to turn our intention to the interior, and that led to conflict with the French, already ensconced in Pondicherry. Our triumph there is due to the flawed but determined genius of Robert Clive – Clive of India – a former clerk who had attempted suicide at least once but now rose to the military and administrative occasion to which fate beckoned him.

After his first successes in India, Clive returned home, but went back to the sub-continent in 1756. At that time he was made aware that the Nawab of Bengal, Suraj-ud-Dawlah, had killed 123 Europeans in the atrocity of the so-called Black Hole of Calcutta. This Clive efficiently avenged, and in doing so broke the power of the French, Suraj's allies, though blame for the atrocity cannot be laid at their door. Clive himself did not earn the gratitude of the British nation, and, in one of the bouts of depression that plagued him all his life, ended it by an overdose in 1774, aged 49.

On the other side of the world another young Englishman was fighting to expand British (and crush French) overseas interests. We were by now embroiled in yet another war with the French, which had spread to their possessions in North America, and in 1759, the last year of George II's reign, the 32-year-old Major-General James Wolfe led his men in a daring ascent of cliffs known as the Heights of Abraham in Canada, thereby surprising the superior forces of the French general, the Marquis de Montcalm. Wolfe and Montcalm both died in or soon after the battle, but Britain won it, thereby securing Quebec, and future British rule of Canada (we already controlled European-occupied North America below the 'fifty-first parallel', but that, of course, was soon to change).

Pitt's belligerency was paying off, increasing British international power with every step he took. But George II died on 25 October 1760 at Kensington, and the grandson who succeeded him had been born in London and was more attuned to the British than either of his two predecessors. He also had a far greater interest in the management of his country.

One of our most popular and successful athletes, Colin's sporting prowess was most recently demonstrated when he was just pipped at the post in the 2005 *Strictly Come Dancing* final. But he's far more accustomed to winning. In his illustrious career, he set a 110 metre hurdles world record of 12.91 seconds in August 1993, which stood until as recently as July 2006, and Colin still holds the indoor world record for the 60 metre hurdles at 7.3 seconds, established in 1994. Colin's sporting achievements have been recognized by the award of an MBE in 1990 and a CBE in 1992. He has retired from the track but is well known these days as an authoritative sports commentator for the BBC.

Born Colin Ray Jackson, in Cardiff, on 18 February 1967, and still living in Wales, Colin feels himself to be a Welshman through and through. Descended from Jamaican immigrants who themselves claim a rich ethnic heritage, Colin was aware of – and fascinated by – this mixture and set off on a voyage of discovery. To find out more, he also decided to take a DNA test to find out where his roots lay. But Colin started his research where everyone who can should: by talking to the family.

The first of his family to arrive in the UK was Colin's maternal grandfather, the splendidly named Everil Emmanuel Augustus Dunkley, known as Dee, who arrived from Jamaica in 1955, settling in Cardiff because of the work opportunities provided by the coal and steel industries. His wife, Maria, who had been born in Panama, returned to Panama to look after her sick father when Angela was three years old. Dee and Maria became estranged and Dee refused to allow the children to move to Panama. Maria tried in vain to get the children back, and lost all contact with them when they moved to Wales. But after 40 years they were finally reunited when Maria visited Colin's family in Cardiff.

Dee, working as a coalman and later in the steel industry, did well and bought a house on Constellation Street, Cardiff, which still stands. In those days it was hard to find places to rent as landlords didn't want to accept immigrants. Dee's four-bedroom home had enough space to house Angela, her sister Winsome and her brother Tony. The spare room was let to fellow immigrants and one of them, Ossie, who came over in 1962, fell in love with Angela. At this time, there was plenty of work: Cardiff was Britain's largest coal-exporting port and expansion meant work for people from Ireland, Scotland, the Caribbean, Africa, Malta and Cyprus. These were the dying days of the British Empire.

Ossie and Angela married and settled down to start a family in Cardiff. Talking to them both about their immediate ancestors, Colin was told that Ossie's mother looked Indian. It's possible that she could have been descended from the Indian indentured labourers who were brought to Jamaica during the peak of the British Empire.

Colin decided to go back to Jamaica to investigate his father's side of the family. He hadn't visited for 15 years but, although a bit nervous, was spurred on by the results of his DNA test, which revealed him to be 55% sub-Saharan African, 38% European and 7% Native American. Colin was shocked that he was only 55% sub-Saharan African and very surprised by the reference to Native American.

Colin Jackson

Colin's maternal grandfather,
Everil Emmanual Augustus
Dunkley, known as Dee.

OPPOSITE
Colin's parents, Ossie and
Angela Jackson, on their
wedding day.

Jamaica was first colonised by the Spaniards, and their arrival spelled the end for the native Taino Indians, some of whom managed to survive inland, but most of whom succumbed to the sword and the diseases brought by the European invaders. Kingston is one of the largest natural deep-water harbours in the world, and its value was quickly recognised. When the British took the island from Spain in 1655, they established sugar plantations and began to import slaves from Africa to work them. Colin's 7% Native American DNA showed that he is descended from the Tainos, which is where he probably gets his high cheekbones, almond eyes and open face.

The Tainos mixed with slaves who had escaped from the Spanish and who made their own 'Maroon' communities, so it's possible that Colin's remoter ancestors were Maroons – or *cimarrones* (from the Spanish *cima*, summit) – runaway slaves who fled to the mountains in great numbers and established themselves there, no doubt intermarrying with the surviving Taino populations. So successful were the Maroons that in 1739 the British drew up a formal treaty with them in order to legitimise their self-government, though rebellions continued throughout the 18th century. Learning this, Colin wondered whether it could be the root of his own rebellious nature and his determination to succeed!

At the Spanish Town Record Office, Colin was able to trace his paternal grandmother, Marie Wilson, and her parents, Jacob and Eugenia. Colin's own father

still has cousins living on the island – Speedy, Alderman and Justin – and they were able to tell Colin a bit more about his great-grandparents, who had ten children. What's more, there was a sporting streak: two close forebears were called Speedy, and one first-cousin-once-removed had been a boxer.

Archives going back earlier than the 1880s in Jamaica are rare, but local genealogist Cynthia Roser was able to track down Colin's great-great-grandfather, Adam Wilson, who died in 1849. He was almost certainly born a slave, but would have become emancipated with the abolition of slavery by the British in 1834.

Colin finds out that his ancestors were Moravian Christians – a Protestant sect

COLIN REFLECTED ON THE TURBULENT TIMES BOTH SIDES OF HIS FAMILY HAD LIVED
THROUGH, AND ON THE RICH CULTURAL AND ETHICAL COCKTAIL THAT HAD SHAPED HIM.

which split from the main Hussite movement in 1450, and was essentially Evangelical
Lutheran in nature. This choice originally expressed rejection of the Catholicism of the
original Spanish colonists and slave-owners. Militant slave rebellions took place very
frequently during the late 17th, and throughout the 18th century in Jamaica, but
as none took place at Greenmount it's unlikely that any of Colin's forebears
were involved.

After abolition, the Moravian Church bought a former plantation at a place called
Maidstone and converted it into smallholdings for freed slaves to work. Colin's great-
great-grandfather Adam had one such plot, proving that he was a member of the

Church; and he worked hard enough on it to be able to buy another.

Colin then turned his attention to his mother's ancestry. He had a photograph of her mother, who was born in Panama, whose skin was strikingly light. From her birth certificate he learned that his great-grandparents were Richard Augustus Packer and Gladys Campbell, the latter born in 1888. The surname Campbell suggested the Scottish link already supposed by family tradition, and a little more research revealed his maternal great-great-grandparents to be Duncan M. Campbell and Albertina Wallace. There was a sizeable Scottish community in Kingston in the 19th century, and after some initial difficulty Colin was able to identify his great-great-grandfather as belonging to that community. Albertina was his maid, so Colin tried to investigate what their relationship was. He found out that it wasn't unusual for white men to have a relationship with a Jamaican and for the couple to bear children. Colin hoped that theirs was a loving partnership. However, the family evidently fell on hard times after the earthquake of 1907 that devastated Kingston.

Colin was unable to trace a death certificate for Albertina, nor was he able to establish for sure why Richard and Gladys moved to Panama, though the most likely reason is that they went there in search of work. Many thousands of Afro-Caribbeans arrived in Panama from the 1880s to work on the construction of the Panama Canal. Of an estimated 85,000 workers, a large number succumbed to malaria or yellow fever, and only 22,000 are recorded as returning home. But despite the risks, Panama and the canal continued to attract Jamaicans and other Caribbean islanders as its construction continued into the early 19th century, because of the much higher rates of pay (from a Caribbean point of view) that were offered.

At the Miraflor Museum in Panama, Colin looked for evidence that Richard and Gladys had worked on the Canal. A search for Gladys drew a blank, but Richard turned up trumps: he was listed as working for six months in 1905 for the canal company as a hospital attendant at $25 a month. He then left its employ, but Colin knew that he and his wife remained in Panama where their daughter, his grandmother, Maria, was born in 1921. She was taken by Gladys to complete her education in Jamaica, but returned to look after her sick father in Panama, leaving her own husband and three children to do so. She was not to see them again for thirty years.

As he laid flowers on his grandmother's grave in Panama, Colin reflected on the turbulent times both sides of his family had lived through, and on the rich cultural and ethical cocktail that had shaped him.

Colin Jackson

CHAPTER SIX

Age of Renewal

(from the Restoration to the early eighteenth century)

A CONTINUATION OF THE REPUBLIC WAS UNFEASIBLE, SO THE LEADERS OF THE COUNTRY, THE LANDED ARISTOCRACY, THE HIERARCHY OF THE CHURCH AND THOSE CROMWELLIANS WHO HAD THE DEXTERITY AND ACUMEN TO ADAPT, DECIDED TO INVITE CHARLES TO RETURN FROM FRANCE AS KING CHARLES II, WITH CERTAIN CONDITIONS INVOLVING RECOGNITION OF PARLIAMENT AND A DISAVOWAL OF THE DIVINE RIGHT OF KINGS. CHARLES ACCEPTED, THOUGH HE STILL HAD FAR MORE EXECUTIVE POWER THAN A MODERN BRITISH MONARCH, AND ASCENDED THE THRONE IN 1660, TO MUCH JUBILATION.

Charles II, who reigned from 1660-1685, was known as the 'Merry Monarch' due to his cheery disposition.

A Golden Age

To many, it was as if the sun had emerged from behind clouds, and indeed the period roughly between 1660 and 1710 would be regarded by many people as the Golden Age of British history, despite the shadows cast over it by the Great Plague in London in 1665 and the Great Fire of 1666. Intellectually, the period was certainly the best we've had. Though inevitably dominated by men, a short list of some who lived between the dates mentioned will give an idea of what a volcano of creativity and thought erupted then.

John Bunyan published *The Pilgrim's Progress* – quickly to become the most-read book in Britain after the Bible – in 1678; the great diarists Samuel Pepys and John Evelyn, whose works have left us with an incomparable record of their times, lived between 1633–1703 and 1620–1706 respectively; architecture is represented by Christopher Wren, the designer of St Paul's Cathedral, who was also an eminent astronomer and mathematician. With his colleague and fellow-scientist Robert Hooke he constructed the Monument which commemorates the Great Fire of London in such a way that it could also double as a mathematical instrument. Robert Boyle pushed forward the frontiers of physics and chemistry, while Isaac Newton dominated the field of mathematics, publishing his *Principia Mathematica* in 1687. William Dampier, the explorer and pirate, was the first Englishman to set foot in Australia, in 1699, seventy years before Captain Cook and without that lesser sailor's technical advantages; Dampier also wrote a study of the trade winds which was still in maritime use in the 1930s. The astronomer Edmond Halley spent a year on St Helena mapping the stars of the southern hemisphere, also wrote on the trade winds, and, with Giovanni Domenico Cassini, in 1680 identified from the observatory at Paris the great comet that bears his name.

Aphra Behn had a double career as a secret agent and our first well-known female playwright and novelist. Peter Lely now adapted his style of painting to the Restoration taste of Charles II. Literature saw the rise of Daniel Defoe, who wrote one of the first books in English that could truly be called a novel, *Robinson Crusoe* (though claims may be made for

Nell Gwyn was known as one of the greatest restoration actresses, with a superb talent for comic acting.

earlier books by John Lyly and Sir Philip Sidney), and John Dryden, whose *Annus Mirabilis* celebrates the triumphs and disasters of 1666 in 304 stanzas.

In the theatre, Restoration drama, with all its self-conscious cleverness, triviality and social bitchiness, was like champagne after the plain ale of the Puritans, who had closed down the playhouses. Charles adored the theatre, granted licences to William Davenant and Thomas Killigrew which gave them a virtual monopoly over productions in London, which flourished in an echo of the glory days sixty years earlier. Charles also confirmed that women should be allowed to act professionally on stage. Indeed, his most famous mistress was an orange-seller turned actress, Nell Gwyn. Restoration drama was more elitist than it had been in Shakespeare's day, and plays more assured and smoother in their construction (comedies were best; tragedies on the whole clunked a bit, and that went on until the 20th century); but it's hard to compare the two periods because they are so different. Theatres now had a form we would recognise, though the style of acting our ancestors went in for would strike us as wildly exaggerated. Most classes of society still attended, though prices, at between 1s. and 4s. a seat, were relatively high. You couldn't book in advance. The upper classes went to ogle each other, young toffs behaved like football hooligans, you might be

John Milton published his epic poem, Paradise Lost, in ten volumes in 1667.

pelted with orange peel or propositioned by a whore, but many of the plays themselves were of an extremely high standard, and are still performed today. What's more, perfectly respectable women could safely attend alone. Pepys, a typical member of the rising prosperous middle and business class, enjoyed going so much that he had to ration himself. A very short list of the best would include *The Man of Mode* by George Etherege, *The Way of the World* by William Congreve, *The Relapse* by Sir John Vanbrugh (also the architect of Blenheim and Castle Howard), *The Beggar's Opera* by John Gay and *The Beaux' Stratagem* by George Farquhar. I am getting a little beyond this chapter's scope with some of these, I admit, but the development of the Restoration stage into that of the eighteenth century is not something I can pursue here. I must, however, mention the truly awful rewrites of Shakespeare that began to appear, which gave such plays as *King Lear* and *Romeo and Juliet* happy endings. Dryden and Davenant managed to transform *The Tempest* into a rather smutty comic opera. It ought to be revived!

In poetry, John Milton, the prominent Puritan, and Latin Secretary to Oliver Cromwell despite having lost his sight in 1652, published his masterpiece, *Paradise Lost,* though its themes had been in his mind since 1641. Since then, Milton had parted from his Royalist first wife, survived her death, remarried, only to lose his second wife after two years, and married again for the last time in 1662. Milton is widely regarded as one of the triumvirate of great English poets, with Chaucer and Shakespeare. John Milton is just one of a number of late seventeenth-century poets, among whom John Dryden, Andrew Marvell and Henry Vaughan perhaps lead the field. But that is a subjective choice. Other poets, Rochester and Sedley for example, wrote bawdy, even pornographic, lyrics that reflected the licentiousness of the court, as did the dirty bits in Restoration comedies. But all that was just part of the overreaction to Puritanism.

The end of the seventeenth century also saw the appearance of many important institutions. The appropriately named Ways and Means Act of 1694 led to the foundation of the Bank of England. The Society for the Promotion of Christian Knowledge, founded in 1698, was instrumental in developing schools for the children of the poor, education for women became more liberal and more profound (though not much); and Charles II, himself keenly interested in science, founded the Royal Society in 1662. Charles also commissioned John Ogilby to undertake the first comprehensive survey of the country's roads (which were dismally maintained). The result, Ogilby's *Britannia*, was published in 1675. Our possessions abroad began to expand. In 1664 we took New Amsterdam from the Dutch. Charles renamed it in honour of his brother, the Duke of York.

Geography, meteorology, hydrography and astronomy were studied not only to advance knowledge, but principally for the very practical reason that such knowledge increased our advantages over the Netherlands and Spain, in both trade and war.

Spanish trading

Though the Golden Age of British piracy was early in the eighteenth century, plenty of our pirates and privateers, some based in the Caribbean, were already picking away at Spanish treasure ships, and many followed Drake's much earlier lead and rounded the Horn to rove the western coast of South America. Gradually the Spanish colonies there became better armed, but they had believed themselves invulnerable on the Pacific for decades. They didn't go round the Horn themselves, but built ships in yards *in situ*. These Pacific galleons

A Spanish chart from
1731 – maps were highly
valuable to seafarers.

brought trade goods back from the Far East, via the Spanish colony at Manila, which were unloaded at Acapulco, where a thirty-day market was held. The ships made the six-month journey once a year between 1565 and 1815, and were regarded by the British as the greatest prize. But they were seldom taken. Thomas Cavendish succeeded in 1587; Dampier and Woodes Rogers took another in 1709.

But there were plenty of other Spanish traders in the Pacific, which docked at Panama, where their goods were unloaded and put on mules for the journey across the isthmus, where they would be reloaded onto Atlantic galleons. One of the most expensive commodities was logwood, which yielded a red dye much in demand in the European textile industry, and which sold at £110 per ton. But more valuable still were the Spanish charts which were sometimes taken. These understandably were rare and vastly prized. The pirate Bartholomew Sharp captured a large 'waggoner' – or collection of charts – from a Spanish galleon, whose crew actually wept to see him take it. Armed with it, he returned to London, which he never would have dared do without it, had his friend the famous seaman-turned-cartographer William Hack re-draw it beautifully, had it translated, and then presented it to Charles II (in 1684) to purchase his pardon. That copy, together with the Spanish original, is now in the Manuscript Room of the British Library. To hold them in one's own hands, knowing their history, gives one an extraordinarily strong sense of the presence of the past.

A growth in knowledge

The extension of knowledge through scientific enquiry, largely pursued for very practical reasons, as we've seen, ushered in a new way of thinking, which makes the last four decades of the seventeenth century crucial in the development of British thought. Rationalism began to take over from superstition. The unknown and the unexplained were things to be

THE UNKNOWN AND
THE UNEXPLAINED
WERE THINGS TO BE
DISCOVERED, NOT
SUPERNATURAL OR
ALIEN PHENOMENA
TO BE FEARED

discovered, not supernatural or alien phenomena to be feared. By James Cook's time, no one intelligent seriously believed in sea-monsters any more. The men of William Dampier's generation were in a state of transition. Dampier himself was an amateur naturalist, and respected the natives of the unknown lands he visited, making notes of their customs and not simply killing them. To an Elizabethan, a giant squid would have been a sea-monster. To a Carolingian, opinion might still have been divided. To a Hanoverian, it would have been a strange large type of marine creature to be examined and dissected.

All this wasn't an overnight process. Despite the impression of intense civilisation and even modernity given by the art, architecture and literature of the time, and the advance of some branches of science, life remained brutal and most people lived in an atmosphere close to death, disease and even torture; and most women were emphatically subject to men. (Added to which even great rationalists like Isaac Newton were prey to strange mental pre-occupations; Newton himself was fascinated by alchemy. In his case, however, his less credible writings may simply reflect a general, and, as his life progressed, increasing eccentricity.)

Charles II was urbane and cultivated, and he behaved graciously (admittedly, he had to) to the politicians who just over a decade earlier had killed his father and taken over his country. Only a handful of them were executed. But he had the bodies of Cromwell and his chief supporters exhumed and dragged through the streets of London, and then had their heads placed on stakes where they remained for the rest of the reign. To be fair to Charles, this was probably to appease the London mob, who had swung behind him as surely as they had swung against his father. It was important to control that mob. Read Shakespeare's cynical *Julius Caesar* to understand how important, and how it was done, for the mob in that play isn't really composed of Romans, but Londoners. Before the days of a standing army, and those days were only just coming now, control of London increasingly meant control of the country. The capital was effectively becoming a city-state.

It's important to remember that most ordinary people were still fearful of the next world, and had literal ideas of heaven and hell. Most of the predominantly rural population was illiterate, and many still drew their spiritual impressions from depictions of an actual hell with burning pits and demons armed with hooks and tongs; and a heaven of the rosy-cheeked Saved singing endless Hallelujahs to an elderly white man on a cloud. Gibbets at crossroads and on the coast held the bodies of hanged highwaymen and pirates for years

Ships battle 1666.

Isaac Newton is renowned as the greatest British physicist, mathetician, astronomer and philosopher, but actually devoted much of his time and wrote far more papers on the subject of alchemy.

after their deaths. Witches were buried at crossroads because it was believed that the heavy traffic always associated with such locations would prevent their souls from rising as ghosts. Suicides were buried in unhallowed ground, and the Catholic Church taught that unbaptised babies went to hell.

There was no police force, though towns had their loosely organised militias, and London had its trainbands (citizen-soldiers), though these were abolished by Charles II for having been too closely associated with the Puritan usurpers. It was therefore believed that punishments should be especially harsh, in order to discourage crime. The death sentence was in place until well into the nineteenth century for crimes (viewed by our ancestors equally and literally as sins) as venial as petty theft. A not uncommon sentence of the day for murder or treason, that most popular of political transgressions, might go like this: 'The Court doth award that you be drawn upon a hurdle to the place of execution and there shall be hanged by the neck, and, being alive, shall be cut down and your entrails to be taken out of your body, and, you living, the same to be burnt before your eyes, and your head to be cut off, your body divided into four quarters, and head and quarters to be disposed of at the pleasure of the King's Majesty: and the Lord have mercy on your soul.'

The state of medicine

Given such knowledge of anatomy, it would be thought that in an age of scientific advancement, medicine would progress too, but it was as if Galen and Hippocrates, let alone William Harvey, had never existed. (Psychology and psychiatry were not to become recognised sciences until the second half of the nineteenth century, and people suffering from mental illness before then and for some time afterwards could expect pretty miserable conditions, but a discussion of them is beyond the scope of this book.)

There was no consensus among doctors, no tradition of passing knowledge on; and if anyone knew anything useful he kept it to himself, only perhaps divulging it in the form of a bequest. Robert Boyle famously remarked that there was so much quackery about that the physician was more to be feared than the disease, but he, rational scientist that he was,

TO CURE THE TOOTH-
ACH. TAKE A NEW
NAIL, AND MAKE THE
GUM BLEED WITH IT,
AND THEN DRIVE IT
INTO AN OAK

believed in some pretty bizarre cures. John Aubrey, the antiquary, a most intelligent and articulate member of London's cultural elite, as well as being a member of the Royal Society, notes various cures, of which I give you two: 'To cure the Thrush. Take a living Frog, and hold it in a Cloth, that it does not go down into the Child's mouth; and putt the head into the Child's mouth till it is dead ...' (The frog, presumably, not the child.) 'To Cure the Tooth-Ach. Take a new Nail, and make the Gum bleed with it, and then drive it into an Oak.'

The list, from all sorts of sources, goes on and nostrums are often a lot madder than these. Added to these snippets of what really amount to folk-medicine is a whole variety of pills and universal panaceas, which were marketed vigorously and endorsed by the great and the good in a completely disinterested way. Some were harmless, some were con tricks, but some were worse than the disease they sought to cure, and patent distillations containing mainly laudanum and alcohol were given to children to quieten them. All this at a time when bubonic plague still ravaged the country, and smallpox was also rife.

It is a miracle that anyone survived. (But, lest we think ourselves too superior, look at the amounts we spend on slimming aids and shortcuts to six-packs. I myself cheerfully bought some 'slimming soap' once, which needless to say failed to counterbalance the more assured effects of Irish whiskey and meat pies on my body!)

The serious medical quackery lasted an unbelievably long time though, well into the eighteenth century and even beyond, taking in such mighty and questioning intellects as Dr Johnson himself. But this book is not a history of medicine, so I won't pursue this, except to say that we weren't the only ones. Probably the poor, who couldn't afford doctors, and had their own herbal cures, fared better than the rich. Here's a tiny sample of what Louis XIV underwent at the hands of his doctors, from Nancy Mitford's superb biography, *The Sun King*: 'The King had excellent health. Like almost everybody he suffered from his teeth; part of his upper jaw-bone had been removed while one of them was being torn out so that he had difficulty in masticating his food, bits of which sometimes came down his nose. He took medicine regularly once a month, a tremendous purge which worked six or seven times. On these days he never left his room. He had gout. But he was not regarded as having real illness.' (I'll spare you the description of Louis' doctor.)

Some of the cures must have been effective though. Unless he was a man who suffered from *chutzpah* to an insane degree, a pharmacologist whose opulent tomb is to be found in Southwark Cathedral has this inscribed on it, and we must presume the product it posthumously advertises was a good one:

Here Lockyer lyes interred, enough his Name
Speaks one hath few Competitors in Fame;
A name so great, so gen'ral, it may scorn
Inscriptions, which do vulgar Tombs adorn;
His vertues and his Pills are so well known,
That Envy can't confine them under Stone;
This Verse is lost, his PILL embalmes him safe
To future Times without an Epitaph.

Surgery was scarcely in a better state, and you took a risk even if you belonged to one of the more fortunate strata of society. Early in 1658 (spring was considered a good time for the operation, being neither too hot nor too cold, and providing good daylight for the work to be done in) Samuel Pepys underwent surgery to remove a stone that had formed in his bladder, a condition he'd suffered from for years. The operation had been performed successfully since ancient times, as many people suffered from the stone; and Pepys had the services of a highly experienced surgeon, Thomas Hollier, who'd been working at St Thomas's and Bart's hospitals in London for three decades. For weeks in advance, acting under advice, Pepys tried to stay in a calm frame of mind, at the same time avoiding alcohol and sticking to a light, bland diet. Shortly before the operation itself, he would have been given a number of warm baths – bathing was quite unknown to our ancestors, so this would have been a novel experience – and kept in a warm bed. He was bled with leeches, rubbed with oils and given mild emetics.

The operation took place late in March in Pepys' own bedroom. He'd been fully apprised of what would take place and of the risks involved, but the pain of his condition was so insupportably harsh that he preferred to face death, rather than live with it. After some final preparations he was bound to a table which had been padded with straw sacking. His genital area was shaved and a group of surgeon's assistants, strong young men, stood round ready to hold him down. There was no anaesthetic, nor for this delicate operation could his senses be dulled with alcohol, as they might have been for a simple amputation, for example.

When all was in readiness Hollier inserted a thin silver probe through the penis into the bladder to locate the stone and hold it in position. Then he made his incision between the scrotum and the anus, just deep enough to cut into the wall of the bladder above. Once open, and as fast as possible, the stone was removed with pincers. The wound was dressed but not stitched – it was believed best to let it heal itself. The recovery period, during which Pepys would have been in constant fear of secondary infection, and in continual pain, usually lasted about six weeks. Pepys, a fit young man of 26, made it in five.

Pepys' stone was about 6cm in diameter. He showed it to John Evelyn, who mentioned it in his diary. On 26 March every year thereafter Pepys threw a party to mark the anniversary, and he had an expensive glass case specially made to keep the stone in.

The Church, still powerful, acted as a brake on scientific enquiry, though its conservative influence was not as pernicious here as it was in Catholic Europe, where the Inquisition was still a force to be reckoned with. Churchgoing remained popular, but it should be remembered that for our ancestors going to church was as much a social occasion as a religious obligation, and far fewer people were actual believers than was once assumed. The illiterate peasantry understood the cartoon-like frescoes and stained-glass windows, telling biblical stories in pictures; sermons were often seen as entertainments; and, above all, church was a place where friends could get together regularly.

Newgate Prison, in existence on the site since the twelfth century, was run as a private enterprise (the ideas of Thatcher and Blair were nothing new), and conditions inside were as bad as they had been 500 years earlier. It was so full that prisoners slept three to a bed, and so verminous that lice 'crunched underfoot like shells on a beach'. The smell was such that visitors had to hold bunches of violets or pomanders to their nostrils in order to withstand it. Prisoners were bathed in vinegar before making an appearance in court. At the same time, as it was run as a business, prisoners had to pay rent for their cells and the warders charged fees for their services. If you were rich or had rich friends, your life as a prisoner could be bearable.

Socially, sexual liberation (at least among the ruling and middle classes, and probably more in London than elsewhere), which the monarch enjoyed with great energy, was one

On March 26, 1660, Samuel Pepys wrote in his diary 'This day it is two years since it pleased God that I was cut of the stone at Mrs. Turner's in Salisbury Court. And did resolve while I live to keep it a festival, as I did the last year at my house, and for ever to have Mrs. Turner and her company with me.'

indication of how far the pendulum had swung the other way. Under Cromwell, adultery had been punishable by death. Under Charles II, it was almost the done thing. This wasn't unhealthy, in that the Church had for centuries frowned on sexual activity as the unfortunate adjunct of procreation, and avoided addressing the question of why God had made it pleasurable. By the 1660s we hadn't come far, except of course that in practice most people simply ignored the madder teachings of the Church, from the stance of one J. Benedicti, who wrote in 1584 that, even within marriage, the *enjoyment* of sex was sinful: 'The husband who, transported by immoderate love, has intercourse with his wife so *ardently* in order to satisfy his passion that, even had she not been his wife he would have wished to have commerce with her, is committing a sin.' Now, we were slowly moving forward to greater sexual freedom and tolerance, a good by-product of which was an erosion of the authority of the Church in people's private lives. This happy state of affairs would continue until the Victorian era. The pendulum of reaction always at first swings too far in the other direction: as it was with Cromwell, so it was with Charles. But with Charles we see the beginning of a recognisably modern type.

Eat, drink and be merry

As far as food and drink were concerned, Charles brought certain French refinements with him from the continent, such as eating with a fork as well as a knife, and a slightly broader run of wines. Food shops tended to be rare, except for bakers and grocers. Pepys' wife Elizabeth (a Huguenot by the way, and so with her parents and brother a refugee from religious discrimination at home) went with her maid early in the day to buy meat at one of the London markets, which opened at six in the morning and reserved the first two hours of trading for housewives. The better-off among the people, notably the rising middle class, which was at its most apparent in London, ate well, but their diet wasn't one we'd consider exactly balanced. They ate a lot of meat but very little fruit and vegetables. Beef was expensive but not necessarily good, since the breeding of beef cattle had not yet been refined and butchers in the days before refrigeration were unwilling to let the meat hang long before they sold it. A venison pasty was a great treat since you could only get venison if you had a friend who owned a deer-park, and it was often served at dinner parties, which among the middle-class businessmen of London were often given to advertise the host's status, in much the same way as the opulence and ornateness of their wigs (hence the expression, 'bigwig').

Breakfast was unknown, though people would take a mid-morning 'draught' with a snack. Mid-morning, for people for whom a lie-in meant getting up at six or seven, was considerably earlier, however, than we would think it. Dinner, the main meal of the day, was generally taken about noon, and a light supper would be eaten at some point in the evening. Fish was plentiful, and there was a good supply of poultry; turkeys, for example, were bred, then as now, in Norfolk. Flocks of thousands of birds were brought weekly to be sold in the London markets; though Pepys mentions having turkey for Christmas dinner only once.

As for drink, water was not regarded very highly: it was piped into only a few houses and people believed it to be bad for the health, especially if not fresh. Tea and coffee were only just making their appearance, and they were expensive, tea especially, which cost £2.50 (in contemporary money) per 500 grammes, imported as it was from China via Holland. Coffee was cheaper, and coffee-houses were gradually becoming fashionable – in fact, in the second half of the seventeenth century they proliferated about as fast in London as Starbucks. But it wasn't to everyone's taste. In the view of one person it was 'Useless, since it serveth neither for Nourishment nor Debauchery'.

Wine was imported in barrels and served in squat little bottles. Wine in corked cylindrical bottles was as yet unknown, though there was one château-bottled claret, Haut-Brion, sold in London by the French émigré restaurateurs, the Pontacs. There were no burgundies as yet, and white wine came from Germany, Spain and the Canary Islands. The Canaries were usually left out of any war Britain happened to be having with Spain, by the way, as the wine trade was too valuable to be interrupted.

The national drink remained beer, drunk in large quantities at various strengths and believed to be very good for you. All ages drank it and it cost between 1d. and 2d. a quart (c. 0.5 and 1p a litre). It was sometimes mixed with sugar or water or even wine or (hot) with butter. Great fuel for a burgeoning country. By 1688 twelve million barrels of beer, each of 36 gallons, were sold annually – two each for every man, woman and child in the country.

Charles II and his parliament

It isn't my intention to go into the intricacies of the power-sharing deal between Charles and his parliament. Charles still had more power than a modern constitutional monarch, his private sympathies were Catholic, and he can't have spent the better part of ten years in Louis XIV's court without learning a thing or two about monarchic absolutism. Louis was just beginning to create the situation which would lead, just over one hundred years later, to the end of the monarchy in France – permanently, since by then political thinking had become much more advanced, driven especially by Rousseau and Voltaire; and the French monarchy had, because of Louis' conservatism, not really moved out of the Middle Ages. But Charles was more modern than Louis, and he wanted to preserve the monarchy in Britain. Privately, he clung to the idea of the Divine Right of Kings. But he was a canny man, and because of his cosmopolitian background he could take a detached view of his own country. His character is well (though a bit unfairly) summed up in the famous squib of Rochester's:

Here lies our sovereign Lord the King
Whose promise none relies on;
He never said a foolish thing,
Nor ever did a wise one.

Charles was, as we've seen, half-French, a quarter Danish and a quarter Scottish. This is speculation on my part, but he probably spoke and thought in French better than in English. His whole personality and taste reflect French rather than British culture. He'd spent the first decade of his adult life abroad, and his formative years fighting or on the run. He was not quite 30 when he ascended the throne, but people grew up far more quickly in those days, they didn't have our lifespans, and he was experienced beyond his years. He appreciated how vital to stability was religious tolerance. (Again one cannot overemphasise the centrality of religion in people's lives.) He had his grandfather's *nous* and his father's charm.

He needed both. He was short of money. He wanted to continue the Republic's work of rebuilding the navy ('It is upon the Navy, under the Providence of God, that the safety,

RELIGIOUS
EXTREMISTS WERE
QUICK TO IDENTIFY
IT (AS WELL AS THE
FIRE WHICH
FOLLOWED IN 1666)
AS A JUDGEMENT OF
GOD ON A CYNICAL
AGE PREOCCUPIED
WITH 'BLASPHEMOUS
QUESTIONINGS'

honour and welfare of this realm do chiefly attend') – his younger brother James taking a keen, intelligent and hands-on interest – and to establish a proper professional standing army, beginning with a Royal bodyguard, for very obvious reasons. He was a complicated man. Intellectual, cultivated, lecherous, even libidinous, fond of his pleasures, not always vastly interested in affairs of state, physically attractive, very tall for his times (about 1.85m.), athletic, not quite as interested in bloodsports as his forebears, unhygienic and dirty but able to attract and keep an extraordinary number of mistresses (the father of at least 14 children from 13 of these mistresses – five British dukes today are descendants of Charles's bastards); politically at once lazy and astute ... well, one could go on and on.

In May 1662 he married Catherine of Braganza, daughter of the Duke of Braganza, later King of Portugal. Portugal was an old ally, so Catherine's Catholicism was tolerated, especially as she brought with her a fantastic dowry – £300,000 in cash (which actually took some collecting), as well as the ports of Tangiers and (especially good for annoying the Dutch) Bombay (Mumbai). They had no children. She loved him dearly, put up with his horrible treatment of her and his many infidelities, mourned his death deeply and only returned to Portugal seven years after it.

Charles II still had the power to call and dissolve parliament, but the one he gathered round him in 1660 was broadly sympathetic. He himself was, on the whole, a negotiator not a dictator, the wheeling and dealing probably amused him a lot of the time; and it was in everyone's interests after the uproar of the last 20 years or so to usher in some stability. Charles and his parliament therefore trundled along together more or less amicably but not without the odd upset for 18 years.

Charles had two great advantages at the start. The Republic had never existed in law, it was decided, so Charles had been legally king since the moment of his father's death. All laws passed since then and actions taken as a consequence were therefore null and void. Thus Church and Royal estates seized by Cromwell were restored. This was a popular move, and mollified the Church, which was slipping gradually into a secondary role. There would be no more Archbishops of Canterbury or York serving as active and leading ministers of state. The second advantage was in Charles's choice of chief minister.

Edward Hyde, Earl of Clarendon, had been loyal to Charles I, and remained so to Charles II in exile. He was just over 50 in 1660, and an experienced politician. He was what we'd call a safe pair of hands and Charles was wise to appoint him, as his ministerial skill and gravitas guided the country through the first still-uncertain years of the new reign. However, Hyde became too powerful for the liking of others, and ended up mistrusted by Cavalier and Puritan alike. At the end of his seven years in power, he was a rich man, but isolated; he was envied and hated, and had even been blamed for the Great Plague and the Great Fire. Charles's lack of funds meant that he was almost always in hock to his wily old protector Louis XIV, and Clarendon's stock was lowered by the sale of Dunkirk (Dunkerque) to France for £400,000 to drum up funds. Charles knew that it was time to let him go, if government was to remain stable. The usual trumped-up treason charge was invoked, and Clarendon left for exile in France, where he died in 1674. He did leave an important legacy: his daughter Anne married the Duke of York and had two daughters by him, Mary and Anne, who would succeed each other as queens of England after the debacle of the reign of James II.

Despite the fall of Clarendon, Charles effectively stayed in Louis' pocket for his entire reign. The downside of the era was that we became a sort of vassal of France. And we spent a large amount of time and money bickering with our close neighbours, natural allies and

Following his exile in France, Edward Hyde, Earl of Clarendon, is buried in Westminster Abbey.

co-religionists, the Dutch. All, as is usual with most wars, for nothing in the end, for James II was to cede the British throne to a Dutchman after all.

After Clarendon's departure, Charles ruled in consultation with five close associates, who were already in place in the Privy Council. From 1668, his closest associates – almost a forerunner of a modern Cabinet – were Clifford, Arlington, Buckingham, Ashley and Lauderdale – and I mention their names because their initials in that order spell out a word that has passed into our language – cabal. With them he ruled more or less firmly for some time. They were far from perfect, but at least there was no major internal dissent during the reign, and when individuals tried to foment disaster, they failed. The two major events of the early part of Charles's rule are as well known to us as the Battle of Hastings and the signing of Magna Carta.

Plague and fire

Plague was still an occasional visitor to these shores and people had learned to live with it, but the epidemic which hit London in 1665 was without recent precedent. Religious extremists were quick to identify it (as well as the fire which followed in 1666) as a judgement of God on a cynical age preoccupied with 'blasphemous questionings'.

The plague struck London in June 1665 and peaked in September. At the time, people thought it was carried on the air. Tobacco was thought to be a useful protection against it, and wise men invested in tobacco stocks. One Etonian later remembered that he had the severest flogging of his school life for neglecting to smoke. We now know that a flea specific to the medieval black rat – whose numbers were soon to be reduced in a losing competition with the European brown rat – carried the disease. Black rats lived in close proximity to man and their fleas could and did transfer from rat to man as hosts.

This was the last serious eruption of bubonic plague in Britain, and it hit hard. London's

The Great Fire of London made homeless over 100,000 people (approximately one-sixth of the population of London).

Sir Christopher Wren, who was responsible for the rebuilding of 51 churches and numerous other buildings in London during the 35 years it took to rebuild St Paul's Cathedral.

official death-roll from all causes in 1665 was 97,306, of which number 28,710 are supposed to have died of causes other than the plague, but the latter figure is still more than double the death-rate in the capital over the previous five years. Add to that the fact that many deaths went unreported, so that the true figure for the plague's mortality rate is nearer to 100,000 – about a quarter of London's population at the time.

The hardest-hit were the poor. The court, the major prelates and the rich burghers all pulled out of town to safety until the storm passed, as did other members of the British *nomenklatura*, like Dryden and Milton, who both sheepishly devoted a few lines to the disaster in poems written later. The medical profession was generally useless, except for rare individuals. Dr George Thomson performed an autopsy on a plague victim and wrote a treatise on his findings. He caught the disease himself, but survived, despite his own self-prescribed treatment of putting a dried toad on his chest.

Facilities for those struck down were minimal, but in fairness it was hard to organise sufficient bed-space for them. The hero of the hour was the Lord Mayor, Sir John Lawrence, who stayed with his aldermen and did his best to keep the town functioning. Samuel Pepys stayed too, though he moved his family from the City to Woolwich; and rather than say more here about that terrible visitation, which needs (and has) books to itself for a real discussion, I'll let him give a short first-hand account of how it felt to be there at the time: 'But Lord, how empty the streets are, and melancholy, so many poor sick people in the streets, full of sores, and so many sad stories overheard as I walk, everybody talking of this dead, and that man sick, and so many in this place, and so many in that. And they tell me that in Westminster there is never a physician, and but one apothecary left, all being dead – but that there are great hopes of a great decrease this week: God send it' (16 October 1665).

The Great Fire of September 1666 lasted four days and did more damage to London than any other conflagration apart from the Blitz of 1940–41, when Germany firebombed our capital early in the Second World War. But life went on, horrifying though the effects were, and London's recovery was remarkable. But the devastation was unutterable. Most of the City was destroyed, including the great cathedral church of St Paul's, with its magnificent Inigo Jones portico. Eighty-four parish churches disappeared, as well as countless homes. Mercifully few lives were lost. There was no fire brigade in those days, and the houses were mainly half-timbered buildings dating from the last century, and constructed along narrow streets, their upper storeys almost touching, so that once begun the fire could spread easily.

Afterwards, there was the usual cock-up. Christopher Wren and his brilliant assistant, Nicholas Hawksmoor, put forward plans for a neo-Classical London with broad boulevards, designed to keep buildings far enough apart for fires not to jump from one to another, but complicated restitution arrangements meant that the owners of destroyed edifices could rebuild on the same plots and along the same old street lines. Nevertheless, Wren and Hawksmoor gave us some beautiful churches (some of which survive in horribly insensitive late-twentieth-century development areas along the Thames), and a sense of what might have been. (Though of course it all might have been destroyed by the Germans anyway. The great neo-Classical city Paris survived because the general in command of it towards the end of the Second World War (1939–1945) refused to obey Hitler's orders to destroy it, as Warsaw and much of London had been razed, and gave it up without a fight. Thank God for civilised people. And the Great Fire of London gave rise to the appearance in our increasingly bureaucratically driven lives of fire insurance. It also marked the last time buildings were erected on bridges in London.)

Pepys survived the fire, burying his best wine (and his *Parmezan* cheese) in the garden to protect them, and stashing his cash and his papers in iron chests in his cellar. Here's a sample of his take on it:

By and by Jane [one of the Pepys' maids] comes and tells me that above 300 houses have been burned down tonight by the fire we saw, and that it was now burning down all Fish Street by London Bridge. So I made myself ready presently [at once], and walked to the Tower and there got upon one of the high places, Sir J[ohn] Robinson's little son going up with me [Robinson was Lieutenant of the Tower]; and there I did see the houses at that end of the bridge all on fire, and an infinite great fire on this and the other side the end of the bridge – which among other people did trouble me much for Michell and our Sarah on the Bridge. So down, with my heart full of trouble, to the Lieutenant of the Tower, who tells me that it begun this morning in the King's bakers house in Pudding Lane, and that it hath burned down St Magnes Church and most part of Fish Streete already. So I down to the waterside and there got a boat and through the bridge, and there saw a lamentable fire. Poor Michells house, as far as the Old Swan, already burned that way and the fire running further, that in a very little time it got as far as the Stillyard while I was there. Everybody endeavouring to remove their goods, and flinging into the river or bringing them into lighters that lay off. Poor people staying in their houses as long as till the very fire touched them, and then running into boats or clambering from one pair of stair by the waterside to another. And among other things, the poor pigeons I perceive were loath to leave their houses, but hovered about the windows and balconies till they were some of them burned, their wings, and fell down.
(extract from entry for Sunday, 2 September 1666)

The Dutch wars

As if all this wasn't enough, the Dutch wars simmered on, and in 1667 we were obliged to suffer a serious humiliation at their hands.

Like his forefathers, Charles II was tight with money. He had to be, to be fair, but he should have spent more on the country than he did on himself. The navy, which Pepys and the Duke of York among others were trying to reorganise, was beginning to reform, but it was a slow process, and in the meantime experienced seamen were left unpaid, being fobbed off with a kind of promissory note. This far from satisfied many of them, and they defected to the Dutch, who paid cash. It was pretty shortsighted of us to let men who knew how to navigate our shorelines and rivers go over to the enemy, however superior we thought ourselves to be, but we underestimated Dutch naval power. If Admiral Robert Blake had still been alive, things might have been different.

We need to look very briefly at what had been going on in Holland. After years of struggle, by the mid-seventeenth century the northern part of the Spanish Netherlands, whose people had converted to Protestantism in the Reformation, finally shook off their Spanish overlords to create the Dutch Republic (modern Netherlands) under their own leaders, the Stadtholders. (The Spanish retained hegemony over the southern part of their possessions for the time being. Some 200 years later these would become the Kingdom of Belgium.)

Britain and the Netherlands had always maintained friendly relations, there had been marriages between the chief families and we had a lot in common. But as we've seen, the Dutch began to muscle in (as we saw it) on our maritime supremacy. This led in the latter

PEPYS SURVIVED THE FIRE, BURYING HIS BEST WINE (AND HIS *PARMEZAN* CHEESE) IN THE GARDEN TO PROTECT THEM, AND STASHING HIS CASH AND HIS PAPERS IN IRON CHESTS IN HIS CELLAR

half of the seventeenth century to a number of little wars between the two countries, resolved when William of Orange, Charles II's nephew and married to James II's daughter, was invited to come over to Britain as its king when James II was booted out. But for a time we didn't like the Dutch at all. Andrew Marvell had this to say about them:

Holland, that scarce deserves the name of land,
As but th'off-scouring of the British sand:
And so much earth as was contributed
By English pilots when they heaved the lead;
Or what by th'ocean's slow alluvion fell,
Of shipwrecked cockle and the mussel shell;
This indigested vomit of the sea
Fell to the Dutch by just propriety.

I'm not going to go into all the intricacies of these wars here, but at the time of the plague and the fire we were also fighting the Dutch. They are close neighbours, and for the first time since the Armada enemy ships were at our gates. Gunfire from some of the battles could even be heard in London, and worse was to follow.

In August 1666 we managed to get into the Dutch anchorage of the Vlie and there destroyed with fireships almost the whole of the Dutch East India merchant fleet, recently returned from the East Indies, and still laden. The following year the Dutch retaliated so successfully that any smug smiles were wiped definitively from our faces. Using the expertise of English sailors, who mockingly waved their 'Treasury tickets' or promissory English notes for payment at us, they sailed up the Medway. Admiral de Ruyter managed to set fire to Chatham dockyard, burning some of our best warships, towing away the first-rate *Royal Charles* for their own use. The Dutch also sent ships up the Thames and threatened London. This was a great victory for the Dutch, and a serious blow to our national esteem.

Pepys and his master, Sir William Coventry, were partly to blame for this (Pepys' diary entries for mid-June are frantic), since they failed to heed the advice of experienced military men like General Monk and Sir Robert Holmes (who'd made the attack on the Vlie), but it was really the fault of parliament for not voting sufficient funds to the navy, and the matter dented Charles's popularity. Many were looking on him as a frivolous lecher who was more French than English, and began to feel nostalgia for Cromwell. In Cromwell's time, they said, such a thing could never have happened. And they were probably right. There was also a good deal of disquiet at the increasing toleration of Catholics, at least at court.

Anti-Catholicism

Soon afterwards, peace was declared and treaties drawn up to form a northern Protestant alliance. France under Louis was looking more solid than ever, and there was a need to bury differences and balance the Catholic power. But at home rumblings against Catholicism continued, and the Protestant faction was not reassured when the Duke of York, following the death of his first wife, Anne Hyde, in 1671, declared his conversion to the Church of Rome. Two years later he remarried, his new wife Mary being the Catholic daughter of the Duke of Modena. Charles II's policy had always been for religious tolerance but the upheavals of the middle years of the century were well within living memory and prejudice dies hard. Various

Louis XIV, under whose reign, France achieved political, economic and cultural dominance in Europe and beyond.

acts were passed to protect the Anglican communion, and in 1673 the Test Act provided that Catholics should not hold key offices. This meant that the Duke of York was obliged to resign the office of Lord High Admiral – in turn ironical, since he was good at the job. But still Charles remained under the perfectly justified suspicion that he was being bankrolled by Louis XIV. And he was. Louis knew that Charles had Catholic sympathies. Louis didn't want to see another revolution in Britain, this time leading perhaps to a permanent Republic; and Charles even connived with him in an abortive plan to attack Holland together and split it between them.

So Charles trod a delicate line. A good politician and a sensitive man, but unable in the end to escape, diplomatically speaking, the bad things in his blood: belief in Divine Right, instinctive Catholic leanings and need for money at all costs. At least he had the sense not to try to follow his father's example in his treatment of parliament – but by this time we had moved on from that kind of behaviour anyway. Or so we thought.

Because of this situation the country became, if not unstable, increasingly uneasy, and things weren't helped when in 1678 an opportunistic and hysterical mythomane of psychopathic character, the disreputable cleric (he was kicked out of a naval chaplaincy for sodomy) Titus Oates, dreamed up and managed to sell the idea that a demonic Popish plot was afoot amongst the Catholics to rise up and murder the Protestants, kill the king and invite the French to invade. The fact that he succeeded at all with this madness is an indication of how jumpy people had become. Oates was discredited within a very few years of his allegations, but not before three dozen prominent (and entirely innocent) Catholics had been executed. Oates himself, though imprisoned and subjected to unbelievably savage floggings, survived and died a natural death in 1705.

Parliamentary changes

Meanwhile parliament itself was evolving. There was an increasing feeling, fuelled by the mistrust of the Catholics, that the king's powers should be further curbed. This feeling was not shared by everyone, and two opposing sides emerged. The Court Party, led by the Earl of Danby, protected Charles's interests. Opposing them was the Earl of Shaftesbury, who wanted to see parliament free of any royal interference. He also opposed the idea of a standing army, which he felt could take over the country (which still happens in many parts of the world). Shaftesbury saw the Popish plot as an opportunity to pass an Act which would prevent the declared Catholic James from succeeding his older brother Charles, who had no legitimate heir and by now seemed unlikely ever to produce one.

Over this matter three elections were fought, leading to the development of two distinct parliamentary groupings – the Democrats with Shaftesbury (an old Republican who'd survived because of his great expertise, and Charles's chancellor), and the Royalists with the mildly corrupt but very astute Danby. The two new parties needed some form of identification. Both derived their appellations from derogatory nicknames: Shaftesbury's lot were called Whiggamores after a group of Scottish rebels who marched on Edinburgh in 1648 (the name derives from *whig* [drive] and *mere* [mare] – hence horse-drovers); Danby's bunch were called *toraidhes* – an Irish word denoting terrorists who attacked English- and Scottish-owned estates in Ireland.

Whigs and Tories: the first two British political parties and the beginning of truly modern government. Even so, Charles retained the right to summon and dissolve, and there was no question of disputing James's succession. But what had been brought about was the right to be in a party that disagreed with the Establishment, without being branded a rebel or a traitor.

Passing of the Merry Monarch

Charles II died in 1685, in his 55th year, of a stroke. He'd been known as the Merry Monarch, and so, to a certain extent, he was. He managed the kingdom well through some difficult times, bringing a civilising and modernising touch to the realm, and our folk memories of him are warm. We all remember his deathbed *bon mot*: 'I am sorry, gentlemen, to be so unconscionable a time a-dying'; and that his last words reputedly were ones of concern for the fate of Nell Gwyn: 'Let not poor Nellie starve.' But he was also a bit of a reactionary, and in the pocket of France. He was adamant that his brother should succeed him, though he must have known the likely effect of that. Perhaps in his heart of hearts he realised that James would quickly hang himself with the rope given him, and that then matters would take their course. Had he ever spoken to his nephew William of Orange? Or did he hope that James would, after all, ensure a new Catholic succession? Charles himself received extreme unction in the Catholic rite. It remains for John Evelyn to give us a contemporary summing up:

Thus died King Charles II, of a vigorous and robust constitution, and in all appearance promising a long life. He was a prince of many virtues, and many great imperfections; debonair, easy of access, not bloody nor cruel; his countenance fierce, his voice great, proper of person, every motion became him; a lover of the sea, and skilful in shipping; not affecting other studies, yet he had a laboratory ...

He loved planting and building, and brought in a politer way of living, which passed to luxury and intolerable expense ...

He took delight in having a number of little spaniels follow him and lie in his bedchamber, where he often suffered the bitches to puppy and give suck, which rendered it very offensive, and indeed made the whole court nasty and stinking.

He would doubtless have been an excellent prince had he been less addicted to women ... He frequently and easily changed favourites, to his great prejudice.

As to the other public transactions and unhappy miscarriages, it is not here I intend to number them; but certainly never had King more glorious opportunities to have made himself, his people and all Europe happy, and prevented innumerable mischiefs, had not his easy nature resigned him to be managed by crafty men, and some abandoned and profane wretches who corrupted his otherwise sufficient parts.

James II and the advance of Catholicism

How unlike this flawed, humorous and sophisticated man was his younger brother. James II was rigid, tactless, cold and arrogant. The best you can say of him was that he'd been a good naval administrator, but it was as much his personality as his Catholicism that damned him in double-quick time.

James knew he wasn't popular, but instead of trying to woo his people, he sought to dominate them. He thought Louis XIV had the right idea, but he didn't have Louis' means, experience or plain power. It wasn't long before a rebellion was raised against him by an illegitimate son of Charles, the Duke of Monmouth, who formed a ragtag army in the southwest. It was still very early in James's short reign – it was still, in fact, 1685; and no one in the Establishment then was going to back Monmouth's hotheaded and disorganised attempt at a coup against the king. And if James didn't have an army as such, he did have the Life Guards and a couple of other regiments at his disposal. He also had John Churchill, later the Duke of Marlborough, an ancestor of Winston Churchill and a brilliant strategist, close to the king partly because he simply had an eye to the main chance, partly because he was committed to maintaining the status quo, and partly because his cousin had been James's mistress. Monmouth's force, going round in idiotic circles in the West Country, was soon wiped out, and he himself was executed. But James then unleashed the pathological Judge George Jeffreys to try the surviving conspirators. This alcoholic sadist presided over a series of arbitrary show trials – known later as the Bloody Assize – and had people executed, transported to the American colonies, or flogged, wholesale. James rewarded him by making him Lord Chancellor, though Jeffreys never turned Catholic himself. He died in the Tower, where he'd been put to protect him from the vengeful London mob, after James's fall. He was 40.

By now parliament was sufficiently entrenched for the king to be unable to shake it, but the Monmouth rebellion had given James the excuse he needed to maintain an army, which he officered with Catholics, and recruited Irish landworkers to man it. But it was an unreliable force, and its existence only served to make James even more disliked. Even British Catholics turned against him, because his behaviour was bringing them all into disrepute. And at this very moment, in October 1685, Louis XIV revoked the Edict of Nantes, which meant that Huguenots were robbed of any protection under the law. This led to a wave of immigrants – James hadn't quite dared to try to impose Catholicism here in the same Draconian fashion – and fresh revulsion at Catholic extremism.

James soon lost the support both of parliament and the people. Although the economy continued to build gradually, Catholicism was feared and hated, and James, who was, as we've seen, not all bad, and probably would have led a good and useful life as Admiral of

The Coronation of James II, the last Roman Catholic ruler of Scotland, England and Ireland.

the Fleet, responded to the dislike with an attempt at ruling with an iron fist. He prorogued parliament. He advanced Catholic cronies. He made nothing but enemies where he should have made friends. As a Catholic convert, he pushed his version of Christianity with a janissary-like zeal. He issued two Declarations of Indulgence, which meant greater freedom and rights for religious dissenters, including, of course, Catholics. It was the freedom for Catholics that stuck in most people's craws. Seven principal English bishops declined to have the Second Declaration read in all churches, as James had commanded. In the face of all advice, James had them sent to the Tower. A face-off couldn't be far away, but James believed he had the support of the armed forces. He lacked Charles's flexibility and diplomacy. He couldn't bend. He was brittle. Only one outcome was possible.

Spain was a spent force by now, but France was far from being so, and France was the new enemy and rival. Clearly, James, also, of course, half-French, had to go. Sedition was already in the offing when the trigger came. On 10 June 1688 Mary of Modena gave birth to a son, James. The boy was quarter-French and half-Italian. A Catholic, foreign heir.

At this point the Earl of Danby and other men of influence wrote a letter to William of Orange, Stadtholder of the Netherlands, and Charles's and James's Protestant nephew, also married to James's Protestant daughter, his cousin Mary. William, though physically frail, was a very tough customer and a good soldier. He'd been watching James flannel about for some time, with interest. At the same time the imprisoned bishops were released: there was no case against them. The populace cheered.

William of Orange

Of course it wasn't that easy, but the long and the short of it is that William was invited to take over the throne of England, ensuring a Protestant succession. This took delicate handling, for the proposition was treasonable, but towards the end of October 1688 William landed an army on our south coast. James did still have a force of perhaps 25,000 at his disposal, but the officers wavered. They had their own backs to protect. Churchill and other commanders went over to William. The jig was up.

James fled from England, thereby abandoning his country and giving the powers there the shaky grounds for declaring that he had abdicated. But he recouped in France, and came back to Ireland with a French/Irish army two years later, intending to invade England; but in Ireland he was met and defeated by William of Orange's forces at the Battle of the Boyne (1 July 1690, and still celebrated by Northern Irish Protestants – you'll have heard of Orangemen). And that was the end of him. He returned to France where he played out his days until his death, in his 68th year, in 1701. Britain had achieved its coup against him almost bloodlessly. It now had a moderate king who exercised religious tolerance. And, aware that James II's son was alive and at his father's court in France, and that he would be the focus of any possible Catholic plot to recapture the throne, parliament would, in the same year that James II died, pass an Act ensuring that the succession would only be through a Protestant line. Given that William and Mary were childless, and that Mary's sister Anne's last surviving child also died in 1701, the succession would pass to the nearest Protestant candidates, who happened to be the Electors of Hanover, through a complicated line of descent from James I.

William, for all his severity of upbringing and his battle with ill-health, was a liberal realist. There were a few constitutional flutters because the throne by succession really belonged to his wife, but in a famous and I think unique compromise in British history they ruled as joint monarchs. They ruled wisely and well, on the whole, the only blot on the escutcheon being perhaps the massacre at Glencoe in Scotland in 1691, when, following a minor insurgency on behalf of James II's son (known as the Old Pretender – the word pretender being used in the sense of one who aspires to the throne – his son James), the Campbell clan, acting on orders from William, massacred the Macdonalds (their inveterate enemies anyway) because the latter had been tardy in reaffirming their loyalty to William. Of course the Campbells exploited the situation. What would William have known of Scottish feuds?

Mary died in 1694 aged 32. William continued alone until his death a few years later. Their reign was one of solidity, and they were adored by their people for that. It has to be admitted that for all his qualities – he could speak six languages and he was a good diplomat – William was a bit of a bore, and even a bit of a boor – but he ruled well. There was, however, another nasty and inconclusive war with France, which is of interest to the family historian because a tax to pay for it was levied on births, marriages and burials in 1697, the burial tax an early appearance of what we now have to shell out as death duty. But it meant that parish registers became very efficient and detailed.

And in those days when wars ended and soldiers and sailors were demobilised, a vast number of men were unleashed as unemployed on the population. Pirates and highwaymen were on the way.

But there would always be another war, and already by 1700 we were muscling up for the next one. Carlos II of Spain died childless in November that year, and he bequeathed his domains (including what was left of the Spanish Netherlands) to the Duke of Anjou, Louis XIV's grandson. At about the same time our spies discovered that the Jacobites (supporters of King James II in exile and his heirs) were plotting a French-funded invasion. A Frenchman ruling Spain wasn't a pleasing prospect, especially i\f he had control of lands as close as Holland as well.

War loomed again, but William didn't live to see it. He died on 20 February 1702, following a fall from his horse. Naturally medical science was unable to save him.

B arbara Windsor MBE is a national treasure. She is also a true survivor, who has seen bad times follow good and back again, and lived through them without losing either her nerve or her sense of humour, as anyone who has read her autobiography *All of Me* could tell you. Following a flourishing stage career, and perhaps her best known cinema roles in the *Carry On* films, she returned to the small screen with the role of Peggy Mitchell in the BBC's *EastEnders*. Barbara, who was born Barbara Ann Deeks in Shoreditch in August 1937, was awarded an MBE in 1999, and was also the inaugural recipient of the Rear of the Year Title in 1976!

Barbara started tracing her ancestors with little knowledge of her family tree beyond her grandparents. A true East Ender herself, she's always felt somehow cut off from it as her mother was such a snob about it, and early on moved the family away to Stoke Newington in North London.

Barbara knows more about her mother's side of the family than her father's.

Although her parents were second cousins, her mother (*née* Ellis) always looked down on the Deeks branch of the family, though she did allow herself to be seduced by Barbara's dad's barrow-boy charm and patter. All the Ellis sisters wanted to better themselves; Barbara's Aunt Dolly even married a man whose surname was Windsor, which is where Barbara got her stage name.

Her parents' marriage wasn't destined to last. Her dad started life as a barrow-boy, served with the army in North Africa and Italy during the Second World War, and returned to civilian life as a bus conductor. When he came home he found his wife's uppishness too much, and sad to say began to knock her about, which led to their divorce.

The house Barbara was born in no longer exists, having been swept away along with the street and most of the district in the slum clearances of the 1950s. Barbara says sadly that her East End no longer exists. So her forebears represent a past of which the physical traces have disappeared.

Barbara's maternal grandfather was Charlie Ellis, a docker who liked his drink – 'and when he was tipsy I always knew he was good for a few pennies for a jam doughnut' – but also entertained in the local pubs as a singer. 'I loved Grandad Charlie. He was a real gent, always well turned out, he never swore, a bit of a local celebrity, and I'm sure that's where I got my entertaining gene from.'

Barbara didn't know exactly what Charlie's day job entailed, so she sought the advice of Chris Ellmers, an expert on the London Docks. It emerged that Charlie had started work as a casual labourer there in 1916 and became permanent staff ten years later, which constituted a move up the social ladder. It was a varied life, the air full of the scent of exotic spices, fine wines and Balkan and Virginia tobacco. Barbara was tickled to find out that her grandad started out with a job which would have been classified as *lower* working class – think how put out her mother would have been about that! Charlie was also evidently politicised because he risked his job, as his work records reveal, to join the 1926 General Strike.

But Barbara still hadn't found out why her mum looked down so much on her dad's side of the family. On her paternal grandparents' side, she has a first cousin

RIGHT
Rose Deeks, Barbara's
mother.

FAR RIGHT
Barbara's great-
grandparents, Emily and
James Ewin.

once removed called Gerald, who lives in Clacton. It turned out that Gerald knew a good deal.

Gerald's mum and Barbara's paternal grandmother were sisters. Barbara's grand-mother was called Fat Nan, but apart from that Barbara didn't know much about her. Gerald told her that Fat Nan had been a chorus-line dancer — a 'hoofer' — at the Britannia Theatre, Hoxton, just before the First World War, when she was about 16. Her husband, Jack Deeks, was a costermonger, selling fruit and vegetables (coster-mongers were the precursors of the Pearly Kings and Queens and wore similar apparel; they had their own slang which prefigured Cockney rhyming slang); and Fat Nan's mother, Emily Ewin (appropriately *née* Bacchus), was a pub landlady. Intriguingly, Barbara discovered that there's a family myth that Emily didn't want *her* daughter to marry a Deeks either.

To follow that line of enquiry, Barbara went to meet Gloria, another first cousin once removed, who also happens to be an amateur genealogist. Gloria and Barbara share a great-grandfather, John Deeks. It emerged that the Deeks men were very handsome and charming, but rather given to drinking, which didn't go down well with parents who wanted their daughters to better themselves.

But the Deeks pretty much held down decent jobs. From Gloria, Barbara learned that her great-great-grandfather, John Deeks, had a skilled job — he was a bricklayer. Why then did the family seem caught in a poverty trap?

To find out more, Barbara visited the London Metropolitan Archive and talked to the economic historian Paul Johnson. Paul explained how the East End of London fell into decline in the course of the nineteenth century as burgeoning industry led to pollution and cramped living conditions, resulting in bad hygiene, poor health and

RIGHT
**Polly Deeks Nan, with
John, Barbara's father.**

high mortality. John Deeks (1834–1909) would have had to face fierce competition for work, and when he got it, it would involve sixty-hour weeks without any security. Back in the 1880s, when there was a mini-depression in the area, people like Barbara's great-great-grandfather became more or less permanently unemployed. By 1889 John was in the workhouse, where he spent much of the last twenty years of his life. None of his ten children seemed able to help him.

Was Barbara's mother's family as poor as her father's? Barbara doesn't do the Internet, so she got her husband Scott to go online to find out more about her maternal grandfather's parents. She has a photo of her maternal great-grandmother, who looks a timid little thing. Was that what she was really like?

It turned out that Mary Ann Ellis was a matchbox-maker, probably at the Bryant & May factory in Bow in the early 1880s. She worked from home, on piecework, with her children helping out. Matchbox-making was tedious work, mind-numbing but requiring concentration too. They would have worked sixteen hours a day to produce

500 matchboxes. Day in, day out. Home was in Old Nichol Street, in one of the worst slums in London. And Old Nichol Street was close to where the Deeks lived. The families probably knew each other.

It's more than likely that Mary Ann was involved in one of the first significant strikes in English industrial history – the matchgirls' strike of 1888. Barbara also learned that 90 per cent of the workers were Irishwomen, and finds out from her grandfather's birth certificate that her mother's maiden name was Collins. She then got Scott to look up the 1871 census online, which confirmed that her great-grandmother hailed from Cork. Subsequent research there revealed that Mary Ann's parents emigrated from Ireland to the East End of London at some point between 1846 and 1850 – a period of mass emigration from Ireland on account of the notorious potato famine. Emigration to the United States, mainland Europe or England was for millions the

BARBARA SAYS SADLY THAT HER EAST END NO LONGER EXISTS. SO HER FOREBEARS REPRESENT A PAST OF WHICH THE PHYSICAL TRACES HAVE DISAPPEARED.

only way to escape death and disease; and even so one million people died in those five years. The Collins family got out in time, but Barbara sadly discovered that her great-grandmother, born in 1857, was named after an older sister, born in 1846, who had died of scarlet fever in infancy in London, ironically having already escaped a scarlet fever epidemic in Ireland.

Meanwhile news came from historian Paul Johnson of an even earlier relative, great-great-great-grandfather Golding Deeks, a bricklayer born in Bures, Suffolk, in 1806. At Bury St Edmunds Record Office, Barbara found out from archivist Sheila Reid that Golding Deeks's father was called William. He was also a bricklayer, and what's more he could sign his name in the marriage register, at a time when most working men were illiterate and would only have been able to make their mark. It seems likely that with the advent of the industrial revolution and the decline of building in the countryside, Golding Deeks made a move to London where there would have been plenty of work. He was probably therefore the founder of the Deeks London dynasty. But as time went on, and his descendant John was forced into the workhouse, the near-neighbouring family of Ellis/Collins came to look down on what they saw as the feckless and even more impoverished Deeks bunch.

Sheila then went on to explain something extraordinary about the name Golding. It turned out that Golding was Golding Deeks' mother's maiden name, and that it was a family tradition to give a boy his mother's surname as his Christian name. The famous landscapist John Constable's father was called Golding Constable, also born in Bures. Sheila explained that Golding Deeks' mother, Elizabeth Deeks, was born in the same year as John Constable in 1776. They shared the same great-great grandparents, who were wealthy. So, Barbara shares an ancestor with John Constable! However, to Barbara's amusement, the wealth went down the Constable line, and not to the poor old Deeks.

Age of Change

(from James I to the Restoration)

QUEEN ELIZABETH I DIED JUST BEFORE DAWN ON 24 MARCH 1603. SHE HAD REIGNED FOR THIRTY YEARS, AND DURING THAT TIME THE COUNTRY HAD GRADUALLY STABILISED, SHAKEN OFF ANY SUBSERVIENCE TO SPAIN AND ESTABLISHED ITSELF THROUGH ITS INCREASING DOMINATION OF THE SEAS AS THE WORLD POWER IT WAS TO REMAIN FOR 300 YEARS. THE ELIZABETHAN ERA IS UNDOUBTEDLY A GOLDEN AGE, WHICH SAW SUCH GREAT MARITIME HEROES AS DRAKE AND RALEIGH, AS WELL AS A BURGEONING OF NATIVE THOUGHT AND ARTISTIC TALENT, MOST OBVIOUSLY IN THE THEATRE, WHERE SHAKESPEARE STANDS AT THE HEAD OF A GROUP OF WRITERS WHOSE WORK IS STILL PERFORMED.

The 'wisest fool in Christendom'

James I was a far more successful ruler of Scotland, than of England, where he laid the foundations for the future English Civil War, which would see his son, Charles I, tried and executed.

Elizabeth died without a direct heir, and the Tudor dynasty died with her. Since 1586 however she had had an agreement with James VI of Scotland, the son of Mary, Queen of Scots, and he now became James I of England as well, uniting the two countries under one king for the first time and founding the troubled dynasty of the Stuarts. He was 37 years old when he travelled down to London, a man well into middle-age by the standards of the time, and set in his ways. His monarchy over both nations was ratified after a little humming and hawing by parliament, and in October 1604 the term Great Britain was used for the first time. But James remained a Scot all his life, and never really attempted to adapt to England.

Not for nothing was James dubbed 'the wisest fool in Christendom' by that astute French observer and financier, the Duc de Sully. The great Victorian historian Lord Macaulay paints a similar picture: 'He was indeed made up of two men – a witty, well-read scholar who disputed and harangued, and a nervous, drivelling idiot who acted.'

Born and raised in Scotland and suffering a narrow and austere Calvinist education, he was an inflexible man of undoubted intellect but boorish manners, who was interested in administration but only on his terms, and a man who combined suspicion and superstition in his character to an extraordinary degree. Fatally, he was a believer in the Divine Right of Kings, that is, that their rule and decisions should be unquestioningly accepted by everyone else, an error he passed on to his son Charles I, who, attempting to rule like him in an increasingly modern world, brought about his own downfall and our first (and, so far, only) Republic, under Oliver Cromwell.

James married Anne, the daughter of the King of Denmark, in 1589, and she seems to have had an altogether more refreshing character, being fond of the arts and particularly of masques, the extravagant music-and-dance court entertainments fashionable at the time, in which she also appeared. James, by contrast, is reputed to have slept through the first performance of *The Tempest*. He was a passionate *aficionado* of blood sports.

SE RIO.

Robert Cecil, 1st Earl of Salisbury, was Secretary of State for both Elizabeth I and then James I, heavily involved in securing the succession.

Although he was guided initially by Robert Cecil (the son of William, and himself an able statesman who remained James's chief minister until his death in 1612), James had a weakness for handsome young men of the decorative rather than the intelligent sort, and this led to a string of favourites, which did not endear him to his people. Nor did his attempt to rule England as autocratically as he had ruled Scotland.

He wasn't helped by an ungainly physique, with spindly legs and a tongue that seemed too large for his mouth. Unpleasant rumours circulated that he never changed his under-garments. He disliked tobacco, which had been introduced by Walter Raleigh during the last reign, so much that he wrote a treatise inveighing against it. (Walter Raleigh's other import, the Virginian potato, though it caught on successfully in Ireland, was avoided by the English for another 150 years or so. The English thought these potatoes could be bad for you, give you colic, and even make you impotent. They were also suspected of making you flatulent, and even of causing leprosy! This despite a most enthusiastic puff from Francis Drake: 'These potatoes be the most delicate rootes that may be eaten, and doe farre exceed our passneps or carets.') The English ignored him and stuck to the sweet variety. The upper classes avoided vegetables altogether.

James's closed mind made him incurious about the English, about whom he knew nothing and to whom he was a foreigner of dubious ancestry. But he knew where he stood on religion and those who abused it. He was especially interested in witchcraft, and had even published a book about it, *Daemonologie*, in 1597.

Burn the witch

With his approval, 'witches' were to endure a savage persecution, which culminated in the work of Matthew Hopkins, who during Cromwell's time was responsible for the torture and deaths of hundreds of elderly women and one 80-year-old vicar between 1644 and

HIS FAVOURED
METHOD OF TESTING
FOR A WITCH WAS
ONE SUPPORTED BY
JAMES I, AND RESTED
ON THE BELIEF THAT
WATER, BEING A
HOLY SUBSTANCE,
WOULD REFUSE TO
ACCEPT SUSPECTS IF
THEY WERE GUILTY

In the 17th century, hanging was the most common form of execution for alleged witches – burning at the stake being more common on the continent.

1647, when he was himself accused of witchcraft and executed. His favoured method of testing for a witch was one supported by James I, and rested on the belief that water, being a holy substance, would refuse to accept suspects if they were guilty. Thus, if they sank (and drowned) they were innocent; but if they floated, or swam, they were guilty, and were therefore executed, either by hanging or at the stake. Witches, usually elderly women living alone, sometimes capable of healing by faith or herbs, often the victims of vindictive neighbours who denounced them, endured formal persecution in Great Britain from the thirteenth century until the laws against them were repealed under George II in 1736. The last execution of a witch in Britain took place at Dornoch, Scotland, in 1722. So despite the ascendancy of science over superstition from about 1650 on, old habits died hard, and our ancestors would have been used to the presence of death and grisly reminders of it in the form, for example, of the heads of traitors stuck on pikes; and highwaymen's corpses hung rotting in gibbets at crossroads until far more recently than one might think.

The 17th-century family

Women who were not witches, although they did not enjoy the same levels of freedom and education as men, and indeed with a few brave and/or privileged exceptions were not to do so for several centuries yet, ran their households.

A huswife good betimes will rise,
And order things in comelie wise.
Her mind is set to thrive:
Upon her distaffe she will spin
And with her needle she will winne,
If such he hap to wive.

This is a good example of what was to be expected. The housewife saw to the brewing and the baking, the servants and (in the country) the care of the animals. Then there was dyeing, spinning and all manner of needlework. But there were recreations too: bowling, fishing and riding for the well-to-do were considered pastimes suitable for women, as well as the care of children.

It was not, however, until much later that our concept of parent–child relationships developed. Children of the poor were set to work as soon as they could walk and fend for themselves, certainly by the age of four, and by the same age children of the better-off were being dressed and treated as little adults. Some had private tutors for their education, mainly learning the Classics by rote, the same system as that used in most schools, where it was firmly believed except by only a very few enlightened men that the only way to impart knowledge was by flogging it into a child, behaviour which alas the parents usually approved of. A parent's authority was unquestioned during his or her lifetime. Grown-up children were expected to stand for however long a parent's visit lasted, or at best kneel on cushions. A father was never addressed familiarly by his son or daughter, but called 'sir'.

Much of the reason for this was the belief people held that children were born in the state of Original Sin and that to redeem them from this their spirit had to be broken. Wilfulness and youthful high spirits were punished with a ferocity that today we would view as sadistically insane. Fifty strokes were nothing, and John Aubrey describes the headmaster of the highly esteemed St Paul's School, Dr Gill (no ancestor of mine, thank God!), working himself into an actual fit while belabouring a child. Nicholas Udall (1504–1556), who was headmaster of Eton until he was dismissed and imprisoned for buggery (he was later pardoned), once gave a boy 53 strokes of the cane. Udall, incidentally, was the author of *Ralph Roister Doister*, a rollicking comedy inspired by his favourite Roman playwrights, Plautus and Terence, which in turn influenced the comedies of the later Elizabethan and Jacobean theatre. Aubrey, who lived from 1626 to 1697, by contrast, was an advocate of liberal education.

The Divine Right of James I

For all his faults, James I managed the country pretty ably for over twenty years, and kept it out of any major conflicts, and though it's possible that sensible policies up to 1612 can be attributed to Cecil, it's also true that James was a stubborn absolutist who was disinclined to take others' advice.

But James's faults were many. He neglected the navy and disliked or mistrusted the prominent men he'd inherited from Elizabeth. By allowing our significance as a sea-power to decline, he left the field of the East Indies, the one not dominated by the Spanish, to be exploited by the Dutch. Only under Cromwell would our fortunes as a sea-power revive. James didn't like working with parliament, either, and unfortunately for the immediate future of the monarchy he'd arrived a little too late in the day to impose his will on an institution that was beginning to get used to flexing its muscles independently of the monarch. James's own views, in his own words, are clear: 'The King makes daily statutes and ordinances, enjoining such pains thereto as he thinks meet, without any advice of Parliament or Estates, yet it lies in the power of no Parliament to make any kind of law or statute without his sceptre be to it for giving it the force of law.'

Parliaments of one kind or another had existed in England for centuries. Originally councils of the leading men in the country – in practice the most powerful landowners – to

BY ALLOWING OUR SIGNIFICANCE AS A SEA-POWER TO DECLINE, HE LEFT THE FIELD OF THE EAST INDIES, THE ONE NOT DOMINATED BY THE SPANISH, TO BE EXPLOITED BY THE DUTCH

determine financial and judicial policies, they developed into more sophisticated forms as early as Henry II's time, and under Magna Carta (1215) the monarch's power was limited. Three committees of the king's court were later established at Westminster Hall to deal with petitions, and these three together formed a consultative body which grew in time into a parliament. With the advent of formal taxation, originally on land, came an obligation, in return for the money collected, to offer wider representation. Parliaments could be called and dismissed, however, at the will of the monarch. Originally held in a single chamber, these meetings gradually developed into what we know as Lords and Commons, self-descriptive titles of an obvious and inevitable division. Henry VIII relied heavily on his parliaments and under him the desire for greater independence from the monarch's will grew. However, the right of the monarch to dissolve or summon parliament was retained for a long time yet.

James, whose work as King of Scots had largely involved breaking the power of the local nobility, had no desire to be told what to do by his subjects. The Divine Right of Kings was a very convenient political doctrine for him. It argues that sovereign power has a divine sanction, and doesn't depend on either the will of the people or the assent of any government. The idea that a monarch can use his power by inherited right took root under the Tudors. Henry VIII, though, took advice from his parliaments, and Elizabeth was a diplomat who was also tactful and popular, so no one worried too much. But then along came James.

The countries he ruled – England, Scotland, Wales and, somewhat shakily, Ireland – had a combined population of about six million, of whom four million lived in England. Economic hardship had seen to it that the population had increased slowly – people

Westminster Hall with the Courts of Chancery and Kings in Session.

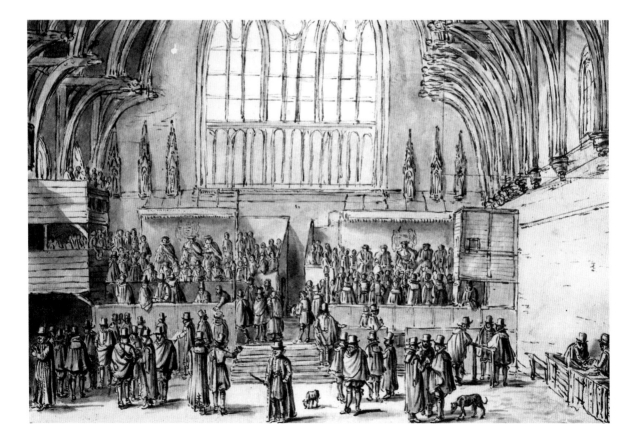

The illustration bears the inscription:

ErGENTLICHE ABBILDVNG WIE ETTLICH ENGLISCHE EDELLEVT EINEN RAHT
schließen den König sampt dem gantzen Parlament mit Pulfer zuvertilgen ·

Bates · Robert Winter · Christopher Wright · John Wright · Thomas Percy · Guido Fawkes · Robert Catesby · Thomas Winter

The Gunpowder Plot conspirators in 1606.

married later and, as life expectancy was shorter, had few child-bearing years. It's been calculated that women actually began menstruation later and that the menopause came earlier than nowadays, families were not large and infant mortality was high. (Loss of children was expected. Even the great humanist and essayist Michel de Montaigne (1533–92) could write, 'I have lost two or three children in infancy, not without regret, but without great sorrow'; and it should be remembered that death was a far more prevalent presence to our ancestors than it is to us; that they feared it less, and that an accommodation with it was necessary if you were going to keep your sanity. It's probably worth stressing here too that although human nature may not have changed a lot, perceptions and habits have. I can remember as a little child having a great-uncle who lived in rural Derbyshire. He hated coming to London because the pollution made his nose bleed. Just as we would recoil from some of the things our ancestors had to put up with – as early as Richard II's day it was said that a traveller could smell London before he could see it – so things we take for granted as something we just have to put up with, such as carbon monoxide emissions, and to which we have adapted, would make our ancestors ill.

Even so, things were improving and the population was slowly increasing, as disease and malnutrition gradually abated. But the economy remained depressed, and any form of nationally organised welfare was still a very long way off. To make matters worse, conflict in Ireland in the last five years of Elizabeth's reign had cost £1,600,000.

It was in this atmosphere that James confronted his parliament. They were a pretty inexperienced lot, sure only of the necessity of protecting their independence from him. James needed his parliament because he had to raise funds, but he cordially disliked its members, especially the lawyers – traditional objects of hatred anyway – who did most of the legwork and were the most vociferous. Luckily in other ways he was a tolerant man, and had no

interest in persecuting any religious minority, though he did dislike extremists, such as the Puritans, and, at the other end of the scale, the Jesuits, whom he decided to evict from the country. Meanwhile, however, the Church Establishment continued to mistrust the Catholics in general, and lobbied the king to keep them under control. At the time there were about 40,000 of them in the country – not enough to raise too much alarm.

Unfortunately, a small group of Catholic extremists, feeling that their co-religionists were under threat, conspired to blow up King James and his parliament. This they attempted to do on 5 November 1605, but their plan was betrayed and failed. The chief members of the Gunpowder Plot, Robert Catesby, Guy Fawkes and the rest were tortured and executed. As for the rest of the British Catholics, James and his parliament came down on them like a ton of bricks. Catholics were banished from London, forbidden to hold any public office, and had to swear an oath of allegiance to the king which was so worded as to make it impossible to comply without at the same time undertaking disobedience to the Pope. For good measure, and no doubt very glad of the excuse to augment his coffers, James confiscated two-thirds of their estates.

In the meantime plans were afoot to prepare a new English translation of the Bible, a standard version to be used in all Church of England churches which would supersede the various Tudor renderings still in use. Committees comprising about 50 scholars in all were set up in Oxford, Cambridge and Westminster to supervise the production of the work, which took until 1611 to complete, and appeared then as the Authorised Version. It is a masterpiece of early seventeenth-century prose and despite recent attempts to put the Bible into more modern, 'accessible' English, it has not been surpassed. This was one of the most important events of the reign. Despite the great flowering of literature in Elizabeth's day, which spilled over into James's (Shakespeare didn't die until 1616, and such luminaries as the poet John Donne were Stuart, not Tudor writers), we shouldn't forget that this upsurge was essentially centred in London, and increasingly aimed at a literate and sophisticated minority. For most people (and levels of literacy were slowly but surely on the rise, at least among the male urban population), the Bible remained the one book available to read, together perhaps with Foxe's *Book of Martyrs*, and it would be another century before any significant number of private individuals acquired libraries.

17th-century culture and science

Culturally, James's reign did not interrupt the development started in Elizabeth's. Francis Bacon continued to explore philosophical and scientific questions, arguing for practical experimental research and the use of logic. In a superstitious age when true science was still in its infancy and far more credence was given to the supernatural, Bacon was well ahead of his time, but the propositions he advanced took root and were not forgotten. Important scientific discoveries were made, too. In 1616 William Harvey, for example, established that blood flows through our bodies. He went on to become James I's personal physician, and late in life published a book which laid the foundations for the science of biology. Both cultural life, and the ordinary life of the farmer and the labourer went on despite all the political upheavals of the first half of the seventeenth century. The period from 1601, beginning with *Hamlet*, also saw the appearance of Shakespeare's finest plays. John Webster, one of the greatest tragedians of the day, wrote his two masterpieces *The White Devil* and *The Duchess of Malfi* in the middle years of James's reign.

The period also saw a continuation of fine music, with the great composer John Bull created first professor of music at Gresham College. Bull also collaborated with William Byrd and Orlando Gibbons in the publication of *Parthenia*, the 'firste musicke that ever was printed for the virginalls'. Music, dance and drama combined in the newly fashionable court masque, which somewhat superseded formal drama as the years passed. These productions involved extravagant set design and spectacle more than complicated plot. The playwright Ben Jonson (1572–1637) and the designer and architect Inigo Jones (1573–1652) collaborated for ten years on masques for James's queen. The partnership must have worked, though God knows how. At his worst, Jonson was a pugnacious drunk, and Jones as vain as he was moody.

Inigo Jones was the first fully professional architect in England, and much of his work can still be admired. In James's day, he was already leaning towards a classical style, and he may well have assisted in the design of Hatfield House, built in Hertfordshire for Raleigh's rival the Earl of Salisbury around 1611. His first truly classical building, though, is the Queen's House at Greenwich, begun in 1616 and twenty years in the building, a villa inspired by the great Italian architect Palladio, and in English terms a century ahead of its time. Not for nothing had Jones accompanied the young Earl of Arundel, one of the first great patrons of art and architecture in England, on a grand tour of Italy in 1612.

Arundel's passion was shared by the Prince of Wales, James's eldest son, Henry, who, though he died very young, started a collection which his brother Charles would inherit and augment, and which would have remained an important national treasure had it not been broken up and sold off under the Republic, the ground for whose arrival was already being prepared by James.

Foreign policy

Abroad, James had to look at a rocky situation. He had inherited a country which was still poor, and he wasn't very popular with his new English and Welsh subjects, who had adored Elizabeth. His best foreign policy was to keep the peace; France was beginning to pull itself out of a long period of instability, and Louis XIII, who came to the throne in 1610 and was to reign for 33 years, soon had one of the ablest politicians ever at his elbow, Cardinal Richelieu.

Added to that, Spain was still an active enemy, though James refused to give in to pressure to help the Dutch, fellow-Protestants, rid themselves of the Spanish yoke. In fact he went to some lengths to mollify the Spanish king (Carlos IX, Philip II having died in 1598). In 1603 one of his first acts as king was to imprison in the Tower those surviving Elizabethans who had been particular thorns in Spain's side. Among them was Sir Walter Raleigh, by then 51 years old, who'd been arrested on a trumped-up charge and sentenced to death, that sentence being commuted to imprisonment because Raleigh remained very popular and conducted his own defence brilliantly. In the Tower Raleigh studied chemistry and wrote a history of the world, but in 1616 James was persuaded to release him, and send him on an expedition to South America to search for gold. Raleigh undertook to do no harm to Spanish settlements, but on arrival at the mouth of the Orinoco he was taken ill, and stayed with the ships while his eldest son and the deputy leader of the expedition went ahead. They failed to find gold, but they attacked and razed the Spanish town of San Thomé. During the fight, Raleigh's son was killed. Raleigh arrived back in England in his one surviving ship in 1618, and without of course bringing any loot with him. To propitiate Spain,

One of the most important houses in architectural history, the Queen's House at Greenwich was the first completely classical piece of architecture in Britain.

James rather shamefully had Raleigh, by then an old man and the last great Elizabethan hero, beheaded on the original charge.

James's daughter Elizabeth, however, had married the ardent German Protestant, Frederick V, in 1613. Frederick became head of the German Protestants, and accepted the crown of Bohemia in 1618 when that country rebelled against the control of the Holy Roman Emperor. Frederick didn't last long, and James took no action to ally himself to his daughter's interests, even though the Holy Roman Emperor was cousin to the King of Spain, and James's own people were anxious at the growing power of the Catholic Counter-reformation. He did try a little diplomacy, but it came to nothing. Meanwhile the quarrel over Bohemia and Frederick's own lands, which the Empire had annexed for good measure, bubbled on, involving Denmark and later Sweden and snowballing into a massive European war between Catholics and Protestants that was to last 30 years.

Meanwhile James, in a policy that added nothing to his already limited popularity, courted Spain, and sent his eldest surviving son Charles, in the company of his latest favourite, the Duke of Buckingham, an abler man than most of the others, though like the rest far from popular, to court the Spanish Infanta. Negotiations for a match began, but the Spanish demanded concessions for English Catholics that James knew he could never wring from his people, who in any case were still lobbying for war with Spain and the Empire.

The next step James took, stage-managed by Buckingham, was adroit. Playing on the continuing rivalry between France and Spain, he managed to arrange the marriage of the Prince of Wales, 25 years old, to the French princess, Louis XIII's sister Henrietta Maria, then 13. It was a calculated risk because Henrietta was a Catholic and therefore deeply resented by the British. But it brought James a powerful ally in mainland Europe, and with France he would be able to satisfy, as he thought, his subjects, by sending military aid to his son-in-law, Frederick, and thus be seen to be doing something to drive a wedge between Spain and the Holy Roman Empire. But the whole plan foundered because, despite the marriage and the political union it brought, Louis XIII trusted James no more than James trusted Louis. The botched campaign saw English soldiers, refused permission to land in France, bogged down in the Spanish Netherlands, where they proceeded to be cut down by disease. In the midst of this debacle James died, aged 59, on 27 March 1625.

Charles I and the Duke of Buckingham

Charles I had been a sickly child, but despite a certain shyness and a stammer which he never got rid of, he was a man of some principle and strength of character, neither alas always sensibly applied. He was in his twenty-fifth year when he came to the throne, but he'd already been running the country with the Duke of Buckingham, who had become his staunch friend, during his father's illness. His marriage turned out to be a happy one, and he and Henrietta Maria had seven children.

Charles inherited a situation that was fraught with difficulties. There was still a great deal of religious tension. Both Catholics and Puritans had left the country to pursue their religious rites in peace. Maryland, named after Henrietta Maria, was founded by Catholic émigrés during Charles's reign; and as early as 1620 the Pilgrim Fathers sailed for the Americas in the *Mayflower*, making landfall in what is now Massachusetts.

'Charles I in Three Positions', by Carlo Maratti.

As Louis XIII's 'Chief Minster', Cardinal Richelieu is often considered the world's first 'Prime Minster'.

The threat of war would not go away either. Richelieu, who'd been consecrated a bishop at the age of 22, was French Secretary of War and Foreign Affairs – a neat twinning – by the age of 31 in 1616. He'd been made a cardinal in 1622 and was chief minister of state in 1624. The following year he'd been instrumental in helping to arrange Charles's marriage, but his motives were more to spite Spain than to form an alliance with Britain. His next task was to break the recovering power of the Huguenots, and by 1628 La Rochelle, a Huguenot stronghold, was under siege. The British Parliament wanted to send armed assistance, a position with which Charles and Buckingham agreed; but they and parliament were already at loggerheads. To understand this we have to go back a bit.

Initially, Charles had been popular with both his people and his parliament, but matters quickly came to a head when parliament made it plain that the Duke of Buckingham – unpopular with them and mistrusted because of the extent of his power – would have to go. Charles refused, and dissolved parliament, but not before it had impeached Buckingham. Then the king had to find money by himself, and with his council's backing tried to enforce taxes without parliament's approval. The judiciary took a dim view of this and wouldn't give its endorsement to the scheme. All this within the first twelve months or so of the reign.

Parliament agreed to drop their pursuit of Buckingham, however, and as a result Charles summoned it again. The members who returned were, however, determined to defend their integrity and oppose what they regarded as any wilful proposals of the king. Charles, who, like his father, was a firm believer in the Divine Right of kings, and had also inherited his father's stubbornness and tactlessness, tried to play along, and parliament voted money for the war with France. However, they attached conditions to their decision and framed them in a Petition of Right. It was drafted by Sir Edward Coke, a brilliant but opportunistic lawyer who had presided over the downfall of Raleigh. It wasn't at all unreasonable in itself; but from Charles's point of view, by agreeing to its terms, he would be signing away far too much power to the people. He prevaricated, but he could see that his refusal to bow to the Petition, which really outlined some pretty basic human rights, was going to make him deeply unpopular. The judiciary told him that signing wouldn't affect his Royal Prerogatives. He got his money, but then at least partially went back on his word. He dismissed both the Lords and the Commons, and with Buckingham set about planning an expedition to relieve La Rochelle. Then a fresh disaster struck: Buckingham was murdered. The La Rochelle expedition foundered, and the Huguenots were defeated.

The arts

Owing to the influence of Arundel and the king, who'd been interested in the arts since his youth, painting in England began to relate itself more consciously to the trends of mainland Europe. Francis Bacon's younger brother, Nathaniel, was a highly talented amateur painter, and the activity would become popular as a pastime. Charles I, who had been introduced to work by Velazquez, Titian and Rubens on his visit to Spain to pay court to the Infanta in 1623 (Philip II had been a great collector himself), began to build on his late brother's acquisitions, and though he failed to tempt Rubens to England with the promise of a knighthood, he did get the famous Flemish artist and diplomat to paint the ceiling panels for the superb Banqueting House designed for the Palace of Whitehall in 1619 as a double cube (he did another at Wilton) by Inigo Jones, which luckily survives, the only part of the palace to do so. Charles was luckier with Anthony van Dyck, who succumbed to a knighthood, a house

and a pension in 1632 and moved to London, where he spent most of the remaining ten years of his short life. His lightly idealised portraits of Charles and the members of his court have immortalised them, and a triple portrait, showing three aspects of Charles's face, was sent to the master sculptor and architect Gianlorenzo Bernini in Rome, who used it to produce an exquisite portrait bust, which in turn triggered in England for the first time an interest in sculpture other than rather stiff traditional church monuments and memorials.

Meanwhile the tradition of the masque continued, and one, *Comus*, was produced for Charles at Ludlow in 1634 with music by Henry Lawes and words by a 26-year-old poet called John Milton. The theatre was coming under increasing attack from Puritans, who had always disapproved of it, but in any case the high standards of the Elizabethan and Jacobean period were in gradual decline. Poetry, by contrast, was in the ascendant, and the religious work of George Herbert, for example, and the amorous songs of Robert Herrick have among them some of the most beautiful poems in the language.

Charles, his council and parliament

Charles ruled by himself for eleven years. (That is, he ruled together with his council – a small group of hand-picked men, usually nobles, to advise him and guide policy.) There were two principal advisers, the Earl of Strafford, and William Laud, Archbishop of Canterbury – the latter an intelligent but ambitious and blinkered man out of his depth in national politics, who managed to alienate the Scots by insisting that they use the English Prayer Book. Charles compounded this imperious action by trying to take for himself former Catholic Church estates in Scotland which had been in the possession of Scottish nobles since the Reformation. This led to a disastrous war with Scotland, at the end of which Charles's standing with many of his people had fallen to an irredeemably low ebb.

In 1640, under huge pressure, he called parliament again, in order to organise taxes to pay for the Scottish war. This convocation, known to history as the Short Parliament, spent

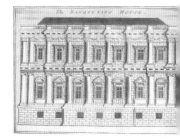

TOP
The siege against the Hugenot stronghold at La Rochelle in 1628.

ABOVE
The Banqueting House in Whitehall, designed by Inigo Jones and with superb ceiling panels by Reubens, introduced the new Renaissance style.

most of its time in disagreement with the king, airing its grievances at having been deprived of a right to have a say in government for over a decade. One powerful member was a Puritan, John Pym, whose resistance to voting funds to Charles resulted in the king once again exercising his unpopular rights and dissolving parliament after three weeks. But in November Charles was forced once more to recall it, and this, the Long Parliament, would make a big impression. It began by impeaching Charles's other main adviser and stalwart, Thomas Wentworth, Earl of Strafford, on a cleverly constructed charge of treason. In 1640 Strafford was executed, and William Laud was soon to follow.

By now, powerful men had control of the reins of government and they were not going to hand them back to Charles, however much he might wish to summon and dissolve parliament at his will. The fact is that Charles had painted himself into a corner. By poor judgement and weakness he had lost control, and the coming men were not only commoners but also Puritans. One of them was the MP for Cambridge, a Huntingdon landowner who would soon find his place in history: Oliver Cromwell. Now, by a narrow majority won by the parliamentarians over the king's supporters, and after a furious debate, a document splendidly called The Grand Remonstrance was passed at Westminster. It was huge, covered everything, and put Charles in his place.

Charles of course was not going to take this lying down, but in his response he made another fatal error. Early in January 1642 he marched to the House of Commons with about 350 men – the original Cavaliers – to arrest Pym and four other of his principal enemies among the parliamentarians on charges of high treason. They'd been forewarned and they'd fled. Unfortunately for Charles, London was staunchly parliamentarian and when the population learned what had happened, they demonstrated outside the Palace of Whitehall. Most of the demonstrators consisted of organised gangs of City apprentices, whose short haircuts later gave rise to the nickname given to the parliamentary forces: the Roundheads.

The Royal Family retreated to Hampton Court. Negotiations trickled on for another few months, but parliament was making demands Charles couldn't accept without suffering personal humiliation and the betrayal of his own beliefs and principles. In the meantime both sides were gathering forces and a civil war was inevitable. It was almost certainly what the Puritan parliament wanted anyway. They had seen a way in which they could get rid of their monarch for good and all.

Civil War

Hostilities began formally in August. Not a propitious moment, for it was harvest-time, and ordinary people were more interested in getting it in than fighting each other. The two causes, however, had kindled strong emotions, even though to begin with the issue was blurred by the parliamentary side who, to legitimise their campaign, claimed to be acting in the interests of the King. By September Charles had an army of about 2000 cavalry and 6000 infantry, which was augmented by troops and trained professional officers sent by the queen from Holland, where she had fled. She would later return to France.

Charles's problem throughout the war was lack of funds. The Roundheads, supported financially by London, by far the biggest and richest city in the country, could command far greater resources, and soon had an army of 25,000 in the field, trained and disciplined by professional German officers, specially imported for the purpose, and infused with revolutionary

Oliver Cromwell was the first commoner to hold the post of the Head of State from 1653 to 1658 – the only other being his son, Richard Cromwell (1653–1658).

zeal. When Oliver Cromwell later replaced the Earl of Manchester as its leader, it became an even more formidable force.

What's especially interesting from the point of view of the family historian researching this period is that the two sides were divided along geographical rather than class lines. It is also true to say that the lines were determined in many cases by principle and ideology. Families and dear friends found themselves at odds with one another, though no doubt too the reasons for splits were personal – the rebellious son choosing to oppose the autocratic father, for example. Many individuals chose their side through self-interest. Others felt the king's sacred position as Defender of the Faith should be supported. But on the whole you could say that most of the larger towns and ports supported parliament. However, Oxford was for the king, while Cambridge was for parliament, York was for the king; Hull, then an important port, changed from being a parliament town to a Royalist one. Bristol, too, supported Charles, and later in the war his cousin Prince Rupert, a dashing character who was to prove himself as able a fighter on land as on sea, and a worthy adversary of Cromwell and his maritime counterpart Admiral Blake, took Liverpool for the Crown. You could broadly say that the south-west of the country, as well as a wide tract between Wales and the Yorkshire Dales, supported Charles, and the rest (and the Scots) sided with parliament.

The first major battle was at Edgehill in Warwickshire on 23 October 1642. It ended indeterminately, with both sides naturally claiming victory. Charles established a kind of government-in-exile at his headquarters in Oxford, while in London the parliamentarians were momentarily fazed by the emergence of a Peace Party. But the war went on doggedly, and as it did, the Roundheads, deploying their famous Ironside infantry (who got their name from the sobriquet given Cromwell by Rupert at Marston Moor), as well as the heavily armoured London cavalry, nicknamed the Lobsters, slowly gained the upper hand. Cromwell was not a soldier by training, nor Robert Blake a seaman. Blake, who'd briefly been an academic and until the age of 40 had led the quiet life of a country gentleman, had already surpassed himself as a land commander before taking over the then broken-down navy at the age of 50. Within two years he had totally transformed it, and honed it into a fighting force with which he would ultimately rout Prince Rupert. (After the war, during the Commonwealth under Cromwell, he took on the Dutch and broke their maritime domination.) Blake is less well known than Nelson, but every bit as great an English seaman. Only Drake surpasses them.

Given how few people were actually directly involved in the Civil War (about 3 per cent of the male population), it is amazing that it was so widespread. Its battles covered the country, extending from engagements at Newbury in the south to Naseby in the Midlands in 1645, to the north of the country, as the Royalists under Prince Rupert and the fat Marquess of Newcastle, who had held York and the north for the king, were routed at Marston Moor in 1644.

All the time parliamentary power waxed. Cromwell, a tough, ruthless and instinctive strategist, in battle as in politics, proud of his plainness of appearance and manner (and actually making rather a thing of them – he asked that his portrait be painted with 'warts and all' included), grew ever stronger among the leaders of the rebellion. And the parliamentary army was developing into a proper, professional, uniformed force. Under Cromwell after the war, this New Model Army, as it was called, would become the prototype for the first British standing army ever.

Cromwell at the head of his troops after the battle of Marston Moor in 1644.

The royalists lost the north at Marston Moor. At Naseby their last significant field-force was crushed. By 1646 it appeared that the war was over; but now a quarrel broke out between the unpaid New Model Army and the House of Commons, which was bereft of some of its strongest members, like Pym, who had died, over tolerance of rites within Protestantism.

Other problems were appearing with the peace: taxes had been raised to pay for the war, hitting the upper and middle classes hardest, but an increased tax on beer affected everyone, since beer was the staple drink of men, women and children, in preference to water, which was deemed unhealthy. Drinks like tea had of course not made their appearance yet. It's worth mentioning another tax – a kind of council tax – called the *scot*, an old word of German origin for a payment. This was a most unpopular tax but if you were astute you could get out of it – you would then be scot-free!

The road to Charles' execution

Seizing his opportunity Charles, down but not out, found renewed support in the north. He was still king, and still a popular figure, and his position was helped by the fact that the New Model Army, some 22,000 men, faced rebellion from factions that had hitherto been loyal to the cause it supported. Landlords and merchants who'd hoped to keep the workers in their place turned against it. London was becoming nervous of its power. The Scottish army, not fully paid for its support, was rumbling, and the Scots in general were unhappy at the way Presbyterianism was being viewed by the English. There was an uprising in the south-west, and a royalist force appeared in Essex. The Welsh rebelled. Even the navy turned against its master.

At its head, Cromwell led the New Model Army, or sent detachments of it, and in the course of 1648 crushed all opposition. The German training and discipline had paid off, and the army stood fast as a coherent force. With it at his back, Cromwell could take overall command, and in the interests of national solidarity and security, he did so. He was effectively a dictator. Later he would affect the title Lord Protector.

Meanwhile Charles had fled to Carisbrooke Castle on the Isle of Wight. From there, at the end of November, he was brought to London. In January 1649 he was tried. Sentenced on 29 January, his death warrant was signed by Cromwell, John Bradshaw, Thomas Grey and Lord Groby. He was beheaded in front of the Palace of Whitehall, outside Inigo Jones's Banqueting House, the following day. Among the crowd who watched the execution were the teenaged Samuel Pepys, and the Puritan politician, MP for Hull, and poet – the greatest of his age after Milton – Andrew Marvell, who, in the following year, wrote the following description of it:

He nothing common did or mean
Upon that memorable scene:
But with his keener eye
The axe's edge did try:
Nor called the gods with vulgar spite
To vindicate his helpless right,
But bowed his comely head,
Down as upon a bed.

GIVEN HOW FEW PEOPLE WERE ACTUALLY DIRECTLY INVOLVED IN THE CIVIL WAR (ABOUT 3 PER CENT OF THE MALE POPULATION), IT IS AMAZING THAT IT WAS SO WIDESPREAD

The execution of Charles I, outside the Banqueting Hall in Whitehall.

THE CIVIL WAR AND
THE CROMWELLIAN
REPUBLIC WHICH
UPSET THE
CONTINUITY OF
ROYAL POWER IN THE
MIDDLE DECADES OF
THE SEVENTEENTH
CENTURY DID LITTLE
OR NOTHING TO
ALLEVIATE THE
POSITION OF THE
POOR

Marvell was a committed Puritan, and became assistant to John Milton, who was Cromwell's Latin Secretary and chief apologist. But there is no doubt that these lines, from a poem which is principally about Cromwell's return from a military expedition to Ireland, strike a great chord of sympathy for Charles. It is thought that the poem, like all Marvell's work unpublished in his lifetime, circulated in Royalist circles. At the Restoration, Marvell was pardoned and successfully interceded (with William Davenant) for Milton's life. Davenant was repaying a compliment. Milton had once during the Commonwealth got him out of the Tower. In hard times, poets should stick together!

Judicial regicide was unprecedented. It took strong nerves and iron commitment to see such an act through. Cromwell had both.

The inequity of wealth

The rise of ordinary people was significant. In France and Germany, the peasantry and farmworkers still had very little freedom, but in England, even humble villagers were able slowly to gain some measure of independence. They also enjoyed the possibility of leaving the country and colonising distant lands, and some, like the Pilgrim Fathers, did so. Slowly the crises of the Tudor era were passing, and some measure of stability, if not actual prosperity, was returning. Small wonder so few welcomed the disturbance of the Civil War.

Until the middle of the nineteenth century, about 80 per cent of the population of the British Isles worked on the land. Or at least they tried to, because the greed of landowners often led them to sequester and fence off for their own use areas of what was once common land. This meant that poor rural labourers lost the benefit of common grazing and were sometimes deprived of what little land they had to tend for themselves. These people made up a significant proportion of the population and the chances of some of us having ancestors who belonged to this class are pretty high.

The Civil War and the Cromwellian Republic which upset the continuity of royal power in the middle decades of the seventeenth century did little or nothing to alleviate the position of the poor. We are able to confirm this by looking at the findings of Gregory King, a pioneer statistician and genealogist who was born in 1648. He made a detailed analysis of the population and relative wealth of Great Britain in the closing years of the century and came up with the following figures: out of a total population of 5,500,520, there were 1,275,000 who could be classified as 'labouring people and outservants', whose annual income per family amounted to an average £15. Below them came some 1,300,000 people classed as 'cottagers and paupers' whose annual income only reached about £6.50 per family. Families were not as large in the old days as is sometimes believed, so that an average household might number around five. After all, people didn't live much beyond sixty and among the poorer classes thirty was a respectable lifespan.

Below what might be classed as the lowest stratum of working poor, King placed the 'vagrants, gypsies, thieves and beggars', whose income was indeterminate, and who totalled some 30,000. This last estimate seems conservative in view of the number of vagrants in London alone, but it gives an indication of how money was dispersed. To give you a bit of an idea, rather than embark on the dubious task of trying to give modern equivalents of the sums of money I've mentioned, a good ticket to a London theatre in 1680 or so would set you back 12 or 13p, and, more cogently still, we can take a look at the cost to the Earl of Bedford of a weekend jaunt to Cambridge (where he'd studied) from London in 1689.

Meals alone at the Red Lion in the city came to £15.20 for one day, not including food for his servants which came to nearly £7.00. One item on the bills that have come to light is £4.85 – 'the bill for wine and glasses broke'. The whole sum paid by the earl for his trip came to twelve times the annual income of his senior footman.

The state did try to make some allowance for the dispossessed poor. There was an Act of Settlement in 1662 which provided that settlement could be acquired by forty days' undisturbed residence in a parish, but also that any newcomer could within forty days be removed to the parish where he was last legally settled by birth, residence or apprenticeship, unless he or she could afford to rent a lodging for at least £10 a year – clearly beyond the reach of the destitute. This left the responsibility very much in the hands of local parishes. The problem was, the local parishes saw the poor as a burden and they did everything they could to shift them physically out of the area of their responsibility. The ploy saved them money. The account books of parish constables of the period and well before reveal the relative expense of relief doled out to the poor. Most such unfortunates were sent back whence they came and no doubt received a very doubtful welcome there:

Given to a poore man and his wife and five Children which lay a day and night in James Bloomer's barn ——————— 1s. 8d.
Given to a cripple woman being sent from constable to constable in a cart being very weake and feeble, she being reliefed with meat and money ——————— 8d.

Rural labourers formed a large proportion of the population until the nineteenth century.

WITH PEOPLE
ACTUALLY BEING PAID
TO GO ROUND
SMASHING IN PANES
OF FOURTEENTH-
CENTURY WINDOWS
AND KNOCKING THE
HEADS OFF SAINTS

Gregory King estimated that a high-ranking aristocrat might make £3200 a year; someone in a position corresponding to a modern senior civil servant, about £240; a successful businessman, £400; a successful artist, £60; and a shopkeeper, £45. Samuel Pepys, who kept his famous *Diary* between 1660 and 1669, was a rising young administrator in the Navy Office during that time. He was a materialistic man, ambitious and almost obsessive about making money. At the beginning of 1661 he tells us he's worth £300 'clear'. By July 1665 he'd saved £2000; and three years later he was able to afford the ultimate status symbol: a coach and horses of his own. Pepys' coach was painted bright yellow.

If one had been descended from Pepys, one would probably not have too hard a time of it tracing oneself back to him. Most of us will be faced with the harder task of finding an ancestor who was far lower down the social ladder, who was probably illiterate, and who would consequently have left no personal written (or indeed any other) memoir or clue about their existence.

To which should be added that, if you are of Jewish ancestry, it's worth noting that Cromwell allowed Jews to live in England officially again in 1654, for the first time since they had been banished by Edward I in 1290 (see Part One). Cromwell needed an injection of financial acumen, and the first Jewish immigrants tended to be wealthy merchants and bankers from the Iberian peninsula. (The following year many left for New Amsterdam, the Dutch settlement on an island on the north-east coast of America.)

Cromwell's Republic

Once in place, Cromwell acted decisively to get rid of all opposition. Dissenting Puritan extremists, such as the ultra-democratic Levellers, and the Diggers, who held that no property should be privately owned, were crushed. The monarchy, the House of Lords and the Anglican Church were abolished. All official attributes of royalty were done away with. Anyone declaring the slightest doubt about the rectitude of the execution of Charles would be imprisoned. Anyone supporting the Prince of Wales, also Charles, would be declared a traitor and, if caught, suffer execution. Government was to be by a Council of State.

There was no way of resisting the power of the army. Ireland, which still housed Royalist sympathisers, suffered defeat and massacres in a bloody campaign of 1649. Ireland, as a Catholic country, was to suffer greatly under Cromwell. Most of the land passed from Irish to British ownership, and the power of local leaders was destroyed. Ironically, it was the priests of Ireland who kept the spirit of nationalism alive.

In September 1650, rebellious Scots were defeated at the Battle of Dunbar and 3000 of them slaughtered. When the survivors retaliated, after Cromwell's withdrawal, by declaring the Prince of Wales King Charles II and crowning him at Scone (he had sought refuge in Scotland after his father's fall), the dictator bided his time. He knew any force that rallied around Charles would be doomed to failure if it marched on England, and that the English Royalists were definitively stripped of any power.

Charles's army duly crossed the border and made its way south. Cromwell allowed them to come on, and met them at Worcester, by which time their lines of supply were long, in the late summer of 1651. Once again he was victorious, but Charles escaped, by hiding in an oak tree according to tradition (hence the number of Royal Oak pubs there are), and made his way to Holland. He would spend the next nine years either there or at the French court, where Louis XIV, whose long reign would stretch to 1715, was already concentrating his power.

Cromwell did not maintain his stern rule alone. Robert Blake, as has been mentioned, strove to curb Dutch maritime power, and an expedition to the West Indies in 1655 under the command of Admiral William Penn (father of the famous Quaker who founded Pennsylvania) and General Robert Venables took Jamaica from Spain and established a lasting British toehold in the Caribbean. In fact the expedition had been ordered to take the then far more important and better defended island of Hispaniola, so when Venables and Penn returned, a furious Cromwell slung them in the Tower for a month. The expeditionary force left behind to occupy Jamaica was all but abandoned, though it hung on, and many would never return home, some later swelling the ranks of the buccaneers, pirates and privateers who were soon to throng the Caribbean seas, among them men still wearing the now-faded red uniforms of the New Model Army.

Culture under Cromwell

The arts during the Commonwealth did not have much of a time. Puritan zealots destroyed much of the beautiful medieval church statuary and stained glass that had survived the iconoclasts of the English Reformation, with people actually being paid to go round smashing in panes of fourteenth-century windows and knocking the heads off saints.

All royal patronage of painting and architecture ceased, though portrait-painters like Robert Walker, who painted a wartless and rather noble-looking Cromwell, survived (as well, to be fair, as Samuel Cooper, whose miniature of the Lord Protector is almost overgenerous with the warts). William Dobson succeeded van Dyck, who died in 1641 aged only 42, as Cromwell's unofficial 'court painter'. Dobson's style was more solid and naturalistic than van Dyck's, suitably enough, but he is genuinely good, and John Aubrey thought him 'the most excellent painter that England hath yet bred'. And the Dutchman Peter Lely, who had worked for Charles I, survived under Cromwell, and under Charles II became not only court painter in his turn, but was given a knighthood.

Another area of the humanities untouched by the Puritans was the field of philosophy, a term used more broadly then than it is today. The principal new work of this period was Thomas Hobbes's *Leviathan*, published in 1651; a book which started a more than century-long evolution of philosophy in Britain, to which such great thinkers as John Locke (1632–1704) and the Scotsman David Hume (1711–1776) were major contributors. Hobbes is thought of today as the father of English moral and political philosophy. He took Francis Bacon's ground-breaking premises further, and drew advantage from the fact that travels abroad Europeanised him and brought him into contact with Descartes and Galileo. The tenets dealing with statehood in *Leviathan* didn't entirely please the exiled Charles in Paris, as Hobbes was opposed to any idea of the Divine Right of Kings, something which Charles was unwilling to let go of; but his general conceptions are ones we would probably agree with today: that the state is a kind of giant composed of innumerable people; that the natural human condition is one of 'war of every man against every man', and that consequently an ordered society is a form of self-defence. This leads to one of the most famous quotations, often taken out of context, that without such a society life would be 'solitary, poor, nasty, brutish and short'.

On a pragmatic level Hobbes, essentially a materialist and a cynic, prudently left England in 1640 and stayed in Paris until 1651. (Hobbes counted among his close friends William Davenant and John Aubrey, who wrote biographies of them both. There were fewer of us in those days, there was less privacy, snobbery and insecurity, and our circles crossed more. By the way, do read Aubrey's *Brief Lives* – see Part Three for details – it is a beautiful book, and a valuable resource for the sixteenth and seventeenth centuries.)

The area of the arts that suffered most was drama. The theatres were closed in 1642, not to reopen until the Restoration. As we've seen, Puritans had always been opposed to plays. As early as 1576, when James Burbage built the first theatre in London, unpleasant, even hysterical comments were being passed: 'Satan hath not a more speedy way ... to bring men and women into his snare of concupiscence and filthy lusts of wicked whoredom, than those plays and theatres ... 'And in 1630 William Prynne let fly with: 'Stage-plays, the very pomps of the Devil, are sinful, heathenish, lewd, ungodly spectacles ...' Unfortunately for Prynne, Queen Henrietta Maria not only enjoyed the theatre, but herself played in masques, so he had his ears lopped off by the public executioner; but in the end his fellow-zealots saw to it that there was no more spoken drama for eighteen years. Many actors were put out of work. Some troupes left for the Continent. But however rigorous they were, the Puritans couldn't police the whole country, and small groups of strolling players survived and continued to practise their profession, at fairs and in inn yards, throughout the Republican period.

There was, however, one extraordinary chink in this armour. The Puritans had nothing against music. Milton had contributed to a masque, and was himself an accomplished player. John Bunyan, during his twelve years in Bedford Gaol following his arrest for unlawful preaching in 1660, relaxed when he was not writing by playing a home-made flute. And Cromwell himself had the organ of Magdalen College, Oxford, dismantled and moved to

Sir William Davenant, the playwright and poet, who was the godson of William Shakespeare, and was rumoured to be his biological son though this is thought unlikely.

Hampton Court, where he had set up his palace. Under the Commonwealth, apart from what they saw as the flowery cadences of the Anglican Rite, music, including secular music, was encouraged, and continued to be played and published.

The playwright and theatre manager William Davenant was well aware of this. An energetic self-publicist who claimed descent from Shakespeare, he was a resourceful man who'd been made Poet Laureate in 1638 at the request of Henrietta Maria, as successor to Ben Jonson, who'd just died. Davenant's plays were, on the whole, pretty poor, but he was not a bad poet. He had also recently suffered a cruel fate: the loss of his nose through the pox – venereal disease – which misfortune excited mockery from court wits and poets like Sir John Denham. (There wasn't really such a thing as delicate feelings in those days. One of the rules laid out for well-behaved courtiers by Castiglione is, 'When you meet a blind man, do not say to him, How many fingers am I holding up?')

Davenant became manager of the Cockpit Theatre (later Drury Lane) in London; but at the outbreak of war in 1642 he was relieved of his job by the rebels and flung in the Tower. He quickly escaped to France, returning to fight on the king's side and earning himself a knighthood (conferred by the Earl of Newcastle) in 1643. This didn't prevent him from getting into trouble with the Puritans again, resulting in two more years in the Tower.

While in France, Davenant had visited Paris, and there he'd seen a performance of the Italian opera, very little known in England at the time. As he knew that the government had no objection to music, he managed to get permission to perform his play *The Siege of Rhodes* with the words sung 'in recitative musicke'. This was in effect the first notable English opera (Richard Flecknoe had composed one called *Ariadne* two years earlier), performed at Rutland House in 1656, at the height of Cromwellian power. It was designed by Inigo Jones's pupil, John Webb (Jones died in 1652), in the style of a masque. It featured moving scenery, another first, which Davenant was to exploit after the Restoration. But the best is yet to come: Davenant was allowed to use female actors to play the women's roles. *The Siege of Rhodes* featured Mrs Coleman, the first actress that ever appeared on an English stage.

The production wasn't a one-off. In 1659 the other famous diarist of the age, John Evelyn, a sophisticated writer and lawyer who kept a journal for 60 years, went to see Davenant's propaganda piece, *Cruelty of the Spaniards in Peru*. Evelyn, a travelled man, found the production 'much inferior to the Italian composure and magnificence'.

Death of the Republic

Cromwell's Republic lasted seven years. The Lord Protector, who had always refused to reign as king, died on 3 September 1658, aged 59. He had not made a huge impact overseas, though his Caribbean venture and the efforts of Blake, who died from wounds fighting the Spanish the year before, had re-established us as a sea-power. At home, Cromwell's overly tough policies in Scotland and Wales, and his atrocious treatment of the Irish, coupled with a quasi-military method of domestic government, meant he left behind few to admire him and many to hate him. His son Richard, an amiable enough man, took over the reins of power, but he hadn't the force of personality or even the interest to control the conflicting factions which quickly grew up. Known as Tumbledown Dick, he lasted about six months, surrendering power in May 1659 and going to live abroad under the name John Clarke, and to continue his favourite country pursuits. He returned to England in 1680 as a private individual, and died unremarked at Cheshunt in 1712.

'SATAN HATH NOT A MORE SPEEDY WAY … TO BRING MEN AND WOMEN INTO HIS SNARE OF CONCUPISCENCE AND FILTHY LUSTS OF WICKED WHOREDOM, THAN THOSE PLAYS AND THEATRES …'

PEPYS WAS AMONG
THOSE WHO, WITH
MOUNTAGU, SAILED
IN LATE MAY 1660 TO
COLLECT CHARLES
FROM THE
CONTINENT

The country was falling into chaos and the parliament was in tatters. Ordinary people were fed up with Puritan supremacism and autocracy, and with the damper that had been put on the pleasures of life. Luckily the army, as a force for maintaining some kind of stability, stood firm behind its commander-in-chief, General George Monk, a sensible and cool-headed man without the ambition to rule himself. He was able to restore order in London and arrange for new parliamentary elections, a process everyone recognised and welcomed with relief. It was, however, quite clear that the republican experiment had now failed, perhaps above all because there was no one to take it forward. The only way to dispel the chaos and bring back stability was to restore the monarchy, though the people had no intention of restoring to the king-in-exile the same rights as his father had possessed, or at least tried to assert, over the government.

Return of the monarchy

To preside over this the Rump Parliament was restored. This had been the tail-end of the old Long Parliament (hence its name), which had been dismissed by Cromwell finally in 1653. It wasn't much good, but it could at least maintain continuity, and that was what Monk was most interested in doing in the period of transition and negotiation with Charles.

We are very fortunate that it was on 1 January 1660 that Samuel Pepys, then rising 27 years old and embarking on a career in naval administration, should have decided to start his *Diary*. This wonderful account, which he kept daily for almost a decade, gives us a unique flavour of how life was lived in the latter half of the seventeenth century. Among the day-to-day entries for early 1660 there creeps in an increasing sense of excitement. Pepys was fairly close to the action, too, since his cousin and employer, Edward Mountagu, had been a Cromwellian politician and was a naval commander. Mountagu (1625-1672) had had nothing to do with the arraignment of Charles I, but he had been close to Cromwell in the early days. Now disaffected, he was closely allied to Monk, and one of those responsible for the plans to bring Charles II back. Owing to his family and professional connections, Pepys was among those who, with Mountagu, sailed in late May 1660 to collect Charles from the Continent. A flotilla of warships was sent over for the job, but they all still had their parliamentary names. Charles was welcome to return, but the message had to be stressed that this would be on certain conditions. Mountagu and Pepys travelled on the *Naseby*, a name that would not be without significance for Charles, who on the 23 May 1660 was just under a week shy of his 30th birthday. Pepys' entry for that day is long and ecstatic. Here is some of it:

The King, with the two Dukes, the Queen of Bohemia, Princesse Royalle and Prince of Orange, came on board; where I in their coming kissed the Kings, Queen and Princesses hands ... Infinite shooting off of the guns, and that in disorder on purpose, which was better than if it had been otherwise.

After dinner, the King and Duke [of York, the future James II] upon the [quarter-deck] altered the name of some of the Shipps, viz. the Nazeby into the Charles – The *Richard, James*; the *Speaker, Mary* ...

... we weighed Ancre, and with a fresh gale and most happy weather we set sail for England – all the afternoon the King walking here and there, up and down (quite contrary to what I thought him to have been), very active and stirring.

The House of Parliament
in session in 1641.

Upon the Quarter-deck he fell into discourse of his escape from Worcester. Where it made me ready to weep to hear the stories that he told of his difficulties he had passed through. As his travelling four days and three nights on foot, every step up to the knees in dirt, with nothing but a green coat and a pair of country breeches on and a pair of country shoes, that made him so sore all over his feet that he could scarcely stir.

On 25 May they arrived on the English coast and transferred to a barge to take them ashore. Pepys continues:

I went, and ... one of the King's footmen, with a dog that the King loved (which shit in the boat, which made us laugh and me think that a King and all that belong to him are but just as others are) ... and so got on shore when the King did, who was received by General Monke with all imaginable love and respect at his entrance upon the land at Dover. ... the shouting and joy expressed by all is past imagination.

29 May was Charles' 30th birthday. A very new age indeed was about to begin.

avid 'The Duke' Dickinson is the television antiques expert whose flamboyant charm and popularity turned him into a cult figure following his success on BBC's *Bargain Hunt*. He was born in 1941 and grew up in Stockport. His wife of over thirty years is the international cabaret artist Lorne Lesley. David's ancestral quest has been especially meaningful for him, because he was adopted.

David's parents, Jim and Joyce Dickinson, adopted him as a baby – something he wasn't to find out until he was about 12 years old. But he had always felt 'different'. From an early age he showed a sharp business instinct, but he didn't immediately go into antiques. When he left school at 14 he first worked as an apprentice in an aircraft factory, though he left after only six months for a job in the textile industry, following – though he didn't know it at the time – in his real grandfather's footsteps.

Once he had discovered – by chance – that he was adopted, Jim and Joyce admitted it was true, and Joyce explained that they had taken him from a Barnardo's Home. They also told him that his birth mother was an Armenian called Eugenie Gulessarian, who had lived locally. David was neither distressed nor even particularly surprised by these revelations, and it wasn't until he was in his twenties that he made any attempt to track Eugenie down. He loved his adoptive parents and his grandmother (who'd nevertheless wondered whether he might not turn out to be a bit of a spiv), and felt happy and secure with them.

As time passed, though, David became curious about his birth-family and his Armenian roots. He also wanted to find out why Eugenie had let him go. When he acquired some photographs of his birth-mother Jenny (as she was known) and her parents, Hrant and Marie-Adelaide, he was struck by how similar in appearance they were to him. And not just in appearance. Hrant was a successful textiles entrepreneur in Manchester.

But what had brought Hrant to Manchester from the city of Istanbul where he'd grown up? At the end of the nineteenth century, Istanbul was the centre of the Ottoman Empire, a vast empire ruled by the Sultan, which included Anatolia, parts of the Middle East and most of South East Europe. As a consequence it was a rich mix of many cultural groups. In a city like Istanbul, Turks lived side by side with Greeks and Armenians. However, by the mid-nineteenth century the political situation was shifting. Previously subjected peoples began to gain their independence and the empire was losing its power. During the reign of Abdul Hamid (1876–1909) resentment towards the Armenians by the Turks was growing. Massacres occurred in 1894 and 1896, in which thousands of Armenians died. When the secular Young Turks government came to power in 1908, they perpetuated this persecution. Further massacres of the Armenians occurred during the First World War. These massacres of 1915 and 1916 are known as the Armenian Genocide, in which two million Armenians are thought to have perished.

This persecution within the Ottoman Empire caused many surviving Armenians to flee. Although it's likely that the political situation in Istanbul contributed to Hrant's

MARIE SHOWED DAVID A LETTER JENNY HAD WRITTEN TO HIM: 'I HOPE YOU CAN FORGIVE ME, BECAUSE I CAN NEVER FORGIVE MYSELF ...'

ABOVE
Jim and Joyce Dickinson, David's adoptive parents.

ABOVE RIGHT
David's birth mother, Eugenie Gulessarian.

OPPOSITE
David looking at family photos with his half-brother, Ken.

departure from the city, it was trade links and the family textile business that brought Hrant to Manchester. Manchester had had close trade links with Turkey through the textile industry since the 1840s, and when Hrant arrived there in the early 1900s there was already an established Armenian community. Hrant joined an uncle who already lived in Manchester and was running a family textiles business, exporting cotton and other fabrics to Turkey. By coincidence, the address of grandfather Hrant's business turned out to be just a stone's throw from where David worked when he was in the textile trade. The local Armenian church, Holy Trinity, built in 1869, is still a centre for the Mancunian Armenian community. There David found records of the baptism of his mother Jenny, and her brother and sister, John and Marie, as well as an entry for Hrant and Marie-Adelaide's marriage. He also found the address of Hrant's family home – Warford House in the village of Great Warford, only twenty minutes' drive from David's own home. He paid a visit, and was shown round by the present owner.

Hrant was not particularly happy, however. His marriage to Marie-Adelaide (who was French, according to family tradition) was stormy, and there were terrible rows. Finally Marie-Adelaide left Hrant for a man with whom she'd been having an affair, but Hrant gained custody of the children. When David checked in the Manchester Records Office, he found that his grandmother was born Marie-Adelaide Jackson, the daughter of a Moss Side baker. There was no hint of French blood. The records further showed that Hrant

divorced her for adultery with a man called Frederick Williams. David remembered that in all the photographs he'd seen of his grandmother she looked unhappy.

There was more to come. Through his cousin, Mark Gulessarian, the son of David's uncle John, David learned from Hrant's will that at the time of his death in 1963 his fortune had declined radically, perhaps on account of the slump in trade that followed the Second World War. He died a relatively poor man.

David wanted to find out more about his adoption. Research into Barnardo's Homes records for 1941 showed no trace of his having been through their hands. Why should his adoptive mother not have told him the truth? Was it possible that he had been privately adopted? (Such arrangements were not uncommon during the Second World War.)

David's research led him to his birth-mother Jenny's younger sister, Marie. Marie is almost the last link with that generation, and although David made contact with his birth-mother in the late 1960s, and exchanged letters and talked on the telephone with her, at her request he never met her. She died in 1989. David only knew about Marie because after his mother's death her husband told him she had a sister. Marie told David that it was very likely he had been adopted privately. Joyce Dickinson had been Jenny's hairdresser. Jenny had had an affair with a married man and when she discovered she was pregnant she hadn't wanted to risk breaking his marriage up. She didn't dare admit her condition to her parents, as her father Hrant was a strict traditionalist, and, it emerged, a heavy-handed father. So she was obliged to take the painful step of having her baby adopted. Marie showed David a letter Jenny had written to him: 'I hope you can forgive me, because I can never forgive myself …'

Jenny started a new life. Shortly after giving David up, she met a dance-band pianist called Bert Moss, whom she married, going to live with him in Jersey. Together

ABOVE
Hrant Gulessarian:
Eugenie's father was
a successful textiles
entrepreneur who moved
from Turkey to Manchester
in the early 1900s.

TOP
A school portrait of David.

they had a son, Ken. Jenny told David about his half-brother Ken before she died, but Ken only found out about David's existence some time after her death. David decided to go to Jersey to meet his half-brother. Interestingly, it turned out that Ken and David share similar looks.

Ken lives with his wife Sue in the bungalow that belonged to Jenny and Bert. Ken told David that Jenny never acknowledged her Armenian roots, wasn't close to her parents, and, once in Jersey, seems to have wanted to cut all links with her past. But David took comfort from the fact that his mother found happiness in her marriage and her new life.

Meanwhile David's cousin Mark had been doing more research into the family's history, and told David that grandfather Hrant had arrived in England in 1904. Mark had also discovered that Hrant's father, Boghos, was buried in Istanbul in 1919. A funeral notice gives the location of the cemetery, and provides a list of other Gulessarian family members. David decided to travel to Istanbul, where he enlisted the help of local Armenian historian Ani Degirmenioglu to look for the family grave. Sadly, the plot no longer existed. There had been no one to tend it, so at some point it had been sold to another family.

Ani explained to David that Armenians were treated as second-class citizens by the Turks, and many were buried in unmarked graves. In Istanbul at least, where the Western press was well established and there was a strong European influence and presence, Armenians could live in relative safety; the massacres took place in the remote east of the country. However, officially Turkey still fails to acknowledge what took place, and discourages research into the genocide.

The trail of great-grandfather Boghos didn't go cold with the missing grave. In Holy Trinity church in Istanbul, Ani found a funeral certificate for him, from which she learned that Boghos had died aged 63 of dysentery at the holiday resort of Yenimahalle on the Bosphorus. His home address was 64 Sakizagac in Istanbul, in those days a prosperous district, but now run down and neglected. The family house itself is deserted and locked up.

David decided to check out the resort where Boghos died, and where it is believed he had a summer house, or *yali*. Back in Istanbul David and Ani paid a visit to the church where Hrant was baptised to consult the records there. Psamatia church records revealed a mass of Gulessarian ancestors of whom David had no inkling, listing great-great-grandparents and their children, down to baptismal records for grandfather Hrant, born in 1888, a younger brother, Vahe Suren, and possibly the uncle whom Hrant joined in Manchester, Sdepan.

David enlisted the help of local historian Edhem Eldem to find out more about that end of the family business, and discovered that the premises used by his family still exist and are still used by textile traders, though the Gulessarian business petered out in the late 1920s. Armenian records at the Holy Trinity Church revealed that Sdepan, who had returned to Turkey, died there in 1919. Another uncle concerned with the business died in 1926. Both men were in their late 50s, and there appears to have been no one to carry on the business after them. Only Hrant worked on alone in Manchester, his son John having no interest in textiles.

DAVID DICKINSON

One final revelation was in store for David – a surprise meeting with a relative in Istanbul. The chances of any of the Gulessarian family remaining in the city was slim, but David decided to place a series of adverts in the local Armenian newspaper. Initially there was no response, but towards the end of David's visit a gentleman called Hacik Guleser contacted the newspaper. He turned out to be David's third cousin. The family had dropped the name Gulessarian in the 1930s and adopted the more Turkish sounding name of Guleser. So, through David and Hacik, the Gulesssarian family line continues.

CHAPTER EIGHT

Age of Strength

(from the middle of the sixteenth century to the beginning of the seventeenth)

SCHOPENHAUER, THE CELEBRATED GERMAN PHILOSOPHER, WRITING IN THE MID-NINETEENTH CENTURY, POINTED OUT THAT 'HOWEVER MUCH THE PLAYS AND MASKS ON THE WORLD'S STAGE MAY CHANGE, IT IS ALWAYS THE SAME ACTORS WHO APPEAR. WE SIT TOGETHER AND TALK AND GROW EXCITED, AND OUR EYES GLITTER AND OUR VOICES GROW SHRILLER: JUST SO DID OTHERS SIT AND TALK A THOUSAND YEARS AGO: IT WAS THE SAME THING, AND IT WAS THE SAME PEOPLE: AND IT WILL BE JUST SO A THOUSAND YEARS HENCE. THE CONTRIVANCE WHICH PREVENTS US FROM PERCEIVING THIS IS TIME.' (TRANSLATED BY R. J. HOLLINGDALE, FROM HIS PENGUIN EDITION OF SCHOPENHAUER'S ESSAYS AND APHORISMS)

ABOVE
A portrait of Cardinal Thomas Wolsey c. 1520.

OPPOSITE
Henry VIII's accession was one of the most peaceful for many years, leading Henry to focus on the need to provide a secure male heir. This was to define much of his reign.

As we go back to the last half-century this book deals with, it is for you to judge; but when researching ancestors – and anyone who does so must wish to know what they were actually like – it is as well to remember that however different their perceptions of the world might have been, their superstitions and their manner of living life simply as a day-to-day business – which is more or less all that most of us do with it – they would not be so very different from us in their attitudes to the things that really matter to most of us: love, loyalty, material advancement, friends, hope and a healthy respect for death.

Kings and politicians were no less ruthless or self-serving in the distant past than they are today, either; but their unpleasant characteristics can sometimes serve history or their country for the good, although it is rare that someone somewhere doesn't suffer as it is brought about.

Henry Tudor

Henry VIII certainly saw to it that people who opposed him, even those who had been loyal and useful servants, learned to rue their actions. His political right-hand man for the first twenty years of his reign, Cardinal Thomas Wolsey, made sure that England enjoyed a dominant role in Europe, playing the other two significant powers, France and Spain, off against each other. But when Wolsey, who had already made (in the king's view at least) one or two slips in foreign policy, failed to procure from the Pope any sanction for Henry's proposed divorce from Catherine of Aragon, he was summarily dismissed, then arrested for high treason. He died at Leicester Abbey, on his way to the Tower.

Henry abandoned the balancing act with France and Spain to concentrate on how to deal with the Pope and how to break his power in England. Wolsey died in 1530. The king was then 39 years old and had been on the throne twenty-one years. His wife, a Spanish princess who had been the widow of Henry's older brother, had borne him a daughter, Mary, but in 1530 she was 45 years old and clearly not going to have any more children. By

· ÆTATIS ·   · SVÆ · XLIX ·

the standards of the time she was an elderly woman, and Henry himself was getting on – in fact he lived to be 56. He was desperate to have a male heir to secure the succession of the dynasty founded by his father, and for some time already he'd had his eye on a junior noblewoman of 26 called Anne Bullen (now usually spelt Boleyn).

This was no overnight process. Henry had been angling to get rid of Catherine since 1527, but the Roman Catholic Church forbade divorce, and his wife was the aunt of the powerful Habsburg Emperor, Charles V. However, after Wolsey's fall, Henry lost all patience. With perfect timing there arrived at his elbow a new adviser, a cleric called Thomas Cranmer – yet another Thomas, a most fashionable name at the time – who was a friend of the Boleyn family. He proposed that there might be a way of proving that Henry's marriage to Catherine was not legal, and that this proposal might be examined publicly. Henry, used to getting his own way and stamping on anyone who thwarted him, leapt at the idea.

After debates at an international level, English lawyers in the Commons drafted a succession of Bills in double quick time to ratify the 'divorce', and in 1531 Catherine was banished from the court. She spent the rest of her life in retirement and seclusion in the countryside, together with her daughter Mary, and died a devout Catholic in 1536.

Anne and Henry, who had been having an affair for many years by now, married secretly at last in January 1533. By this time Anne was pregnant. To Henry's disappointment she gave birth to a daughter in September, who would in time and after enormous difficulties become Queen Elizabeth I. She was publicly declared Henry's legal wife by Cranmer (who'd been given the Archbishopric of Canterbury as a reward for his services) in May, and she was crowned amid great celebrations. But it was not to last. Henry's ardour had cooled by the end of the year, and when another pregnancy ended with a stillborn son, at the end of January 1536, it was extinguished completely. On May Day 1536 Henry rode off with his retinue from a tournament being held at Greenwich, leaving Anne in the lurch. The very next day she was arrested and taken to the Tower of London, where she was accused of treason (a favourite ploy of Henry's), and, for good measure, adultery committed with her brother and four commoners. She was beheaded on 19 May and on 20 May Henry married Jane Seymour, who gave him the male heir he craved.

Ecclesiastical revolution

In the meantime, Henry had busily introduced a range of legislation cutting himself and the country off from Catholic interference. Laws were passed making the monarch the supreme head of the Church of England, and any denial of that became a treasonable offence punishable by death. Four hundred small monasteries were dissolved and much of their wealth and lands went to replenish the royal treasure chests. It wasn't really a pogrom: the majority of the monasteries were in decline. Most of the monks were paid reparation, and many were assimilated into the Church of England as parish priests. The Crown, by selling or letting the land it had gained, made a small fortune. And it wasn't even as if the faith practised in England changed very much, though now the Bible and the Prayer Book began to appear in English translations. Hitherto, it had been considered that divine literature should only be accessible to clerics and it was therefore available only in Greek and Latin. Church services were in Latin.

Not everyone liked the changes, and in 1537 a rebellion arose in the conservative, Catholic north of the country. It came to be known rather romantically as the Pilgrimage of Grace, but

TOP

Anne Boleyn (1507–1536), the second wife of Henry VIII and hugely influential queen consort.

ABOVE

Martin Luther, the German monk, priest and theologian, whose writings inspired the Reformation.

it was ill-planned and quickly collapsed. Henry used it as an excuse to crush opposition hard. He had 250 of the ringleaders executed, and started on a campaign of suppression of the larger and more important monasteries. He commissioned a huge print run of the Bible in English to be produced in Paris, and ordered that each parish in England should have one.

In the end, he gutted the monasteries, 560 of them in all; but most of the money he thereby acquired was spent on subsequent luckless campaigns in France and against Scottish rebels. However, he did build up the navy; and he'd established a independence and an international identity for his country which it would retain, and he had founded the Church of England. If his motives for doing the last were a little questionable, he didn't do it without intelligent advice, and he was responding in a sense to the wind of change which the German cleric Martin Luther's Reformation blew across Northern Europe. Protestantism was here to stay.

Edward VI and the Duke of Somerset

Most of this of course would have been way over the heads of our early ancestors. They would have had no part in any of the decisions made and most would probably have just been happy to get through each day without bothering about them much, if at all. But the decisions of their leaders would affect them, whether they liked it or not, and deprivation was coming which would force them to react. Unfortunately, eleven bloody and unstable years were to follow Henry's death in 1547. His son, Edward, had survived, but he was only nine years old when he came to the throne, and he was a sickly child. Although he had quite a strong will, and more than a dash of his father's ruthlessness, he was consumptive, and no one seriously thought he'd last long.

As Edward VI was too young to rule alone, his mother's brother, Edward Seymour, the self-made Duke of Somerset, took the role of Protector. The Seymours were an old family, of Norman extraction (St Maur-Seymour), and by conviction Protestant. Edward's sympathies also lay that way, but the country couldn't change or be changed overnight, and the powerful Catholic noble families, notably the Norfolks, were a force to be reckoned with. Somerset made a fortune and built his town residence, Somerset House, on the banks of the Thames. To make room for it, the Catholic church of Our Lady and the Innocents was knocked down, and to provide stone for it the priory church of St John in Clerkenwell was demolished, though its gate still stands, a little sadly, one of London's more neglected monuments.

Henry VIII is remembered as a strong king and for having six wives, but the country his son inherited was in a parlous financial state. Since the terrible depredations of the Black Death in the mid-fourteenth century, the population of the country had begun to increase again, and now there was more labour available than there was land for the people to work on. Worse, food prices were high and getting higher – and they'd already trebled by the 1550s.

The Duke of Somerset was a good soldier but he wasn't a great politician or tactician. The country was seething. The prominent cleric (and proto-socialist!) Hugh Latimer preached a sermon at St Paul's Cross in London in 1548 which summed up the popular mood. It's remembered now as 'The Sermon of the Plough'. Among other things, Latimer had this to say: 'In times past men were full of pity and compassion; but now there is no pity; for in London their brother shall die in the streets for cold; he shall lie sick at the door … and then perish for hunger. In times past, when any rich man died in London, [he] would

HENRY VIII IS
REMEMBERED AS A
STRONG KING AND
FOR HAVING SIX
WIVES, BUT THE
COUNTRY HIS SON
INHERITED WAS IN A
PARLOUS FINANCIAL
STATE

Rural England was
beginning to show the
consequences of the
country's unfortunate
financial situation by the
mid 1500s.

bequeath great sums of money towards the poor ... Charity is waxen (has become) cold.'

On top of the social crisis, Somerset had to deal with more unrest and rebellion. He'd already crushed the Scots at the Battle of Pinkie in 1547, when his intelligent plan to marry Edward (then ten years old) diplomatically to Mary, Queen of Scots (then five) met with resistance. (Mary was the daughter of James V of Scotland and his wife, the French noblewoman Marie de Guise, and thus a first cousin once removed of Princess Elizabeth and her half-sister Mary of England.) It's of genealogical interest too to note that the English army, outnumbered by the Scots at the rate of 16:23, won largely as a result of employing specialist troops – Italian musketeers. The Scots lost 6000 men. The survivors were sent packing.

Now, in 1549, Somerset faced a Catholic uprising in the south-west and a popular revolt in East Anglia. The former was quickly put down. The latter was a bit more complex. The leader of the rebels, Robert Kett, himself a wealthy landowner, had established an 'army' of about 16,000 peasants outside Norwich. Here he had a kind of legal court and tried landowners who were deemed to have divested poor tenants of their land and/or their livelihood. No one was killed, but the landowners were obliged to return to the people common land seized by enclosure, or to make other restitution.

The Earl of Warwick, John Dudley, marched on Norwich to suppress this outrage to the Establishment. No violence was actually intended, but according to legend a small boy made faces (and probably verbally abused) Warwick's men, and one of them shot him dead. Kett's followers were appalled and a fight started in the course of which 3000 of Kett's men were killed. Kett himself was taken, and hanged on 7 December.

This incident had fatal consequences for Somerset, who had not distinguished himself as a leader or as an administrator. On the other hand, Warwick's cachet had vastly increased. He was seen as the coming man, something which he was quick to take advantage of. It wasn't long before he'd wrested power from Somerset, who found himself without supporters. In January 1552, on trumped-up charges, he was arrested and executed.

Somerset may have lacked certain qualities of leadership, but he had more integrity than Warwick, who now, as the Earl of Northumberland, took control of the Privy Council (the group of powerful nobles who advised the king and directed policy), restructured it and appointed himself its Lord President. Edward VI, meanwhile, was declining in health as consumption (tuberculosis) wore him down. Northumberland clearly had his eye on long-term control of the throne. Basically indifferent to religion, he sought to secure the Crown after Edward's death for Lady Jane Grey, whom he had married (against her wish) to one of his younger sons.

Jane (1537–1554) is remembered famously as the 'Nine Days' Queen'. Serious issues attach to her short reign.

Mary wins favour

Edward VI died on 6 July 1553, probably as a result of primitive medical attempts to assuage his illness. His reign had been short and without distinction, except that during it Thomas Cranmer had produced his masterpiece, a translation of the Book of Common Prayer into the wonderful English used by the Tudors from the late and pretty unpleasant Latin that had hitherto been used. The Act of Uniformity of 1549 required the use of Cranmer's book in churches from then on.

Under Northumberland's influence, Edward VI agreed to block the accession to the natural successor, his half-sister Princess Mary, on the thin legal grounds that she was a bastard (since the marriage of their father and her mother had been proven illegal); also, between the lines, because she was a devout Catholic; and finally and principally because Northumberland saw his son as king in effect and himself (he was only about 50 and, though an old man by the standards of the time, in good health) as the power behind the throne. But he badly miscalculated the mood of the people, and the people made their feelings known. Most of them still adhered to the Old Faith, the one they had grown up in, and short as people's lifespans were in those days, it had after all only been a matter of twenty years since Henry VIII had begun to dismantle the monasteries. There was also a sense of mistrust of Northumberland, whose ambition was naked, and a desire for fair treatment: Mary was the rightful heir, and poor Lady Jane, a scholarly, brilliantly educated 16-year-old who spoke several languages fluently, had the most tenuous of claims to the throne: Henry VIII was her great-uncle.

London, and its population, held the trump card, as it was increasingly to do, and played it in favour of Mary. Ordinary people throughout the country flocked in support of Henry's daughter. The Privy Council promptly abandoned Northumberland, no doubt not without some sense of *schadenfreude*, because ambition makes enemies. Only a month after Edward's death 37-year-old Mary, with her half-sister Elizabeth, entered the capital in triumph.

It was a foregone conclusion. Mary became queen. Though she proceeded with moderation at first, and caution, it was necessary to remove the threat, and Northumberland and

Thomas Cranmer's Book of Common Prayer founded the structure of Anglican liturgy for many centuries.

his cronies were beheaded. So too was poor, put-upon Lady Jane Grey, who would certainly have been happier to remain a scholar than to have been forcibly involved with the crass ambitions of others. She had indeed been queen for nine days only; and she was only 16 when she died. She is buried with her husband, who suffered the same fate of decapitation, in the church of St Peter Ad Vincula in the Tower.

Mary herself had led a reclusive and protected life. She was a good linguist, like Jane Grey and like her half-sister Elizabeth; she loved music, and she was devoted to her mother, whom she considered wronged. Certainly her father had treated her shamefully, first bullying and then ignoring her. She was also a devout Catholic, and with little else in her life, Catholicism became her *raison d'être*. She was half-Spanish, and because she had led a secluded life, she knew little of the country she came to rule at the late age of 37.

Mary's push for Catholicism

Her reign saw a harshly managed attempt to restore the Catholic faith in England. Once she got going, Mary set her face against her people and her actions in restoring hard-line Catholics to positions of power were to bring about, in the end, their permanent fall from grace in Britain. She married the Catholic Philip II of Spain, eleven years her junior, but it was a shaky liaison and failed to produced the wished-for Catholic heir who would have united the two countries in a powerful and almost certainly unbeatable Catholic alliance. (Philip later paid court unsuccessfully to Elizabeth, who played him along with all the finesse of her diplomatic skill. Earlier, he had counselled Mary to have her killed, but Mary drew the line at that, imprisoning her sister instead.) The marriage was so unpopular that it sparked a rebellion in protest against it, led by the aristocratic soldier Sir Thomas Wyatt. It was quickly put down, and its leaders executed.

Mary I, or Mary Tudor (who reigned from 1553 to 1558) was known as 'Bloody Mary'.

Mary released the deposed Catholic Bishop of Winchester, Stephen Gardiner, from the Tower and made him Lord Chancellor. By moving cautiously, she got her people into place before anyone could react, and although this was long before the days of a standing army, she had the power of an absolute monarch to enforce her ideas. The saddest thing of all was that she acted from the best possible motives: she genuinely believed that she was acting in her people's best interests, and that by returning them to the fold of Rome she was ensuring their salvation. No extremist has ever lacked people to do his or her bidding, and Mary, who was rapidly to become our least favourite monarch, was no exception.

Gardiner was hated. He quickly saw to it that everyone toed the Catholic line again, and people who refused fared ill. But there was one thing he could not do for his queen, and that was retrieve the land taken from the monasteries by her father. The nobles simply wouldn't part with it, though they were perfectly happy to pay lip-service to Mary by going back to the Catholic Mass. Their closed ranks were too powerful for Mary to challenge otherwise.

There remained the clerics who'd supported Henry in his secession from what his daughter saw as the One True Church. Mary took her cue from the Holy Inquisition, at its most successful in Spain, that primitive organ of torture and repression which had maintained the Church's interests and control throughout much of mainland Europe by terror since 1248. Those clerics who opposed her, or who had preached or acted in the interests of her father's Protestant English Reformation, she now condemned to be tortured and burnt at the stake. Not only leading prelates whom most of us remember from our schoolbooks, like Latimer and Ridley (Bishops of Worcester and Rochester (later of London) respectively, and champions of the Reformation), burnt at Oxford on 16 October 1555 ('Be of good cheer, Master Ridley, for thou and I this day shall light such a candle in England as shall never be put out'), and poor Thomas Cranmer, who, although an adroit ducker and diver, never really learnt to play the political game properly, but 300 others people, mainly from

The Tower of London saw much activity due to the attempt to restore the Catholic faith.

Castrum Royale Londinense   vulgo   the TOWER

Nicholas Ridley and Hugh Latimer are burnt at the stake in Oxford in 1555 for their refusal to recant their Protestant beliefs.

the south-east and mostly ordinary people, certainly including some of our ancestors – if you have early Protestants in your family you may already be aware of their identity – were burned alive during Mary's five-year reign of terror.

At least Cranmer retained – or regained – his integrity at the end. In an effort to save his life, he had signed several recantations of his true beliefs. At the last, he repudiated them, and, tied to the stake, held his right hand, which had put his name to them, firmly into the flames.

Burning at the stake was a punishment the Catholic Church had devised as a merciful end for those who had sinned against it. The thinking was that if a person was burned here, he or she would not have to burn in hell. Quite often the executioners would pile quick-burning bundles of faggots onto the fire to hasten the end, or manage to strangle the victims before the flames reached further than their lower limbs; and though the chief cause of death was suffocation from the smoke, the pain felt by those sentenced would be excruciating for at least five minutes before release came.

Mary, as we have seen, led a narrow life. Sexually unfulfilled, and unworldly, her only solace was her religion. She and Edward VI had, through no direct fault of their own, gone a good way to destroy what their father had striven to create. When she died of cancer in November 1558, knowing the throne would pass to her thoroughly English and Protestant-leaning half-sister, and having lost the last English possession in mainland Europe, Calais, to the French, she left her successor a broken state, which had all but become a vassal of Spain.

It's pretty much beyond dispute that the good old days were really only good if you were rich, though gradually over the centuries and especially in the last hundred years the standard of living of ordinary people – especially working-class people – and their entitlement to rights have improved immeasurably. But for a section of the common people of England in the mid-sixteenth century, whose lives had not changed radically since the Middle Ages, and had always been pretty hard, things were about to take a turn for the worse.

Henry VIII, as we have seen, had broken the power of the Roman Catholic Church in England and dissolved its monasteries. Mary had failed to re-impose her Church on this country. She didn't have time, she was too much of a foreigner, and she failed to see that brutal force is not the best means of persuasion. She had also failed to manage the country's economy, or to do anything about the material welfare of her people.

A changing landscape

Elizabeth inherited a troubled country, and yet under her sway and partly because of her personality, we entered our first phase of true greatness.

THE VERY FIRST WHISPERINGS OF THE INDUSTRIAL REVOLUTION WHICH MUCH LATER WOULD CAUSE HUGE SOCIAL CHANGE AND A RADICAL SHIFT FROM COUNTRY TO TOWN WERE BEING HEARD

The rolling English landscape, with its vast tracts of forest, was about to change. It had been the same since the late Middle Ages at least – open land, with few hedges and fences, divided into strips where the peasant farmer grew his wheat and barley, or open grazing for pigs to forage. But new methods of farming were coming in, and the nascent wool industry required large fenced-in acreages for pasture. And sheep required fewer men to look after them than arable farmland required workers.

Most of the land appropriated from the monasteries went to landowners who were already established. Two-thirds of the peers of the realm were either granted or bought the old abbey estates, for example. Only a little of what had passed from Church to state went to the new class of private entrepreneur, and they shared the same ambition as the Establishment: to make as much profit out of their new-found gains as possible. Coal and copper mines were being developed. Near Bath, zinc ore, which could be mixed with copper for the making of brass, had been discovered, and a wireworks was established successfully at Tintern. The very first whisperings of the Industrial Revolution which much later would cause huge social change and a radical shift from country to town were being heard. Ironworks, paper-mills and salt-pans were set up, manufactories (or factories, as they came to be known) for that relatively new arrival, gunpowder, were established (such a one made the father of the famous English antiquary John Aubrey, whom we've already met, an even richer man than he already was); and forges for steel were being constructed, some in what had once been monastery refectories or guest-houses. In agriculture, enclosure of arable land for pasturing large flocks of lucrative sheep and changes in the pattern of farming saw thousands of poor tenant farmers and serfs turned off land and out of villages which their families had occupied in some cases for centuries.

This was a time of great upheaval for our ancestors. A yeoman who had previously rented a farm for £3 or £4 a year could keep one hundred sheep and above two dozen cows, and still have room for enough arable land to employ six labourers and more than support his family, to the extent of being able to pay for his children's education. Now those days were gone. Rents quadrupled, and unemployment soared. Many a man considered himself lucky to have a roof over his head, an acre of ground and a few 'cabbages, radishes, parsnips and carrots, melons and pumpkins by which he and his poor household liveth as their principal food, sith they can do no better.'

This state of affairs led to a huge rise in the number of people 'on the road', and as there was no sort of police force, law being generally enforced by the local parish and lord of the manor, there was little that could be done to control them. Disaffected men, cast out of work and forced into beggary and vagrancy, and deeply angry at their lot, became a cause for national concern. In 1594, when London – already a vast metropolis – had a densely packed population of about 200,000, the Lord Mayor reported nervously that there were 12,000 beggars in the City alone. Inevitably a proportion of these people had no alternative but to turn to crime and prostitution to earn a crust. They attracted the attention of writers like Thomas Harman and Robert Greene who were interested in social affairs, and who have left us vivid descriptions of their type and their thieves' slang. A coney-catcher was a conman; a dell 'is a young wench, able for generation and not yet

THIS WORK
DEMANDED
EXPERTISE, AND TO
PROVIDE IT WE
SOUGHT THE ADVICE
OF NORTHERN
GERMANY, FROM
WHERE IN 1565 A
CONTINGENT OF
FIFTY SKILLED MINERS
TRAVELLED TO THE
NORTH OF
ENGLAND.

known or broken by the upright man ... These are broken very young. When they have been broken by the upright man, then they be doxies, and no dells.' A Patriarch Co 'doth make marriages, and that is until death depart the married folk, which is after this sort: when they come to a dead horse or any dead cattle, then they shake hands and so depart, every one of them a several way'.

Writers could feel some sympathy with these people, forced into self-employment, being self-employed themselves and often strapped for cash, especially when let down by a patron. Shakespeare was rich because he had shares in a successful theatre company, rather than on account of the quality of his writing. Actors, traditionally known as 'rogues and vagabonds', though of course most of them were neither, formed troupes of strolling players if they had no patron or belonged to none of the small number of theatre companies. And there was the great throng of quacks, acrobats, jugglers, pickpockets, tinkers, pedlars and gypsies – the last particularly leant on by the forces of law and order – who one contemporary described vividly thus: 'Their apparel is old and phantasticke, tho it be never so full of rents: the men wear scarfes of calico, or any other base stuffs having their bodies like Morris dancers and bells and other toyes to entice the country people to flock about them, and to wonder at their fooleries or rather rank knaveries.'

One cannot help thinking of Shakespeare's itinerant pedlar Autolycus, defined in the cast-list of *The Winter's Tale* as 'a rogue', and his lines: 'Ha, ha! What a fool Honesty is! and Trust, his sworn brother, a very simple gentleman! I have sold all my trumpery: not a counterfeit stone, not a ribbon, glass, pomander, brooch, table-book, ballad, knife, tape, glove, shoe-tie, bracelet, horn-ring, to keep my pack from fasting...!'

His customers could have been the more fortunate workers whose skills were in demand. In the south and the east, there were many prosperous farming enterprises. Flax in Lincolnshire, hops in Kent and Suffolk, hemp through the counties of the south coast. Suffolk was renowned for its horses, Devon for its apples, Cheshire for cheese.

With these new agricultural programmes and the increase of industry, the forests which covered Britain in olden times were receding. Wood and charcoal were needed for fuel, though the developing but still small-scale coal mines were making a start at taking over supply. No one of course thought of replacing the felled trees, or wondered about the consequences of drawing on what at least appeared to be an inexhaustible supply. This is a lesson that has never been learned, however, as we continue to do the same thing today.

The textile industry was very successful, and apart from the mining industries already mentioned, and tin mines, which had been in existence since Roman times, lead and copper were also being excavated. This work demanded expertise, and to provide it we sought the advice of northern Germany, from where in 1565 a contingent of fifty skilled miners travelled to the north of England. Their arrival was the result of some negotiation, because at first the Germans had been reluctant to share their trade secrets, but once they were settled, they began to produce good copper, married local girls, bought property and became assimilated. Are you originally from the north of England and do you have a north-German surname? Maybe you're a descendant of one of these men.

Coal was another product of the north, shipped south by coasters, some of whose mariners honed their seafaring skills for greater voyages as the sixteenth century progressed. That's why you still sometimes hear references to sea-coal. Coal fuelled not only newly hatched industries, but also domestic fires. In roughly the last thirty years of the century the amount shipped south rose from 33,000 tons to 163,000.

The other nursery for our seamen was the fishing industry which grew up in the southwest. It isn't by chance that most of the great Elizabethan mariners were West Countrymen. The fishing fleets sailed far and wide, bringing cargoes of cod (salted) from the teeming fisheries of Newfoundland on the north-east coast of North America.

On the land, there was still high unemployment. When Elizabeth came to the throne the attitude to poor relief had hardly changed since her father's day. Her parliaments defined such things as the occupations a man could legitimately follow, periods and terms of apprenticeship, and changes of trade. Vagrancy was feared and detested, and punishments meted out to beggars were harsh. People were whipped and/or branded. But the laws might seem capricious to us: an Act of 1572 defined as vagrants not just what we might call tramps or professional beggars, but workmen on strike, poor scholars and shipwrecked sailors. Harvest workers, and servants who'd been sacked or whose masters or mistresses had died, were regarded as legitimately unemployed, however.

Poor Laws at the very end of the century did define the duties of the Overseers of the Poor, and sought to make some money raised from taxes available for the relief of the destitute, but such people still had a rough ride. No parish they turned up in wanted them on their charge, as we've seen, punishments for vagrancy remained harsh and it was difficult to prove that you were involuntarily on your uppers. But at least the publicity given to the plight of the poor gave rise to widespread acts of individual charity, largely by rich merchants, which kept the problem containable. The other 'advantage' was that the poor didn't live long.

If you were in employment on the land, an ordinary unskilled labourer might expect to earn about 2d. a day, a ploughman would earn 1s. a week with board and a thresher of grain up to 7d. a day. These were miserable wages even by the standards of the times, but there was less work than there were people.

Religious tolerance

Mary had left a legacy of religious intolerance and resentment against Catholics. Elizabeth was far too sensible to care about religious extremism one way or another, and she and her advisers recognised from the first that the only way for the country to progress was through religious tolerance. Catholics were not completely free, and limits were set on what professions they could follow, but on the whole they fared better than they might have expected to after the example set by Queen Mary. They were allowed to practise their rites, and there were even some Catholics at court, notably the Queen's Organist of the Chapel Royal, William Byrd. Byrd was one of a number of talented musicians who flourished in the Elizabethan and Jacobean age. Others were Thomas Tallis, John Dowland and Orlando Gibbons.

Elizabeth herself was what we might call 'high church'. Catholic proselytising was frowned on, but in the nine years between 1581 and 1588 just over eighty people were executed for religious offences, most of them priests – a figure which, if it sounds brutal, still compares favourably with the number Mary had killed. The main problem was not so much religious as political anyway. Elizabeth had no intention of remaining under the thumb of Spain.

ABOVE
Bess of Hardwick, whose
various marriages gave her
a fortune of over £60,000
per year – millions in
today's money.

ABOVE RIGHT
Hampton Court, the
former royal palace, in
the London borough of
Richmond upon Thames.

Building for the future

The collapse of the monasteries meant that in some circles fortunes were made. These Tudor *nouveaux riches* were great show-offs, and spent their money on grand country houses as well as vastly expensive dinners and incredibly costly clothes. The polarisation of wealth makes today's unfair dispersal look very tame. Glass was an expensive commodity, too, and in the last decade of the sixteenth century Bess of Hardwick, Countess of Shrewsbury, several times over the widow of wealthy husbands, built her great house in Derbyshire. She only had half a dozen books – expensive items too in those days but evidently of little interest to her – but the style of her architecture was extravagant, and gave rise to a little rhyme – 'Hardwick Hall, more glass than wall'. Bess was 70 when work started – a mark of a more optimistic attitude, at least among the well-heeled, to life-expectancy. She lived to be 88, an exceptional age for the time.

This style supplanted the fortress-like building of the Middle Ages, though Hampton Court had already shown the way great houses would be designed in the future. Castles were certainly a thing of the past, on account of changes in the way war was waged and the decline of civil conflict. Stone for the new country houses came from the defunct monasteries, ready-cut and easy to get at. Earlier, brick had been used, and typical 'Tudor' domestic architecture features wood frames and wattle-and-daub walls.

It's interesting that this revolution in building style came about without any sort of prompting by design pundits. The profession of architect was as yet unknown, but master-masons conferred with their employers on the style they sought to achieve. Bess of Hardwick's mason is not known for sure as the surviving papers don't mention him, but he was almost certainly Robert Smythson. He was the Norman Foster of his day, the designer of several stately homes including Longleat and Burton Agnes. He died in 1614, by which time the profession he pioneered was recognised. He is described as an architect in an inscription on his tomb at Wollaton: 'Architector and Survayor', it says.

The great and the good who built these houses sometimes found themselves ruined by them. This was partly because they overreached themselves, and partly because of the additional expense sometimes occasioned by the possibility that Queen Elizabeth would come and stay during the course of one of the many Royal Progresses she made around the country in order to show herself to her people (and in all her long life she never left England). William Cecil, Lord Burghley, vastly extended one of his properties, Burghley House in Northamptonshire, to accommodate Elizabeth and her entourage, which was considerable. She travelled with 2000 horses and 300 carts. Each visit to Burghley House – and she made several, and also to another property of his, Theobalds – cost Cecil in the region of £2500. It was of course a great honour to have the queen as one's guest, but it was always a gamble whether she would come or not. Sir Christopher Hatton, who attracted the Elizabeth's attention by his skill at dancing, and rose to become Lord Chancellor, built Holdenby House, also in Northamptonshire. The cost of its construction was crippling, let alone its running costs, for it had to be fully staffed with an army of servants. But in ten years the queen never went to stay once. Hatton died a bachelor in 1591, in his fifty-first year. A nephew inherited Holdenby but couldn't afford to run it and so sold it. By the 1640s it had been demolished.

With the new houses came elaborate gardens, also great status symbols and carefully designed, and as architecture became more sophisticated the corridor was introduced in deference to an increasing fashion (which has stuck) for privacy. But that was rather later. Before that time, rooms simply ran one into another, as you can see in surviving Tudor and Jacobean stately homes. In time, too, rooms came to have a set function, but this was all still some time in the future.

One refinement that didn't catch on was the flushing toilet, devised by Queen Elizabeth's godson, Sir John Harington, in 1596. He invented a valve which, when pulled, would release a flow of water from a water-closet. He recommended flushing once or twice a day.

BELOW
Hardwick Hall, one of the earliest example of the Renaissance influence on the architecture of the country house.

BELOW LEFT
William Cecil, Baron of Burghley, whose home – Burghley House – was built in the shape of an 'E' in honour of Elizabeth I.

The Virgin Queen

Elizabeth was 25 years old when she came to the throne. Fluent in Latin, Greek, Spanish, French and Italian, she also spoke some Welsh – a big diplomatic advantage, given the Welsh pride in the dynasty founded by one of their own. She was a skilled musician and dancer, had a keen interest in the arts and sciences, and read avidly and widely. She greeted the not entirely unexpected news of her sister's demise and her inheritance, according to tradition, by quoting, in Latin, lines from Psalm 118: 'This is the Lord's doing. It is marvellous in our eyes', and falling to her knees under an oak tree. If true, it's an early example of the showmanship she grew to be most adept at. She used it, together with the considerable force of her personality, to break free of the control of her advisers – though she was blessed in them – and to manage the country according to her own will. She understood the importance of having the common touch, and made herself both a popular figure and an icon to her people, a living symbol of nationhood under which they could unite. She was also blessed in presiding over a time when the nation flowered. There have been few other ages in English history when there has been such a burgeoning of the arts, particularly in music and literature, but in painting too – and of exploration.

And it was a long reign – 45 years.

As we've seen, it didn't have a very good start. The nation's morale was low, the treasure chests were bare, Antwerp bankers were charging the country 14 per cent on loans, the coinage was debased and relations with Spain were shaky. But Elizabeth was a survivor. She'd been imprisoned, put under house arrest, had narrowly escaped losing her head and she was a woman, which in the thinking of the time might have put her at a distinct disadvantage. We haven't had many queens down the centuries – Boudicca (if we can stretch a point and count her), Mary I, Elizabeth I, Mary II (with her husband William III in executive control), Victoria, Elizabeth II – but three of them left their mark, and Elizabeth I was the most distinguished of the lot.

That wasn't all to her credit. She had from the first some scintillating male advisers. The first was her tutor, Roger Ascham. The second was her chief minister, William Cecil, 38 when she came to the throne and still at her right hand when he died forty years later. A lawyer, theologian, historian and genealogist by training, he was also a shrew political survivor. His temperament and the queen's matched well, and he must be credited as the builder of Elizabeth's greatness. Lord Burghley, as he became in 1571, was a true Elizabethan of the wealthy *arriviste* class, and spent most of the vast sums he gained on splendid houses. Above all he was an able strategist and it is one of the fortunate quirks of history that he lived when he did, at a time when his country desperately needed his talents.

Catholicism really had to be tolerated, despite the bad name Mary had earned for it. Both the Valois dynasty of France, and Spain, under Philip II, were Catholic nations. So was the Holy Roman Empire, which had split from Spain two years before Elizabeth's accession. Elizabeth was the daughter of the king who'd defied Rome, and the Protestant Anne Bullen, whose marriage to Henry VIII could not be recognised by the Roman Catholic creed. Spain was a close threat to England because of its maritime power and its ownership of the Low Countries; France was a powerful neighbour and, despite close links in earlier days, not necessarily a friendly one, though it wasn't a great sea-power and during Elizabeth's reign was preoccupied with its own problems.

(It was during this period, in 1572, that the so-called St Bartholomew's Day Massacre of

BUT ELIZABETH WAS A SURVIVOR. SHE'D BEEN IMPRISONED, PUT UNDER HOUSE ARREST, HAD NARROWLY ESCAPED LOSING HER HEAD, AND SHE WAS A WOMAN, WHICH IN THE THINKING OF THE TIME MIGHT HAVE PUT HER AT A DISTINCT DISADVANTAGE

BELOW
Elizabeth I, the final monarch of the Tudor dynasty.

OPPOSITE
A portrait of Elizabeth I, later in her reign.

FINALLY A CATHOLIC
PLOT WAS UNVEILED
WHICH IMPLICATED
MARY, AND
ELIZABETH HAD NO
ALTERNATIVE BUT TO
ORDER HER
EXECUTION, WHICH
TOOK PLACE IN 1587

the Huguenots took place. It started on the saint's day, 24 August, but continued until early October. Orchestrated by the Catholic Catherine de' Medici, 25,000 people were slaughtered. Many of the survivors formed the first wave of Huguenot immigrants to England. The massacre was triggered by Catherine's mistrust of Admiral Gaspard de Coligny, Admiral of the Fleet and a prominent Huguenot. Fearful of his power, and of his influence over her son, the French King Charles IX, she had him murdered and with him many prominent Huguenots who were in Paris to attend the marriage of the king's sister. The purge later spread throughout France. In 1598, by the Edict of Nantes, Henry IV of France restored rights of worship and some protection to the Huguenots, but just under one hundred years later Louis XIV revoked the edict in order to curb the waxing power of the Huguenots again.)

Elizabeth and Mary

Elizabeth's lifelong policy was to play the two rival powers of France and Spain off against each other. She toyed with proposals of marriage from each court but never committed herself, overriding Cecil's advice in the early days, for her own counsellors felt it vital that she should have an heir. She also had a serious problem to deal with at home, in the form of Mary, Queen of Scots. Mary was a great-niece of Henry VIII, half-French, and a Catholic. The French and the Scots had long been close allies. Mary was nine years Elizabeth's junior, beautiful and charismatic. She spent ten years in France and was married to the Dauphin (the Heir Apparent), but after his death, and on the death of her mother, returned to Scotland in 1561 to take over the reins of power there. She managed ably at first, despite what was to become a chaotic and dramatic private life, and despite the fact that she was culturally more French than Scots and spoke French and Latin far better than English or Gaelic. The point here is that her existence represented a Catholic threat to Elizabeth. Mary became the focus of various Catholic plots against Elizabeth, though her own ultimate mismanagement of her affairs led her to throw herself on Elizabeth's mercy in 1568, when she lost her throne as the result of an insurrection against her. Elizabeth couldn't bring herself to have Mary killed, but she realised how great a threat she was, so poor Mary spent the rest of her life in various castles and country houses as a prisoner.

Finally a Catholic plot was unveiled which implicated Mary, and Elizabeth had no alternative but to order her execution, which took place in 1587. Her reluctance to get rid of Mary may not have been entirely sentimental. Ironically, because of Mary Queen of Scots' strong links with Philip II's great rival, France, and because she was next in line to the English throne should Elizabeth die, she had actually proffered indirect protection to Elizabeth.

While all this was going on, Elizabeth had to deal with further Catholic rebellions in northern England and put up with an edict of Pope Pius V not only excommunicating her (something she could shrug off) but stating that loyal Catholics should do their best to get rid of her – a kind of *fatwa* in other words.

Then there was a row with Spain because we had intercepted and taken a fleet of treasure ships on their way to the Netherlands. Relations with Spain simmered nastily from then on, and in 1585 Philip II seized all the English ships in his ports. Our spies reported that he was making plans to invade, with a vast fleet.

These alarms and excursions cost money. We led the world in wool production, and 80 per cent of our exports were in textiles, but for all its perceived greatness from the distance

Phillip II, King of Spain
(1527–1598).

of centuries, Elizabethan England was a poor country, with annual revenues of around £500,000, and sometimes far less.

One way of making money was through trade, and English maritime experience was put to good use in this respect now. Men like Walter Raleigh, Francis Drake, Martin Frobisher and John Hawkyns explored new areas of the globe, towards the East Indies, Russia, China and Africa and, in defiance of Spain, the Americas. There was a pressing desire to colonise as well, since one way of solving the unemployment problem would be to encourage emigration. Less gloriously, English mariners were beginning to exploit the slave trade. Hawkyns in particular did business with Spanish Americans, selling them shiploads of Africans he had captured in foraging expeditions along the Atlantic coast of the African continent.

Conflict with Spain

But the English rovers are best remembered for what amounted to a long, unofficial running sea-battle with Spain and skirmishes in the Spanish American settlements. Drake, Hawkyns and the rest were accomplished pirates, and the Spanish treasure ships sailing home from America were attacked over and over again. Elizabeth quietly supported these enterprises and enjoyed her share of the booty they brought. Tough, ruthless and vain, as well as learned and cultivated, her best card of all was her common touch. She was the perfect monarch for the time, but she didn't succeed alone. Her other great adviser after Cecil, Sir Francis Walsingham, counselled her to encourage the rovers. They were a useful thorn in Philip's side, and Spain could never be trusted. Enmity between the two countries was tacit, though Philip had stayed his hand from open war. Nevertheless he had been simmering ever since Francis Drake had successfully rounded Cape Horn on his bound-breaking round-the-world voyage in the *Golden Hind*, and harassed the Spanish colonies on the Pacific coast.

By the late 1580s, Philip had had enough. England would have to be taught a lesson. An army was gathered in the Spanish Netherlands under the Duke of Parma, and a fleet collected in the western Spanish ports, which when it was ready amounted to about 130 ships, carrying 2500 cannon and 30,000 troops. This Armada was generally thought to be invincible, though that quality had already been called into question by Drake in 1587, when he sailed into Cadiz harbour and pounded the ships at anchor there to pieces, seriously delaying Philip's invasion plans. This incident Drake is said to have referred to later as his having 'singed the King of Spain's beard'.

The Spanish plan was to sail up the Channel, rendezvous with Parma's army and pick it up, sail across, land the entire Spanish force and rout the English, while the galleons of the Armada crushed the English fleet.

The English gathered their own forces and their ships on the coast and prepared for battle. The country was united in the face of this threat, and Queen Elizabeth rose to the occasion, addressing the army in a speech which remains famous:

My loving people ... I am come amongst you, as you see, resolved, in the midst and heat of the battle, to live or die amongst you all, to lay down for my God, and for my Kingdom, and for my people, my honour and my blood, even in the dust. I know I have the body of a weak and feeble woman, but I have the heart and stomach of a king, and of a King of

Sir Walter Raleigh, the English navigator.

Elizabeth I knighting Sir Francis Drake on board his ship, the Golden Hind.

England too, and think foul scorn that Parma or Spain or any prince of Europe should dare to invade the borders of my realm ...

Stirring stuff, but she and everyone else knew that it was going to be a close-run thing. And with Mary's reign fresh in people's minds, the thought of being placed under Spanish rule was too terrible to contemplate. One of the most popular books to appear after Mary's death was the *Book of Martyrs* by John Foxe, which found its way into virtually every parish church in the country. It was a chronicle of Mary's atrocities, and extremely influential.

Near the end of July 1588, the Armada appeared at the mouth of the Channel, off Cornwall. Drake attacked from behind but the Spanish held course. When they reached the point of rendezvous, off the French coast opposite Dover, however, the first disaster struck them. Their ships were too big to put into the ports. They simply drew too much water. And as they lay at anchor, on the nights of 28 July and 7 August, the English sent in small, old vessels loaded with pitch and gunpowder and set on fire, which wrought havoc with the galleons. Disaster then followed disaster. The Spanish captains panicked and fled, putting themselves at the mercy of the English, whose smaller, faster and more easily navigable ships picked off the giants as a fierce south-west wind forced the Spanish to sail in the very last direction they wanted to – north. To get home, what remained of the Armada had now to sail right around the north coast of Scotland and back down, out into the Atlantic skirting the west coast of Ireland. Many more ships were lost in that homeward voyage, and only a few made it back.

Spanish power wasn't broken by this disaster, but England had shown the world that as a naval power it was a force to be reckoned with. And though the Spanish didn't give up completely – they tried to foment trouble in Ireland, where the Counter-reformation had worked, and which therefore remained Catholic except in the North – from now on England could look forward to several decades of relative peace and stability.

Culture in bloom

The second half of the sixteenth century was turbulent, but it saw a great flowering of the arts. And although the country was poor, there were plenty of rich patrons, as we've seen, to support this burgeoning. This was a period, too, where skilled artisans flourished in the service of the wealthy, who wanted the best for their homes and gardens. Flemish tapestries covered their walls. Hans Holbein, born in Germany, had arrived from Basel via the Low Countries early in the century as an already renowned portrait-painter, and was to immortalise, among others, the family of Thomas More. A few years earlier, an Italian sculptor, PietroTorrigiano – who as a young man broke Michelangelo's nose in a punch-up – produced his masterpiece, the tomb of Henry VII and his wife Elizabeth of York, which can be seen still in Westminster Abbey. Miniature portraits became fashionable, as these could be carried, encased in lockets. The genre was pioneered by Holbein and the Dutch portraitists who'd settled here, and brought to perfection by the greatest English artist of the period, Nicholas Hilliard, who was born at Exeter in 1547.

Refinement in the art of living was encouraged by the appearance in 1561 of an English translation, by Sir Thomas Hoby, of an Italian manual of etiquette, *Il libro del Cortegiano*, by the courtier and diplomat Baldessare Castiglione. Castiglione covers all aspects of sophisticated and decent behaviour, and the rough and ready English, especially those who had acquired wealth rather than merely inherited it, were keen to learn. The soldier-poet Sir Philip Sidney (1554-1586) typified the appearance and manner which any aspiring Elizabethan would take as his model.

Among the virtues recommended is an understanding of the arts, and within the arts,

The defeat of the Spanish Armada was declared by the English as their greatest victory since Agincourt.

music plays a large part. Musical instruments for domestic use were produced, such as the lute and the virginal (a kind of early harpsichord). Both Queen Mary and Queen Elizabeth played the virginal well, and the instrument was perhaps so called because it was designed to be used primarily by ladies. The lute found its place as the instrument used to accompany lyrics and poems set to music. The great composers of the day wrote for both lute and virginal, and for the small secular orchestras composed of viols (early versions of the violin), hautboys (an early oboe) and recorders. There was also a forerunner of the guitar, called a cittern. But perhaps it was for its theatre that the Elizabethan (and Jacobean) age will best be remembered.

Drama as we know it developed from the religious Mystery Plays which dealt with Biblical and other religious subjects and were performed by members of guilds rather than professionals at important Christian festivals such as Christmas and Easter. The Italians developed what we could call modern professional acting companies with their *Commedia dell' Arte*, but we were slow to follow suit, and although drama was being produced in the early part of Elizabeth's reign and she showed a lively interest in it, the early plays are rather wooden and rarefied, and are seldom produced today. There had always been pageants, involving music, dance and 'dumb-shows', and there had been strolling players performing juggling and acrobatic tricks on makeshift stages or flatbedded waggons.

But then, in London in 1576, something very striking happened. The first theatre was built. Its creator was James Burbage, a carpenter and amateur actor who was also a canny businessman. It was built outside the confines of the City of London, as the City Fathers looked askance at theatrical activities: they were suspicious of them and considered them

Following the defeat of the Armada, the political stability allowed London to grow and culture to bloom.

William Shakespeare's reputation was largely intensified since his death, though various records show that he owned property in central London and the second-largest house in Stratford upon his death.

immoral. However, the new form of entertainment quickly became popular, and following this building – called simply 'The Theatre' – came others – The Swan, The Curtain, The Rose, The Fortune, and, most famous of all, The Globe, built on the south bank of the Thames next door to the Bear Garden, where bear- and bull-baiting took place.

To staff these theatres professional companies were formed, though women were not to tread the boards until the mid-17th century, their parts being taken by boys. Burbage's company was the first, but it was quickly followed by that of Philip Henslowe. Henslowe had originally made money from bull- and bear-baiting, having started life as a dyer and starchmaker. His diaries and some of his accounts survive – they are kept at Dulwich College – and give a fascinating glimpse into the theatre and business practice at the end of the sixteenth century.

Plays were performed in the afternoon, and prices ranged from 1d. for standing in the 'pit' in front of the stage, which projected into a circular space surrounded by roofed galleries. Seats under the roof cost up to 3d., not a bad price when a quart of beer would set

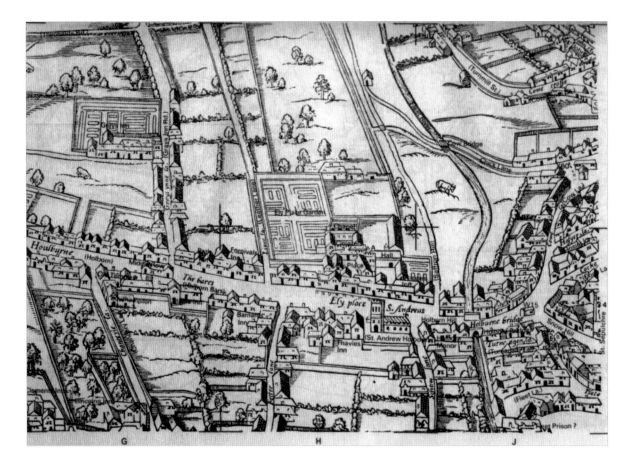

A page from the A-Z of
Elizabethan London.

you back 4d., and an hour with a tart, 6d. Playgoing became immensely fashionable and
popular with both sexes and all classes. By 1605 about a seventh of Londoners were going
to see a play each week. The performances were designed to contain elements that would
appeal across the social board; to compete with bloodier entertainments, often scenes of
extreme violence featured, as well as low comedy and bawdy repartee, alongside the more
sophisticated passages.

The success of theatre fuelled rapid development in drama itself, and the decades
between about 1580 and 1620 saw a flourishing of playwriting that has probably never been
matched anywhere else at any other time in history. An original play could fetch its author
around £5, but for that he sold all rights to it, so that to make a living he would have either
to be very prolific or own shares in the company he worked for. It would be tedious to list
here the dozens of writers at work in the theatre at the time, but chief among them, whose
work is still worth reading if for no other reason than to enjoy the flavour they give of how

Actors became stars. Philip Henslowe's leading man, partner and son-in-law, Edward
Alleyn, was able to retire before he was 40, and made enough money to found and maintain Dulwich College. It's been estimated that the Manor of Dulwich alone, on which the
school was built, cost £10,000. Alleyn's chief rival, James Burbage's son, Richard, was able to
leave his family land worth £300 and shares in two successful theatre companies. Of course,
then as now, rich actors formed a tiny minority of their profession, but it's a measure of how
people eagerly flocked to this form of entertainment that fortunes could be made.

life was lived then, are Christopher Marlowe, Ben Jonson, John Webster and – of course – William Shakespeare.

Shakespeare worked for Burbage's company. He needs no description or discussion here, but it's worth noting in passing that not only are his plays in themselves still tremendous examples of how to construct a drama well, they are also masterpieces of innovation. Shakespeare's work, and to a lesser degree, but in many cases not much less, those of his fellow-playwrights, restored drama to a degree of sophistication it hadn't known since the days of Euripides in Athens and Terence in Rome. But he transcended their work in complexity, both of character and plot, and in him we can boast perhaps the greatest genius in the arts ever known. If he seems a bit inaccessible to us at times nowadays, it's because the allusions in the jokes have become obscure, and because the complexity of women's characters was not fully appreciated, but also because, great instinctive observer of human nature that he was, there was no formal study of psychology then. It's hard, however, to imagine no speculation at all on this subject. There was certainly awareness. Bacon hints at it in his *Essays,* and Macbeth says to the Doctor of Lady Macbeth (arguably Shakespeare's best female character): 'Canst thou not minister to a *mind* diseased?' But as a great recent Shakespearean critic and director once said: 'When you do Shakespeare, forget Freud.'

Stow's Survey

Before leaving the Elizabethan era it is well worth noting the beginnings of a true modern self-consciousness, in the sense of an interest among 'ordinary' people in their history and their surroundings. Francis Bacon, the son of an English Protestant statesman under Henry VIII and again under Elizabeth, himself rose to high political office, but is remembered as the author of a series of philosophical essays in which he explores themes of a psychological nature – a good example of a new approach to thinking in the secular sphere. (He has also been suspected by one or two eccentrics of being the true author of the plays of Shakespeare!)

By 1600 London had a population of about 200,000. It was now among the most important European cities and trade centres, and it was the capital of a fast-emerging power. Appropriately at this very moment a Londoner called John Stow published his *Survey of London.*

Stow was one of the first and greatest English antiquaries. By profession a tailor, he seems to have retired from work when he was about 40, to concentrate on his literary and historical pursuits. The *Survey* is not his only work, but it is his masterpiece, and it is of prime interest to the genealogist and family historian whose research is concerned with the capital because it is the first painstakingly researched history of the town to appear. There are myths and inaccuracies in it, of course, but there is much touching and arresting detail along with extensive lists of local dignitaries and officers and their trades or professions, of prisons, schools, the city gates, churches, bishops' houses, hospitals, notes of public holidays, sports and other pastimes, and so on. It's not an easy read, but it rewards effort.

Stow published his *Survey* in 1598, towards the end of a long life. He'd been born in Henry VIII's reign and died aged 80 in 1605, two years into that of James I, the first king both of England and Wales, and Scotland, of which he was already king as James VI. As Elizabeth died without an heir, James, the son of Mary, Queen of Scots and thus Elizabeth's first cousin twice removed, succeeded her.

With Elizabeth the Tudor dynasty came to an end. James was the first of the Stuarts.

The John Stow Memorial in the Church of St Andrew, London.

The food writer, author and television personality Nigella Lawson is the daughter of former cabinet minister Nigel Lawson and the Lyons grocery and catering heiress Vanessa Salmon. Though born into a life of wealth and privilege, Nigella's life has been touched by tragedy many times: She lost her mother, sister, and her first husband, journalist John Diamond, to cancer.

It comes then as no surprise that Nigella is wary of looking back. She says she has a 'scorched-earth policy' towards the past, associating it with difficult times; but recently she decided that she was interested to know more about her family history. As there were more initial leads, the decision was made to concentrate on her mother's line, the Salmons.

At first the line was easy to trace. The Salmon family are well documented as entrepreneurs from the Lyons catering empire. For most of the 20th century Lyons owned and ran hundreds of high street Tea Shops as well as a string of hotels and restaurants. Lyons had in fact got its name from Joseph (later Sir Joseph) Lyons, a man who had married into the family in the 19th century.

Nigella's grandfather, Felix Salmon, was born in 1908 as Lyons was entering a period of huge growth. As an adult, and despite a reluctance to wholeheartedly embrace the world of business, Felix was made Joint Chief Executive of the company and put in charge of the Tea Shops.

The business had its origins in the merger of two lines, both descended from European Jewish families who emigrated to England in the 18th and 19th centuries. The key moment came in 1863 when Nigella's great-great-grandfather, Barnett Salmon, married Helena, the daughter of one Samuel Gluckstein.

Both Samuel and Barnett had been small-time tobacco traders making a living from the tobacco boom at the turn of the 19th century. They were also friends, but the marriage of the 34-year-old Barnett to Samuel's 17-year-old daughter greatly strengthened their bond and subsequently encouraged them to start a business together: the Salmon & Gluckstein tobacco company.

Launched in 1873, S&G initially produced hand-rolled cigars and cigarettes. But with the dawn of mechanization the company expanded fast. By the turn of the century they had 140 retail outlets, mainly in London. All were supplied by a Whitechapel factory which turned out 1.5 million cigarettes a week. S&G boasted it was the biggest tobacconist in the world.

Barnett Salmon, a child of London's poverty-stricken East End was to make his fortune from Salmon & Gluckstein. But sadly success came too late for his partner and founding father Samuel Gluckstein, who died at the age of 52. Nevertheless, two of Samuel's sons, Isidore and Montague, hooked up with Barnett and, together with newcomer Joseph Lyons, they decided to move out of tobacco and into catering. The men had spotted a gap in the market for quality ready-made food supplied to big public events, business conventions and even garden parties.

A network of Tea Shops and restaurants soon followed. In all, several hundred were opened, and all staffed by the famous Lyons waitresses, known as 'Nippies'. At the peak of the Tea Shop phenomenon Lyons had nine separate premises simultaneously trading in London's Oxford Street. They were joined by huge flagship grocery and restaurant complexes. Sited in prime central London locations, these so-called 'Corner Houses' were the pride of Lyons, a company which soon became a household name.

The importance of both the Salmon and Gluckstein families to Lyons continued long after a controlling interest in the tobacco business was sold to Imperial Tobacco in 1903. Indeed after Joseph Lyons' death in 1917 (he died childless), the chairman of the Lyons board was virtually always a Gluckstein or a Salmon.

Grandfather Felix died when Nigella was only 9 years old. And her memories of him were vague compared to those of his wife Rosemary who gave Nigella some of her earliest cookery lessons as the young girl stood on a chair beside grandma's cooker.

But life was not always good. As Jews, the Salmons feared Nazi invasion during the Second World War. They were right to be scared. Their names, and in some cases even their addresses, were listed along with those of other prominent British Jewish families in a bizarre Nazi publication entitled 'The SS Guide to England'. Family myth has it that Felix's wife Rosemary gave the children suicide pills to be taken in the event of capture by the Nazis. Rosemary is also famed for carrying round a Henry Moore sculpture in her handbag during the war, finally burying it in the garden lest the Germans arrived to steal it.

Felix loved art, and would scour London galleries looking for art works which the company could buy and display in its many buildings. However, Felix is remembered by some as a withdrawn sometimes even melancholic man. Why should this have been? One theory is that Nigella's grandfather may have been actively involved in the liberation of the Nazi concentration camp at Bergen-Belsen in April 1945. The discovery of Belsen by British troops was one of the Second World War's darkest moments.

But was Felix there? His war record is ambiguous. As a Major attached to the Catering Corps not only did he have specialist catering knowledge but, crucially, he was stationed in north-western Europe at the time of the camp's liberation. Ultimately there is no definitive evidence that Felix witnessed the horrors at Belsen, but his known expertise in food provision, together with his war record and anecdotal evidence from Nigella's family left a strong feeling that he did.

To find out when Felix's ancestors came to London and from where, Nigella consulted the 1841 census and found that her great-great-grandfather Barnett, then 12 years old, was listed as 'Barnell Solomon'. His father, Aaron, is entered as 'Aarin Solomon', and according to the record was a clothes dealer born in England and a resident of Bell Lane, Spitalfields, London.

Barnett was the oldest of five children, a younger brother and sister both dying in infancy, as Nigella learned from death certificates provided for her by the Family Records Centre. The baby boy – Asher – died of dropsy, an accumulation of the watery part of the blood in the tissues and cavities of the body; rare in the developed world today, the illness is often due to poor nutrition. The baby girl died of water-on-the-brain.

Nigella had no idea that Barnett Salmon had been born into poverty. It was he who had helped to make the family's fortune. Had he been driven to succeed by a desire

to escape that background? Had the fate of two of his younger siblings moved him to do so? Certainly he made an advantageous marriage. Barnett and Helena Gluckstein were married at the West London Synagogue. There, Rabbi Geoffrey Shisler showed Nigella a copy of the 1863 ketivah – marriage contract – between her maternal great-great-grandparents. How did Barnett flourish thereafter? A glance at the 1871 census revealed that by then, eight years into their marriage, they had three children, but that Barnett's work was listed as 'commercial traveller'. He was then still in a relatively modest line of business, but the seeds of his future success were already sown.

When Nigella checked the 1901 census, four years after Barnett's death, she found that great-great-grandmother Helena was in comfortable circumstances and quite the matriarch, with a large house, servants, surrounded by her growing children and with some sons already in the family business. Barnett had in fact left a substantial legacy, in today's money estimated at several million pounds. Helena would, however, only enjoy the benefits for a further six years. She died, aged 60, in 1907.

Throughout its history both the Salmon & Gluckstein and Lyons businesses were a closely run family affair. As there wasn't a lot of money to spare in the early days, Barnett was actively involved with the idea of a Family Fund – a kind of mutual protection system whereby all profits from the business were pooled and distributed to members as need dictated. It was a kind of mini-socialist economy, in effect, but only operating within the Salmon–Gluckstein families. In many cases, the Fund owned members' homes and paid their salaries. The women of the family were not allowed independent wealth in order to prevent them from marrying outside the family and

RIGHT
Nigella's grandparents,
Felix and Rosemary
Salmon.

OPPOSITE
Baby Horatia with her
Mother, Vanessa.

Their names, and in some cases even their addresses, were listed along with those of other prominent British Jewish families in a bizarre Nazi publication entitled 'The SS Guide to England'.

thus leaking the mutually held capital away. However, on the occasion of a fiftieth wedding anniversary a husband was allocated £1,000 to buy a pearl necklace for his wife. The system also supported women of the family in widowhood.

Apart from the business interests of Nigella's forebears, there was the question of where they might originally have come from. Because of her mother's vaguely Hispanic appearance, Nigella wondered if her roots might ultimately have been among the Sephardic Jews of Portugal and Spain rather than the Ashkenazi Jews of Northern Europe. Family records throughout the 19th century all pointed to North European origins. Samuel Gluckstein's family came from Rheinberg in Prussia, where Samuel was born in 1821.

However, others within Nigella's family were traced to Amsterdam, a city which more than any other had welcomed the migrating Sephardic Jews when they fled Catholic Spain during the Inquisition. Could this family, which included the future wife of Samuel Gluckstein, Hannah Joseph, have been descended from noble Spanish stock? As it turns out, the answer is almost certainly no. Nigella discovered that Hannah's father Conrad Joseph was originally called Coenraad Sammes, the name deriving from a Hebrew word which means 'one who looks after a synagogue'. Remarkably Conrad came to England in 1830 almost certainly as a fugitive after he was convicted of stealing a red leather wallet filled with Dutch state lottery tickets.

The dramatic events of Conrad's trial in Amsterdam present a curious end to

Nigella's story. Witness statements offer claim and counter-claim in a bitter contest to establish the truth. But did second-hand clothes dealer Conrad care? Following the original trial in which he was sentenced to eighteen months in prison he at first appeared to be on a mission to secure justice. He lodged an appeal. However, original handwritten statements from the court bailiff describe his failure to execute a summons at Conrad's Amsterdam home. The appeal judge would uphold the verdict. But Conrad was not even present at the hearing in The Hague. The court heard that he had fled to England.

The rest is, as they say, family history. By settling in England it was made possible for Conrad's daughter Hannah to meet and marry Samuel Gluckstein. The subsequent marriage of Conrad's teenage granddaughter Helena to Barnett Salmon marked the all important joining of the Salmon and Gluckstein clans – a union which formed the starting point for a huge business empire, the great British institution that was Lyons. This empire would go on to shape and mould Nigella's maternal line for the next hundred years.

PART THREE

WHERE TO
GO NEXT

Introduction

This is the Directory part of the book, which will give you the basic tools to carry on your search. The websites, addresses, booklist and so on are not comprehensive but they are designed to give you the essentials. If you want to go further, the websites, addresses and booklist will show you how – because, for example, each of the recommended books carries its own bibliography, so that you can take it from there. One thing leads to another, in other words. This just gives you the essential kit, plus a tiny bit of light relief.

Always be aware that addresses can change and books can go out of print. Check especially e-mail addresses and websites. If books you want are no longer in print, try *abebooks* on the web or any reputable bookseller who may be able to trace the books you need. They aren't necessarily going to be expensive. All information here is given in good faith and is believed to be correct at the time of writing (June 2006).

WEBSITES, ETC.

This is a short list. You'll find other websites in the ADDRESSES section, below.

Genealogical Information Service for the UK and Ireland:
genuki.org.uk

Cyndi's List (Cyndi Howell) – which offers about 65,000 worldwide links in over 120 categories:
cyndislist.com

Familia – lists the family history resources held in local-studies libraries:
earl.org.uk/familia/

UK and Irish records:
ancestry.com

1901 Census online:
census.pro.gov.uk

Association of Genealogists and Researchers in Archives:
agra.org.uk

British Library Newspaper Library:
bl.uk/collections/newspaper

Church of Jesus Christ of Latter Day Saints (family history centres):
lds.org.uk/genealogy/fhc

Family history index:
fhindexes.co.uk

Family history online:
familyhistoryonline.net

Federation of Family History Societies:
ffhs.org.uk

Maps and place names:
alangodfreymaps.co.uk
ordsvy.gov.uk
oldmaps.co.uk
gazeteer.co.uk

Guild of One-Name Studies (GOONS):
one-name.org

Huguenot Society:
huguenotsociety.org.uk

Jewish Genealogical Society of Great Britain:
ort.org/jgsgb

Institute of Heraldic and Genealogical Studies:
ihgs.ac.uk

General Register Office (GRO):
(Southport):
statistics.gov.uk/registration
(Scotland): gro-scotland.gov.uk
(Dublin): groireland.ie
(Northern Ireland): groni.gov.uk

National Archives:
(UK): nationalarchives.gov.uk
(USA): archives.gov
(Australia): naa/gov.au
(Canada): archives.ca
(Ireland): nationalarchives.ie
(Scotland): nas.gov.uk

National Army Museum:
national-army-museum.ac.uk

National Maritime Museum:
nmm.ac.uk

Royal Air Force Museum:
rafmuseum.org.uk

Society of Genealogists:
sog.org.uk

Some other useful sites:
familysearch.org
genealogy.tbox.com
rootsweb.com
one-name.org
mapquest.com

Newsgroups
electronic bulletin boards. The one concerned with British genealogy is:
soc.genealogy.britain

CD-ROM data
You can find a large amount of genealogical and family history data published on CDs. Genealogy software uses a standard storage system called GEDCOM (Genealogical Data Communication), which makes it easy to share your information with others who have different software, and that you can upgrade without retyping data.

Helpful Books
Finding Genealogy on the Internet by P. Christian and David Hawgood (1999)
Genealogy On-Line for Dummies by M. and A. Helm (IDG Books, 1998)

ADDRESSES

These addresses are designed to get you started. They will in turn lead you to others.

UK

National Archives
Ruskin Avenue
Richmond
Surrey TW9 4DU
tel: 020 8392 5200
fax: 020 8392 5286
nationalarchives.gov.uk

Family Records Centre
1 Myddelton Street
London EC1 1UW
tel: 020 8392 5300
fax: 020 8392 5307
familyrecords.gov.uk

The Society of Genealogists
14 Charterhouse Buildings
Goswell Road
London EC1M 7BA
tel: 020 7251 8799
fax: 020 7250 1800
sog.org.uk

Federation of Family History Societies
The Benson Room
Birmingham and Midland Institute
Margaret Street
Birmingham B3 3BS
ffhs.org.uk

Catholic Family History Society
45 Gates Green Road
West Wickham
Kent BR4 9DE
feefhs.org

General Register Office for Scotland
New Register House
3 West Register Street
Edinburgh EH1 3YT
tel: 0131 334 0380
open.gov.uk/gros/groshome.htm

Scottish Record Office
HM General Register House
Princes Street
Edinburgh EH1 3YY
tel: 0131 535 1314

The Scottish Genealogy Society
Library and Family History Centre
15 Victoria Terrace
Edinburgh EH1 2JL
tel: 0131 220 3677
fax: 0131 220 3677
sol.co.uk/s/scotgensoc

Welsh Archives Council
National Library of Wales
Aberystwyth
Ceredigion SY23 3BU
tel: 01970 632857
fax: 01970 632883
llgc.org.uk/cac/cac0051.htm

Public Record Office for Northern Ireland
66 Balmoral Avenue
Belfast BT9 6NY
Northern Ireland
proni.nics.gov.uk

REPUBLIC OF IRELAND

The Genealogical Office
2 Kildare Street
Dublin 2
tel: 01 661 8811
scripts.ireland.com

AUSTRALIA

Each state or territory has its own set-up. Enquire at the Australian High Commission for details of where you want to search:

Australian High Commission
Australia House
Strand
London WC2
tel: 020 7379 4334

SOUTH AFRICA

National Archives Depot
Private Bag X236
Pretoria 0001

ARGENTINA

Archivo General de la Nacion
Avenida Leandro N. Alem 246
1003 Buenos Aires
archivo.gov.ar

ARMENIA

Armenian Genealogical Society
PO Box 1383
Provo, UT 84603 1383
USA
distantcousin.com/Links/Ethnic/Armenia.html

AUSTRIA

Austrian State Archives
Nottendorfergasse 2
A-1030 Vienna
oesta.gv.at/engdiv/geneal.html

BELGIUM

Les Archives Générales du Royaume
rue de Ruysbroeck 2
1000 Brussels
arch.arch.be/AGR_F.HTML

CANADA

Each territory has its own setup. Enquire at the Canadian High Commission for where you want to search:

Canadian High Commission
Macdonald House
1 Grosvenor Square
London W1
tel: 020 7258 6600

CHILE

Archivo Nacional
Miraflores # 50
Santiago
dibam.renib.cl/ISC145

CHINA

Universities Service Centre
The Chinese University of Hong Kong
Shatin
NT
Hong Kong
usc.cuhk.edu.hk

CZECH REPUBLIC
Archivni Sprava
Ministstva vnitra CR
Mlady Horakove 133
166 21 Prague 6

FRANCE
Fédération Française de Généalogie
3 rue Turbigo
75001 Paris
tel: 0033 (0)1 40 13 00 88
genefede.org

GERMANY
Abt. Deutsche Zentralstelle für Genealogie
Sächsisches Staatsarchiv Leipzig
Schongauer Str. 1
04329 Leipzig
tel: 0049 (0) 341 25 5555 1
fax: 0049 (0) 341 25 5555 5
bundesarchiv.de

HUNGARY
National Archives of Hungary
PO Box 3
1250 Budapest
natarch.hu/english/mol.htm

INDIA
National Archives of India
Janpath
New Delhi 110001
tel: 0091 (0) 755 540017
nationalarchives.nic.in

ITALY
Archivio Centrale dello Stato
Piazzale degli Archivi
27 00144 Rome
0039 06 545 481
archivi.beniculturali.it

JAMAICA
Registrar General's Office
Twickenham Park
Spanish Town
Jamaica
West Indies

LDS Family History Center
48 Gore Terrace
Kingston
Jamaica
tel: 00 1 876 925 8492

NETHERLANDS
Centraal Bureau voor Genealogie
Prins Willem Alexanderhof 22
Postbus 11755
2502 AT The Hague
tel: 0031 (0) 70 315 0500
cbg.nl

NEW ZEALAND
Archives New Zealand
10 Mulgrave Street
Thorndon
Wellington
tel: 0064 (0) 4 499 5595
archives.govt.govt.nz

PAKISTAN
National Archives of Pakistan
Admin. Block Area
'N' Block
Pak. Secretariat
Islamabad
tel: 0092 9202044

POLAND
Polish Archives
00-950 Warsaw
PO Box 1005
ul. Dluga 6
tel: 0048 22 831 54 91
ciuw.warman.net.pl/alf/archiwa/index.eng.html

PORTUGAL
Arquivo National da Torre do Tombo
Largo de S. Bento, 1200
Lisbon

SLOVAK REPUBLIC
Matica Slovenska
Ustav pre zahranicnych Slovakov
Frantiskanska 2
Bratislava
matica.sk

SPAIN
Archivo Histórico Nacional
Serrano, 115
28006 Madrid
tel: 0034 (0) 915 807 891
mcu.es/lab/archivos

TRINIDAD AND TOBAGO
National Archives, Trinidad & Tobago
Ministry of Education
195 St Vincent Street
Port-of-Spain

PO Box 763
Port-of-Spain
tel: 00 1 868 625 2689/2834

website for National Library:
nalis.gov.tt/library.html

UNITED STATES
Each state has its own set-up.
Enquire at the US Embassy for
the particular area you want to
search in:

United States of America Embassy
24 Grosvenor Square
London W1
tel: 020 7499 9000

BOOK LIST

This is divided into three sections: Genealogy, History and Contemporary Authors. The first section gives you what we believe to be the essential books on the subject – there are many, many more. The second section suggests basic background reading in British history as covered by this book. The third section gives you an idea of whom to read among those writing at different periods of history, writers who will give you a flavour of their times. We haven't always mentioned more than authors and titles here, where the books are available easily in various popular editions.

We read or consulted over 100 books to write this one. Many of those mentioned in the following list have very good and very full bibliographies.

Genealogy

There are two books which may be said to be the 'bibles' of genealogical research as it concerns us here. They are both weighty volumes and cost about £20 each, but they are well worth the money:
ANCESTRAL TRAILS by John Herber (2nd edn, 1997, Sutton Publishing/Society of Genealogists) – also has excellent websites list, and a superb bibliography.
TRACING YOUR ANCESTOR IN THE NATIONAL ARCHIVES by Amanda Bevan (7th edn, 2006, National Archives) – also has superb useful address section.

Two shorter volumes which still contain a wealth of information, would probably be good to make a start with, written by leading genealogists, are:
TRACING YOUR FAMILY TREE by Jean Cole and John Titford (4th edn, 2003, Countryside Books) – also contains extremely useful bibliographical information and is particularly informative on early records and Record Offices.
READER'S DIGEST: EXPLORE YOUR FAMILY'S PAST (2000, Reader's Digest) – editorial consultant, Mark Herber; contributors include Jean Cole, John Titford and Cecil Humphery-Smith.

Two more books which I found useful were:
GENEALOGY ONLINE by Elizabeth Powell Crowe (McGraw Hill, 2003) and
THE ESSENTIAL GUIDE TO GENEALOGY by Ellen Galford (Apple Press, 2002) – this has a terrific international directory of addresses.

Two more specialised publications which may interest you are:
HOW TO READ LOCAL ARCHIVES 1550–1700 by F. G. Emmison (1988)
SIMPLE LATIN FOR FAMILY HISTORIANS by E. McLaughlin (5th edn, 1994)

Last but not least come the two books which accompany the first and second series of WHO DO YOU THINK YOU ARE?, and which complement this one:
WHO DO YOU THINK YOU ARE? – THE ESSENTIAL GUIDE TO TRACING YOUR FAMILY'S HISTORY by Dan Waddell (BBC Books, 2004)
WHO DO YOU THINK YOU ARE? – DISCOVERING THE HEROES AND VILLAINS IN YOUR FAMILY by Dan Waddell and Nick Barratt (Harper*Entertainment*, 2006)

History

These are some of what we consider to be among the most useful general history and reference books covering our period (and beyond):

Eric R. Delderfield (ed.): KINGS AND QUEENS OF ENGLAND AND GREAT BRITAIN (3rd edn, 1981, David & Charles)
F. E. Halliday: AN ILLUSTRATED CULTURAL HISTORY OF ENGLAND (Thames & Hudson, 1968)
Christopher Hibbert: THE ENGLISH – A SOCIAL HISTORY 1066–1945 (HarperCollins, 1994) – a wonderful book with a superb bibliography.
Christopher Hibbert: THE STORY OF ENGLAND (Phaidon, 1992) – a very useful short history of our nation from Neolithic times to the 1980s.
Christopher Lee: THIS SCEPTRED ISLE – 55BC–1901 (Penguin, 1998) – this derives from a Radio 4 series and draws heavily on contemporary material, as well as Winston Churchill's *History of the English-Speaking Peoples*.
Lawrence Stone: THE FAMILY, SEX AND MARRIAGE 1500–1800 (Penguin, 1990)
G. M. Trevelyan: A SHORTENED HISTORY OF ENGLAND (Penguin, 1988; but first published by Longman in 1942)
G. M. Trevelyan: ILLUSTRATED ENGLISH SOCIAL HISTORY (Pelican Books, 4 vols, 1964; but first published by Longman in 1944) – English social history in exhaustive depth from 1340 to 1901.

Here are one or two more specialised books which may interest you:
Dorothy Hartley: FOOD IN ENGLAND (Macdonald & Jane's, 1954)
Gertrude Jekyll & Sydney R. Jones: OLD ENGLISH HOUSEHOLD LIFE (2nd edn, Batsford, 1944–45)
Henry Mayhew (ed. Peter Quennell): MAYHEW'S CHARACTERS (Spring Books, 1965)
Anne Savage (ed., trl., coll.): THE ANGLO-SAXON CHRONICLES (Bramley Books, 1997)
Lytton Strachey: QUEEN VICTORIA (Penguin, 1984; originally published in 1921)

Stella Tillyard: ARISTOCRATS – CAROLINE, EMILY, LOUISA & SARAH LENNOX, 1740–1832 (Chatto & Windus, 1994)

Ben Weinreb & Christopher Hibbert (eds): THE LONDON ENCYCLOPAEDIA (revised edn, Macmillan, 1992)

Jennifer Westwood & Jacqueline Simpson: THE LORE OF THE LAND – A GUIDE TO ENGLAND'S LEGENDS (Penguin, 2005)

And here are two spoof histories simply for fun and because everyone needs to take a break:

Caryl Brahms & S. J. Simon: NO BED FOR BACON (Hogarth Press, 1986; but first published by Michael Joseph in 1941) – Elizabethan London as it ought to have been.
W. C. Sellar & R. J. Yeatman: 1066 AND ALL THAT (Methuen, 1930) – 'A memorable History of England, comprising all the parts you can remember, including 103 Good Things, 5 Bad Kings and 2 Genuine Dates.'

Contemporary Authors

We have listed this selection in alphabetical order, with a note on roughly what period they lived in, identified either by monarch or sobriquet. They have been chosen because they reflect their period so well. They appear in various editions, all easily available today. Some specific volumes conclude the list.

Jane Austen (Regency)
George Borrow (early Victorian – particularly interesting on gypsy lore)
James Boswell (George III – but read his *London Journal, 1762–1763* (Penguin edn, 1966)
Lord Byron (Regency)
Daniel Defoe (Anne/George I)
John Evelyn (Charles I, Cromwell, Charles II) – selections from the *Diaries*.
Henry Fielding (George II)
Elizabeth Gaskell (Victorian)
Oliver Goldsmith (George III) – look especially at his long poem *The Deserted Village* and at his novel *The Vicar of Wakefield*; but he also wrote interestingly on a huge range of subjects.
Samuel Johnson (George III – any biography of him will also be of interest for the period)
Ben Jonson (James I)
Andrew Marvell (Cromwellian/Charles II)
John Milton (Cromwellian/Charles II)
Samuel Pepys (Charles II) – selections from the *Diaries*.
Alexander Pope (Queen Anne)
Jonathan Swift (Queen Anne)

And here are some specific books which may interest you:

Joseph Addison & Richard Steele: SELECTIONS FROM 'THE TATLER' AND 'THE SPECTATOR' (ed. Robert J. Allen; Holt, Rinehart & Winston, 1966) – early 18th-century journalism.
John Aubrey: BRIEF LIVES (ed. Oliver Lawson Dick; Penguin–Peregrine, 1962) – 17th-century short biographies of famous contemporaries; plus a superb introduction by Oliver Lawson Dick. Originally published in 1949)
Bede: A HISTORY OF THE ENGLISH CHURCH AND PEOPLE (trl. Leo Sherley-Price; Penguin Classics, 1962) – written c. 730, one of the earliest English works of record.
George Borrow: THE ZINCALI (John Lane, 1902) – of special interest to those of you researching gypsy ancestry; written in 1840.
Baldesar Castiglione: THE BOOK OF THE COURTIER (trl. George Bull; Penguin Classics, 1967) – 16th-century primer on how to behave in polite society.
William Cobbett: COBBETT'S ENGLAND (ed. John Derry; Folio Society, 1968) - early 19th-century socio-political observations.
Daniel Defoe: A JOURNAL OF THE PLAGUE YEAR (first published 1722; Penguin English Library, 1966, annotated by Anthony Burgess & Christopher Bristow) – Defoe's take on the Great Plague, written sixty years later.
John Dryden: ANNUS MIRABILIS – THE YEAR OF WONDERS (in *Poems of John Dryden,* (Nelson, n.d.) – You'll find this in almost any Dryden anthology or selection; it celebrates the ups and downs of 1666.
Henry Fielding: JONATHAN WILD (first published 1743; now available in an Oxford World's Classics edition) – 'biography' of a real London master-villain (think the Krays) of the time.
Robert Greene & Others: CONY-CATCHERS AND BAWDY BASKETS (ed. Gamini Salgado; Penguin English Library, 1972 – from texts first published between 1552 and 1592) – low life in London (mainly) in the 16th-century.
Richard Hakluyt (ed.): THE TUDOR VENTURERS (first published 1589. Ed. John Hampden; Folio Society, 1970) – contemporary accounts of maritime exploration and adventure.
John Stow: THE SURVEY OF LONDON (first published 1598. Intr. H. B. Wheatley [no ed. cred.]; Everyman/Dent, 1970) – a milestone in early English records.
Izaak Walton: LIVES (biographies of contemporaries; first published 1640–1678. Intr. George Saintsbury [no ed. cred.]; OUP World's Classics, n.d.) – and also see his THE COMPLEAT ANGLER for 17th-century rural life (available in an Oxford Classics paperback)

IMPORTANT PEOPLE

Here's a list of monarchs up to our present monarch (2006); and prime ministers from the time the office became official until Queen Victoria.

MONARCHS UP TO GEORGE VI
(NAME AND WHEN ASCENDED THRONE):

Tudors
Henry VIII	1509
Edward VI	1547
[Jane Grey]	1553
Mary I	1553
Elizabeth I	1558

Stuarts
James I (VI of Scotland)	1603
Charles I	1625
REPUBLIC (Cromwell)	1653-1659
Charles II	1660
James II	1685
William III & Mary II	1689
Anne	1702

Hanoverians
George I	1714
George II	1727
George III	1760
George IV	1820
William IV	1830
Victoria	1837

House of Saxe-Coburg
Edward VII	1901

House of Saxe-Coburg ['Windsor']
George V	1910
[Edward VIII]	1936
George VI	1936

PRIME MINISTERS UP TO QUEEN VICTORIA
(NAME AND WHEN TOOK OFFICE AND AFFILIATION)

Sir Robert Walpole	1721 (Whig)
Earl of Wilmington	1742 (Whig)
Henry Pelham	1743 (Whig)
Duke of Newcastle	1754 (Whig)
Duke of Devonshire	1756 (Whig)
Duke of Newcastle	1757 (Whig)
Earl of Bute	1762 (Tory)
George Grenville	1763 (Whig)
Marquess of Rockingham	1765 (Whig)
– a great horseman	
Duke of Grafton	1766 (Whig)
Lord North	1770 (Tory)
Marquess of Rockingham	1782 (Whig)
Earl of Shelburne	1782 (Whig)
Duke of Portland	1783 (Coalition)
William Pitt	1783 (Tory)
Henry Addington	1801 (Tory)
William Pitt	1804 (Tory)
Lord Grenville	1806 (Whig)
Duke of Portland	1807 (Tory)
Spencer Perceval	1809 (Tory)
– only British PM so far to be assassinated	
Earl of Liverpool	1812 (Tory)
George Canning	1827 (Tory
Viscount Goderich	1827 (Tory)
Duke of Wellington	1828 (Tory)
Earl Grey	1830 (Whig)
Sir Robert Peel	1834 (Tory)
Viscount Melbourne	1835 (Whig)

What's in a Name?

Abbot(t)
Derived from the Syriac term 'Abba' or Aramaic 'Aba', meaning father, Abbot is an occupational name for the chief ruler of an abbey or for someone employed in the household of an abbot.

Abner
Father or Light.

Abraham
From the Hebrew, the father of a great multitude.

Acheson
Of Cornish origins, meaning an inscription or memorial.

Ackerman
From Acker (oaken/made of oak) and man. The brave, firm, unyielding man.

Adams
From the Hebrew personal name Adam which was born, according to Genesis, by the first man. Possibly from the Hebrew word 'adama' meaning 'earth', connecting to the Greek legend that Zeus fashioned the first human beings from earth.

Agnew
From the town of Agneau in Normandy, whence the family originated. Agneau, in Normandy French, signifies a lamb.

Alcock
From Hal or Al, a nickname for Henry; and cock, a termination meaning little. So Wilcox is little Will.

Alexander
Helper of mankind, defender of men. Of Greek origin, but most commonly found in Scotland. McCallister is a common derivation.

Allen (or Alan/Allan)
Of Scottish origins. From 'aluinn' meaning fair or handsome.

Anderson
Patronymic surname meaning 'son of Andrew'. Andrew (man, manly) was the first of Jesus' disciples, and was a revered name in medieval times due to its church connections. Many Danes, Norwegians and Swedes who emigrated to America with the last name Andersson or Anderssen dropped the extra 's' after their arrival.

Andrews
Greek name meaning 'manly or warrior-like'.

Arkwright
A chest-maker in original English. In the north of England flour bins are still sometimes called arks.

Arrowsmith
A maker of iron arrow tips.

Ash or Asher
Dweller near an ash tree.

Asquith
Someone from Askwith in Yorkshire meaning 'dweller near an ash tree'.

Atkins
Son of Anthony.

Arthur
'Strong man', from 'Ar', meaning man and 'thor' meaning strong. Or 'bear man' from the Welsh 'arth', meaning bear and 'ur' an ending meaning 'man.'

Ayres
Derived from a river, town, and district of the same name in Scotland. It may come from 'Iar', meaning west – the course in which the river runs, or 'Air' meaning slaughter, the place of battle.

Bailey
A crown official or officer of the king in county or town. Keeper of a royal building or house, a person of high rank. From the old French for 'bailiff' and/or the Scottish term 'bailie', a municipal

officer corresponding to an English alderman.

Baker
Occupational name which originated in medieval times from the name of the trade, baker. From the Saxon 'bacan', to dry by heat.

Baldwin
A brave friend.

Ball
Nickname for a bald man.

Banks
Someone who lives near a riverbank, or Irish for corpulent.

Barker
A tanner of leather, derived from Middle English 'bark', meaning to tan. Or from the old French 'berquier, berchier, bercher, berkier, berker', meaning shepherd. Or a variant of the German surname Berger, used to describe a man who lived on or by a hill or mountain, from the Old High German 'berg', meaning mountain.

Barnes
Of the barn (barley house), this British surname is often derived from a significant barn in the local region.

Becker
From the German 'becker', meaning baker, or one who bakes bread. Or one who created wooden vessels such as cups, mugs, and pitchers, derived from Middle High German 'becher', meaning cup or goblet, and Greek 'bikos', meaning pot or pitcher. Or a derivative of the Old English 'becca' meaning mattock – used to denote a maker or user of mattocks, digging tools with a flat blade set at right angles to the handle.

Bell
The name may derive from the French 'bel', meaning fair, beautiful, or handsome.

Bennett
From the medieval given name Benedict, originating from the Latin 'benedictus' meaning 'blessed'.

Bernard
Strong or brave as a bear. From a first name of Germanic origin, Bernard was originally Bernharding from 'beran' meaning bear and 'hardu' meaning brave, hardy or strong.

Bertrand
A medieval French form of the given name Bertram, the Bertrand surname means 'bright raven', derived from the elements 'beraht', meaning bright or intelligent and 'hramn', meaning raven.

Black (Blake, Blakey)
Either one who is black haired or dark complexioned, or a cloth dyer who specialized in black dyes.

Bloggs
A maker of blocks as in shoemaking.

Bonnet
An occupational surname from the old French 'bonet', used to describe a maker of bonnets.

Booth
Someone who lived in a hut or bothy, probably a shepherd.

Boyle
A variant of O'Boyle, from the Irish Ó Baoghill. Of uncertain derivation, but considered by most to be connected to the Irish 'geall', meaning 'pledge' or 'vain pledge'.

Brooks
Derivation of 'brook', or a small stream. Also a name given to those who came from Brooksbank, the name of several places in England derived from Middle English 'brokes' for brook and 'bank' for bank.

Bruce
From Bruy or Bruys, a place in Normandy where the family originated or from the old French meaning 'brushwood thicket'.

Bryant
A variation of the English surname Bryan, from the Celtic given name Brian, containing a Celtic element, 'bre,' which means 'hill'.

Buchanan
One who came from the district of Buchanan, a location near Loch Lomond in Scotland. From the Gaelic elements 'buth', meaning 'house' and 'chanain', meaning 'of the canon'. Or an anglicization of the German 'buchenhain', meaning 'beech wood'.

Burns
This geographical surname comes from the Middle English 'burn', meaning 'stream or creek', usually referring to someone who lived close to a river or stream.

Bush
Dweller near a bush or a thicket of bushes, from the Middle English 'bushe', meaning 'bush.'

Butler
An occupational surname derived from the Old French 'bouteillier', meaning servant in charge of the wine cellar. In Normandy, descendants of Theobald Walter (who died in 1206) took the surname of De Boteler or Butler, to mark his service as chief Butler of Ireland, an office conferred upon him by Henry II for his services to the kingdom.

Cameron
The Cameron surname is thought to be derived from the Gaelic 'cam-shron', meaning 'crooked or hook nose'.

Campbell
Crooked or wry mouth, a man whose mouth inclined a little on one side. From the Gaelic 'cam' meaning crooked or distorted and 'beul' for mouth.

Carter
An English occupational name for the transporter of goods by cart or wagon. From the Anglo-Norman French 'caretier', a derivative of old French 'caret' which originally meant 'carrier'. Another possible derivation comes from 'cairtear,' a Gaelic term for tourist or sojourner.

Chandler
From the old French word 'chandelier', this occupational surname referred to a person who made candles – and extended to chandlers who fashioned wax items that were used in church offerings, to ones who made soap, and to ship's chandlers who made and sold candles, as well as other items, to ships.

Christie
A diminutive form of the first name Christian (meaning 'follower of Christ') and possibly also of Christopher (meaning 'Christ carrier', the Christie name eventually grew into popular use as a surname in Scotland.

Clark
Cleric, clerk, or scholar – one who can read and write.

Clayton
Place in the clay or place with good clay for pottery.

Clement
From the late Latin given name 'Clemens', meaning merciful and gentle.

Cleveland
One who came from the district of Cleveland in Yorkshire, a corruption of 'cliff lane', from the steep, hilly terrain of the region.

Clinton
One who came from Clinton, Northamptonshire, an old English place name meaning 'settlement on the summit'.

Cole
An abbreviation of Nicholas (people's victory). Especially common among the Dutch. Or coal-black and swarthy or top-knot, crown of the head.

Coleman
A charcoal burner.

Collins
A double diminutive of Nicholas (in England). Or from 'cuilein', darling, a term of endearment applied to young animals. In Welsh, Collen signifies a hazel grove, and the Gaelic version of the name Collins is O' Coileáin, which means a young dog.

Cook
An English occupational name for a cook, a man who sold cooked meats, or the keeper of an eating house. Derived from Old English 'coc'.

Cooper
An English occupational name for one who made and sold casks, buckets and tubs.

Cox
Form of cock (little), a term of endearment, often used to denote a leader or chief man. Or possibly originated from the Welsh word 'coch', meaning 'red.' Could also be a locality descriptive surname for heap, haycock, or hillock.

Crawford
Derived from the Gaelic 'cru' meaning bloody and 'ford' meaning 'pass or crossing', the Crawford surname is believed by most to mean a crossing of blood.

Cruise
A bold or fierce man.

Cunningham
A place name from the Cunningham area in the Ayrshire district of Scotland, which, in turn, got its name from the words 'cunny' or 'coney' meaning rabbit and 'hame' meaning home (rabbit's home). Another possible translation is that the name derived from 'cuinneag' meaning 'milk pail' along with the Saxon 'ham' meaning 'village'.

Curtis
Someone courteous, whose manners are suitable for the royal court.

Dangerfield
Originally from a French town called Angerville.

Dalton
Locality derived from the town of Dalton, in Lancashire; a corruption of Dale-ton, the town in the dale, or D'Alton, abbreviated to Dalton, that is from the high or rocky hill.

Daniels
In Hebrew Daniel signifies the judgment of God; the 's' added is a contraction of son – the son of Daniel.

David
From the Hebrew name David, meaning 'beloved'.

Davidson
Patronymic name meaning 'son of David'.

Dawson
Said to be a corruption of the Normandy French D'Ossone, from the town of Ossone, in Normandy. Or a contraction of Davison, the son of David.

Dean
From a valley.

Decker
Occupational in origin, this surname most likely derived from the Old High German word 'decker', denoting one who covered roofs with tile, straw or slate. The meaning of the word expanded during the Middle Ages to encompass carpenters and other craftsman and was used to refer to one who built or laid the decks of vessels.

Delgado
A crippled or deformed person; a thin person. Originated in the mountains of Santander, Spain.

Dench
Descendant of a Dane.

Dewhurst
A wet wood.

Dexter
A male dyer.

Dickson
The son of Dick. The given name Dick is a short form of Richard, meaning 'brave power', derived from the German 'ric' for power or rule and 'hard' for brave and hardy.

Dimbleby
A settlement near a ravine.

Docherty
From the word 'dochartach' meaning 'obstructive'. Docherty is the most common Scottish form of this surname, while Doherty and Dougherty are usually of Irish derivation.

Donaldson
The son of Donald. The given name Donald derives from the Gaelic name Domhnall meaning 'ruler of the world' (from 'dubno', world and 'val', rule).

Douglas
From the Gaelic 'dubh' meaning black and 'glas' meaning water, this surname was usually used to refer to someone who dwelled by a dark stream.

Drake
'Dragon' or standard bearer.

Draper
Cloth maker/seller.

Driscoll
Celtic and Gaelic origins. From 'dreas and coill', a thicket of briars, the place of wild roses.

Duncan
Derivation of the Gaelic name Donnchadh which means 'brown warrior', from the Gaelic 'donn' meaning brown and 'chadh' meaning warrior. Or a powerful chieftain;

strong-headed, from 'dun' meaning fortress, and 'ceann' meaning head or chief.

Dunlop
Muddy hill.

Duran
Son of Durant.

Dymoch
A corruption of 'Dia Madoc', that is, David, the son of Madoc, Dia being the diminutive of David among the Welsh. Madoc is derived from mad, good, with the termination 'oc' affixed, which has the same effect as the English termination 'y.'

Eager
Sharp-set, vehement, earnest. The name may be local, from the river Eger, in Bohemia, or Egra, a city on the river Eger.

Edison
Descendant of Edith, meaning prosperity and strife.

Edmead
Humble minded person.

Edmonds
Old English name meaning prosperity and protector.

Edridge
Prosperity/happiness and powerful.

Edwards
Of Saxon origin. Son of Edward, happy keeper.

Efford
Ford useable at ebb tide. Also place names in Cornwall, Devon and Hampshire.

Eggleston
From 'egles', a church, and 'tun' or 'dun', a hill – the church on the hill.

Eisenhower
An occupational surname meaning iron cutter or iron worker.

Elliman
Oil maker, seller.

Ellinger
Dweller at the alder trees.

Elliot
Supposed to signify the son of Elias; Heliat, Welsh and Cornish British, a huntsman, a pursuer.

Ellis
Contracted from Elias.

Emerson
From the Saxon Emar (Ethelmar) noble, and son – the son of the noble.

Enfield
Open country with lambs.

Erwin
Friend of a wild boar.

Escott
Eastern cottage.

Evans
The Welsh for John, the same as Johns. Evan, 'eofn', means fearless, bold.

Everett
A corruption of Everard meaning well reported, ever honoured, or from Eberhardt, meaning ever hard or enduring. Some writers are of opinion that we have Ebers, Everard, Evered, and Everet, from the word 'Eber', a boar.

Ewell
Ewhill, in Cornish British, signifies high or tall.

Ewer
Water bearer.

Eyton
Place on a river.

Faber
A workman, a smith.

Fairfax
Fair-hair; 'faex' meaning hair.

Fanshaw
'Fane', a temple or church, and 'shaw', a small wood or grove, a thicket – the church in the grove.

Farraday
From 'farraideach' meaning inquisitive, prying, curious.

Ferdinand
From 'fred', peace, and 'rand', pure – pure peace.

Ferguson
Patronymic name meaning 'son of Fergus'. The given name Fergus comes from Fearghas, derived from the Gaelic 'fear' meaning man, and 'gus' meaning vigour.

Fernandez
The son of Fernando, with Fernando being a given name meaning 'journey, venture'. Found throughout Spain and the Hispanic world.

Fielding
This family trace their descent to the Earls of Hapsburgh, in Germany. Geffery, a son of Edward of Holland, served with Henry III in the wars of England, and because his father had dominions in Lauffenburgh and Renfelden, he took the name of Felden or Fielding.

Fillmore
From the old English given name, 'filmore', meaning very famous.

Findlay
From the Scottish name 'Fionnlagh/Fionnlaoich', meaning fair hero. From the Gaelic elements 'fionn' meaning white or fair and 'laoch' meaning warrior or hero.

Fisher
An occupational name from the old English 'fiscare', meaning fisherman. Fischer is a common German spelling.

Fitzgerald
The son of Gerald. Fitz, a son, and Gerald, all-surpassing, excellent. This ancient and honorable family is traced from Otho, a Baron in Italy, descended from the Grand Dukes of Tuscany. Walter, son of Otho, came into England with William the Conqueror,

and afterwards settled in Ireland.

Fleischer
Of German origin, meaning butcher.

Fleming
Deriving from the French, 'Le Fleming', the Fleming surname literally means 'from Flanders.' The first people who bore the surname were 12th century merchants who hailed from Flanders.

Fletcher
A maker of arrows, or superintendant of archery. From the French 'flèche', an arrow.

Floyd
Welsh meaning brown, gravy, hoary.

Forbes
From the Gaelic 'forba' meaning field.

Ford
One who lived near a ford or river crossing, from the Old English ford, meaning 'pass or crossing.'

Forsythe
Of Gaelic origin. From 'fear', a man, and 'syth', upright, honest, stiff.

Foster
Either a foster-child or foster-parent, a forester, or a shearer or scissors maker (from the old French 'forceter').

Francis
From the Saxon, 'Frank', meaning free. The Franks were a people who anciently inhabited part of Germany and, having conquered Gaul, changed the name of the country to France.

Fraser
Said to derive from 'fraises', the French word for strawberry because the Fraser arms display three silver strawberry flowers on a field of blue.

Freeman
One who enjoys liberty, or is entitled to a franchise, or peculiar privilege, as the freeman of a city or state.

Frost
Welsh 'Ffrost', a brag.

Fry
A hill, a town or house on the most prominent part of a hill or eminence. From the German 'Frei', free, and Dutch 'Vry' or 'Fry', free.

Fuchs
From the Middle High German 'vuhs' meaning fox. Sometimes used to describe someone with red hair, or someone considered crafty or clever – characteristics attributed to the fox.

Galbraith
A compound of two Gaelic words, 'Gall' and 'Bhreatan', that is, strange Briton, or Low Country Briton. The Galbraiths in the Gaelic are called 'Breatannich' or 'Clann-a-Breatannich', that is, the Britons, or the children of the Britons.

Gallacher
From the Gaelic 'Gallach', meaning valiant, brave, and 'er' for fear.

Garfield
One who lived on or near a triangular field or piece of land. From the old English 'gar' meaning triangular land and 'feld' meaning open country or field.

Gaskell
Of Gaelic origins. From 'gaisgeil', valorous.

Gibson
A patronymic name meaning son of Gibb which in Middle English was a familiar term for a cat.

Giddings
The son of Gid or Gideon.

Gifford
One who gives generously or has a liberal disposition. From

the Germanic given name Gebhardt, made up of the elements 'geb' meaning gift and 'hard' meaning 'brave or hardy'. The Giffard variant of this surname likely comes from the Old French 'giffard', meaning chubby-cheeked, bloated.

Gilchrist
From the Gaelic 'gille', a servant, and 'Chriosed', Christ – the servant of Christ.

Gillespie
The Gaelic for Archibald.

Goldsmith
A name of trade; formerly in England, a banker.

Gomez
Derived from the given name, Gome, meaning man.

Gonzales
Patronymic name meaning Son of Gonzalo. The given name Gonzalo comes from the medieval name Gundisalvus, which was the Latin form of a Germanic name composed of the elements 'gund', meaning war and 'salv' which is of unknown meaning.

Gordon
A Scottish place name meaning 'great hill'.

Gorman
A native of Germany, the same as Germain

Graham
Believed to be derived from an English place name which meant either 'gravelly homestead' or 'grey home,' this surname was first used in Scotland in the 12th century.

Grant
A commoner form of Grand, meaning big, tall or elder, senior.

Gray
Nickname for a man with gray (grey) hair, or a gray (grey) beard, from old English 'groeg' meaning grey.

Green
One who dwelled at, or near, the village green, or other grassy ground. An alternative meaning is immature, inexperienced.

Griffin
A descriptive name given to a man whose qualities or disposition resembled the mythical creature of the same name. Griffwn, in Welsh, means 'crooked nose' or 'hawk's beak.' Griffin may also be a variation of Griffith or Griffeth from the Middle Welsh 'Gruffudd,' where 'udd' means chief or lord.

Griffith
Welsh and Cornish British origins. One who has strong faith, from the Welsh 'Cryf', strong, and 'ffyd', faith.

Hadley
From 'houdt', a wood, and 'ley', a place or field.

Haines
From the Saxon 'ainulph', alone, and 'ulph', help, that is one who needs not the assistance of others. In French Haine, signifies malicious, full of hatred. In German, Hain, a wood, forest, thicket, grove.

Halden
From the Saxon 'halig', holy, and 'dun', a hill; a place where Oswald got the victory of Cadwallader, the Briton, and from this circumstance was called the Holy Hill, and also the Heavenly Field.

Hales
In Cornish British, it signifies low, level lands washed by a river or the sea; a moor.

Hailliday
Holy day. It is said this name had its origin in the slogan, or war-cry of a Gaelic clan residing in Annandale, who made frequent raids on the English border. On these occasions they employed the war-cry of 'A holy-day', every day, in their estimation, being holy, that was spent in ravaging the enemy's country.

Hamilton
Originally Hambleton, from the manor of Hambleton, in Buckinghamshire. William, third son of Robert, third Earl of Leicester, took that surname from the place of his birth, as above. He was the founder of the family of that name in Scotland, whither he went about the year 1215. The name is derived from 'Hamell', a mansion, the seat of a freeholder, and 'dun', an enclosure, a fortified place, a town.

Hammond
Ham-mount, the town or house on the elevation.

Hanley
From the town of Hanley, in Shropshire. The old place or field, from 'Hen' or 'Han', meaning old, and 'ley', a place, a common.

Hanson
The son of Hans or John, same as Johnson.

Harding
The place where an army was encamped.

Harrington
From the parish of Harrington, in Cumberland, corrupted from Haverington, Meaning the town in or surrounded by oat fields.

Harrison
The son of Henry.

Hathaway
Derived from Port Haethwy, in Wales.

Haycock
A name probably given to a foundling exposed in a hayfield.

Hayes
A man who lived near an enclosure (haeg) or (heye), an area of forest fenced off for hunting. The surname may also have been derived from the old English (haes) or the old French word (heis), both meaning brushwood.

Hayward
The keeper of the common herd or cattle of a town, from the Saxon 'hieg', hay, and 'ward', a keeper.

Hicks
The son of Hugh. Hig or Hick being a common nickname for Hugh. Hick, in Dutch, signifies a simpleton.

Hodges
From Hodge, a nickname of Roger, the 's' being added for son.

Holmes
Meadowlands near or surrounded by water; sometimes an island.

Howell
Of Cornish British origin. From 'Houl', the sun; In Greek 'Euhill' means high, exalted.

Hughes
The son of Hugh. Alfred, in the year 900, used Hugh to denote comfort. Hugh in the Gaelic, is 'Aoidh', which signifies affability, a guest, a stranger. Hu suggests the idea of elevation; Ho, Hu, highness.

Hutton
The high town. Hutain, in French, is haughty, proud.

Ince
Living on an island.

Ingham
The town on the low ground, meadow or pasture.

Inglesby
Inglesby, the town of the English, or Angles; perhaps the town was first named at the time the Angles first invaded Britain. Ing-gil-by, in Saxon, means the town near the brook in the narrow valley.

Inglis
Scottish form of English.

Ingram
From the Saxon angel, and 'rein', purity. Pure as an angel.

Inman
An innkeeper.

Irvine (Irving)
From a river and town of the same name in Ayrshire, Scotland.

Isaac
Meaning laughter in Hebrew.

Ives
From a town named St Ives.

Jackson
Patronymic name meaning 'son of Jack'. Jack may be a diminutive of John or James, or a derivation of the old French given name Jacque, the French form of Jacob.

James
Derived from Jacob and usually meaning 'son of Jacob'. In English, Jacob and James are distinctly separate names, but throughout the rest of the world, the two are used interchangeably.

Jarvis
Usually derived from the given name Gervaise, an English form of Gervasius, comprising the Germanic elements 'geri', meaning spear and 'vase', of unknown meaning. Or one who came from Jervaulx (pronounced Jarvis) in Northern Yorkshire, the site of a Cistercian monastery and named for the river Ure and 'vaulx', meaning valley.

Jefferson
Son of Jeffrey, Jeffers, or Jeff. Jeffrey is a variant of Geoffrey, meaning peaceful place (from 'gawia' meaning territory and 'frid' meaning peace.) Geoffrey is also a possible variant of Godfrey, meaning God's peace or peaceful ruler.

Jenkins
Double diminutive of John'.

Jessup
From the Italian Giuseppe, the same as Joseph.

Jobson
The son of Job.

Johnson (Johnstone)
The son of John (gift of God).

Jones
The son of John (God has favoured or gift of God). This is the most common surname in Wales.

Jordan
The river of judgment. In Gaelic, Jardain, the western river, with respect to the Euphrates. The name is derived from its two spring-heads, Jor and Dan.

Joyce
From the medieval name Josse, which was derived from the earlier Joceus or Jodocus, Latinized forms of the Breton personal name Iodac, a diminutive of 'iudh', meaning lord.

Judd
From Juda, meaning praise, confession, and signifies the confessor of God. Jode or Jood, in Dutch, means Israelite, a Jew.

Kaufman
Of German origin. A merchant, a trader.

Kavanagh
Of Celtic or Gaelic origins. 'Coamhanach' meaning mild, benevolent, merciful.

Keeler
One who manages barges and vessels.

Keen (Kean)
Bold, eager, daring; bright, fair.

Kelly
A grove, generally of hazel. Kill or Cille, in Gaelic and Celtic, denotes a church.

Kemp
In old English, a soldier, one who engaged in single combat. The name Kemp is derived from the Saxon word to kemp, or combat.

Kendall
Derived from the town of Kendal, and was so called

from the river Ken, on which it is situated, and dale – the dale on the river Ken.

Kendrick
From the Saxon 'Kenrick', from 'Kennen', to know, and 'ric', rich – rich in knowledge.

Kennedy
From the Gaelic or Celtic words 'Kean-na-ty', the head of the house, or chief of the clan.

Kenyon
Of Welsh origins. A stubborn, strong-willed powerful leader

Kiel
Derived from the town of Kiel, in Lower Saxony.

Kingston
The name of several towns in England – the king's town.

Kinnear
From the Gaelic, a head man or chief.

Kirby (Kirkby)
The name of several small towns in England, whence the surname is derived; so called from 'kirk', a church, and 'by', a village or town.

Kirkpatrick
Patrick's church.

Klein
Of German origin meaning small, little.

Knapp
From the German Knappe, meaning a lad, boy, servant, workman.

Knightley
From Knight, and 'ley', a place or field.

Knowles
Knowl, in Cornish British, is a projection of hilly ground.

Kyle
From a district of the same name in Ayrshire, Scotland. In Gaelic, 'Coill', a wood. The river Coyle runs through the district.

Lacy
Derived from a place in France by that name. Sire De Lacy came into England with William the Conqueror. The Lacys afterward settled in Ireland.

Ladd
From the English 'lad', originally referring to a servant or one of low birth; or from the Welsh 'lladd', meaning to destroy.

Laing
Scottish dialect for long.

Lamb
The name was probably taken from the sign of a lamb at an inn, the young of the sheep kind.

Lambert
Bright land or light of the land, the Lambert surname derives from the Germanic elements 'land' meaning land and 'beraht' meaning bright.

Lang
A descriptive surname given to an unusually tall individual, from the old English 'lang' or 'long', meaning long or tall.

Langton
The long hill or town, so called from its oblong form.

Latimer
An interpreter. This name was first given to Wrenoc ap Merrick, a learned Welshman, interpreter between the Welsh and English. The name of his office descended to his posterity.

Lawley
From the Saxon, meaning a low pasture.

Lawrence
Flourishing, spreading, derived from Laurus, the laurel-tree.

Lawson
The son of Law.

Lehmann
A vassal, serf, or liege man, from the Middle High German 'lehenman'.

Leigh
A pasture or meadow, the same as Ley, or Lea. The frequency of this family name in Cheshire, England, led to the old proverb, 'As many Leighs as fleas, Masseys as asses, and Davenports as dog's tails.'

Lennon
From the Gaelic 'Leannon', a lover, a sweetheart.

Lewis
Derived from the Germanic name Lewis, meaning 'reknowned, famous battle'.

Lincoln
Derived from the Welsh element 'lynn', meaning lake or pool and the Latin element 'colonia', meaning colony.

Livingstone
A barony in West Lothian, Scotland, so named from one Livingus living there in 1124.

Lloyd
Grey or brown in Welsh.

Lonsdale
Derived from the town of Lonsdale, in Westmoreland. So named from the river Lon on which it is situated, and dale – the dale on the Lon.

Lopez
A patronymical surname meaning 'son of Lope'. Lope comes from the Spanish form of Lupus, a Latin name meaning wolf.

Lorimer
A maker of bits or bridles.

Lowe
A hill.

Lynch
A strip of greenwood between the plowed lands in the common field; a small hanging wood.

Maddock
The same as Madoc, a proper name common among the Welsh, meaning goodness, greatness.

Madison
The son of Matthew or Matilda.

Maguire
The son of Guaire, which is the Gaelic for Godfrey.

Mannering
From the Welsh 'Mesnil' or 'Maenol', a farm.

Mansfield
From a town in Nottinghamshire, England, of the same name, so called from the Saxon 'manrian', to traffic, and field – a place of trade.

Marchant
From the French 'marchand', a merchant.

Marshall
A name of office. Anciently, one who had command of all persons not above princes.

Maynard
Of a powerful disposition, stout-hearted. Maynhard was one of the barons who went into England with William the Conqueror, and whose name is in the roll of Battle Abbey.

McAllister
The son of Alister, the Gaelic, for Alexander. In Welsh, Callester signifies a an invincible man. Galluster, in Cornish British, expresses might or power.

McCarthy
The son of Carrthach, an Irish chieftain, who lived in the eleventh century.

McDonald
Somerled, Thane of Argyle, flourished about the year 1140, and was the ancestor of all the McDonalds. He married the daughter of Olans, Lord of the Western Isles, whereupon he assumed the title of 'King of the Isles'. He was slain, in 1164, by

Walter, Lord High Steward of Scotland. Donald, from whom the clan derived their name, was his grandson.

McGregor
The descendants of Gregor, who was the son of Alpin, King of Scotland.

McIntyre
The son of Kintyre. Also meaning headland, from 'Cean', head, and 'tir', land.

McLean
From a Highland chieftain of the name of Gillean, later called Mac Gillean, in all ancient documents, and now of modern date McLeans.

McLoud
From Mac, son, and Clode, from Claudius, the second emperor who invaded Britain.

McNab
The son of Nab. Nab, being the summit of a mountain or rock.

Mercer
One who deals in silks and woollen goods.

Middleton
From Middleton, a small town in Dorset – the middle town.

Miller
One who attends a grist-mill. Or from the Gaelic 'malair', a merchant.

Mitchell
A corruption of Michael, or from the Saxon 'muchel', meaning big.

Monroe
Monadh Roe or Mont Roe, from the mount on the river Roe, in Ireland, whence the family came.

Moore
A great chief, tall, mighty, proud.

Morgan
From 'mor', the sea, and 'gan', born – born on the sea.

Morris
A hero, a warrior.

Murphy
A modern form of the ancient Irish name O'Murchadha, which means descendant of sea warrior in Gaelic.

Murray
Some deduce this family from a warlike people called the Moravii, who came from Germany into Scotland, and affixed their own nomenclature to that district now called the shire of Moray. The root of the name is the same whether Moravian or Gaelic, and signifies the great water, from 'mor', great, and 'an' or 'av', water.

Napier
He in charge of the king's napery or linen at the coronation of English kings, an office held by William De Hastings, in the time of Henry I.

Nash
From the Gaelic, 'naisg', made fast, bound, protected. Probably an old fortress or watchtower.

Needham
From the Danish words for herd and village – the village of cattle.

Nelson
The son of Neil or Nel.

Neville
From the French 'de neuve ville', of the new town.

Newman
Newly arrived in an area.

Newton
The new town.

Nixon
Son of Nicholas. From the Greek name Nikolaos, meaning 'victory of the people'.

Nolan
rish (Leinster and Munster): Anglicized form of Gaelic Ó Nualláin 'descendant of Nuallán', a personal name representing a diminutive of nuall 'famous', 'noble'.

Norris
Norroy, or north-king – a title given in England to the third king-at-arms.

Norton
The north town.

Oakes
From a dwelling near the oak trees.

O'Brien
The descendant of Brien – meaning exalted, noble.

O'Connor
The descendants of Conor or Concovar, an Irish chieftain, who died in the year 971.

O'Donnell
The descendants of Donal, an ancient Irish family, who trace their descent through Donal to Niallus Magnus, the ancestor of the O'Neills, known as Nial Niagallach, Nial of the nine hostages.

Ogden
The oak vale, or shady valley. Ogduine, in Gaelic, signifies a young man, and Ogdyn, in Welsh, has the same signification.

O'Hara
The descendant of Hara. In Gaelic, 'arra' signifies a pledge; 'arr', a stag; 'arradh', an armament. 'Hara' is the Saxon for a hare.

O'Leary
From the Welsh for gentle, easy.

O'Neil
The descendants of Neil, meaning the powerful or mighty.

Ormsby
A place surrounded by elms.

Osborn
From 'hus', a house, and 'bearn', a child – a family-child, an adopted child.

Owen
The good offspring.

Paine
A pagan, unbaptized; a rustic.

Palmer
A pilgrim, so called from the palm-branch, which he constantly carried as a pledge of his having been in the Holy Land.

Parker
The keeper of the park.

Patrick
From the Latin 'Patricius' meaning a noble, a senator.

Patterson
Patrick's son.

Paxton
From the town of Paxton, in Berwickshire.

Payne
From a place called Payne, in Normandy.

Peacock
Taken from the name of the well-known fowl; 'pea', contracted from the Latin, 'pavo' – a name given from a fondness of display.

Pearson
Pierre-son, the son of Pierre or Peter.

Pelham
Either from 'peele', a tower, castle, or from 'pool', a small lake, and 'ham', a village.

Pendleton
Of Gaelic origins meaning the town at the head of the valley.

Perkins
From Peir or Peter, and the diminutive termination 'ins' – meaning little Peter, or the son of Peter.

Perry
If not synonymous with Parry, it is local, from Pierre (French), a stone, signifying a stony place, abounding in rocks.

Phelps
Supposed to be the same as Phillips. The name may come from the Danish, 'hvalp' and Swedish 'valp', a whelp.

Pickering
A market town of north Yorkshire, with the remains of a castle.

Pierce
The same as Piercy or Percy.

Polland
Of French and Dutch origins. To be chicken-hearted.

Poole
A small collection of water in a hollow place, supplied by a spring.

Pope
From the Greek and Latin, Papa, father.

Powell
A contraction of the Welsh Ap Howell, the son of Howell. It may also be deduced from Paul.

Powers
The same as Parson, or a corruption of Power-son, the son of Power.

Prescot
From Prescot, a small town in England, so called from the Welsh 'prys', a coppice, and 'cwt', a cottage.

Price
A corruption of Ap Rice, the son of Rice.

Pringle
From the Welsh for hazel wood, or in Scotland an obsolete Scottish coin.

Putnam
Of Dutch origins. The house by the well.

Quintin
The fifth son, from the Latin 'Quintus'.

Quigley
A thrifty person or one having a body peculiarity.

Quinn
Shortened Anglicized form of Gaelic Ó Coinn 'descendant of Conn'.

Quirke
From a Gaelic word meaning heart.

Radcliff
A cliff of red rock.

Radford
Derived from Cornish meaning the fern way.

Raleigh
'Rhawlaw' in Welsh, signifies a lieutenant, a vicar; and 'rheoli', to govern, to rule.

Ramsden
From the Saxon for the winding valley, or the extremity of the valley.

Ramsey
An island.

Rankin
This name may be derived from a Danish word meaning upright, erect. If the name is Gaelic, it would come from 'roinn', a promontory, share, or division, and 'ceann', head – the head of the promontory.

Rawlings
From Raoul, French for Ralph. The termination of 'ings' indicates Ralph's son.

Reed
From the Saxon word 'rede' meaning advice, counsel, help.

Reynolds
From the old English word 'rhein' meaning sincere or pure love.

Rice
Another form of the Welsh Rys meaning to rush; figuratively, a hero, a brave, impetuous man.

Richardson
The son of Richard.

Richmond
From the Saxon words 'ric' and 'mund'. A rich mouth, an eloquent person.

Riggs
From the Danish 'rig' meaning wealthy or rich.

Ripley
From the Saxon words 'rypan', to divide or separate, and 'ley', uncultivated lands.

Roberts
Famous in counsel.

Robinson
Son of Robbin or Robin. Also derived from the Polish word 'rabin' (rabbi).

Romero
A Spanish nickname meaning pilgrim, originally 'pilgrim to Rome'.

Roswell
Either Rosveldt, the rose-field, or Rosville, the town on the heath.

Rothschild
From a town in Denmark, which is said to take its name from a river with which it is watered that drives several mills. 'Roe', in the ancient Danish language, signifies a king, and 'kille', a stream of water or brook – i.e. the king's brook.

Rowe
A river that overflows its banks.

Rowntree
Rowan-tree, the mountain-ash.

Ruiz
From the Spanish personal name Ruy, a short form of Rodrigo – son of Rodrigo.

Russell
Of French origin. Meaning red-haired.

Ryan
A shortened form of O'Ryan, an Anglicized form of the Gaelic Ó Riagháin 'descendant of Rian'. Ryan is one of the common surnames in Ireland.

Salisbury
The old town of Salisbury anciently stood upon a hill where there was no water, but it is now situated in a valley, and a little brook runs through the streets. The name was sometimes written Salusbury, that is, the healthy hill or town.

Saltzman
A German occupational name – one who processed and sold salt.

Sanchez
A variant of Basque Zaraitzu, a habitational name from a town so named in Navarre.

Saxton
An under officer of the church, the same as Sexton. Or Sax-town, a town of the Saxons.

Schmidt
A German occupational name – a blacksmith or metalworker.

Schultz
The village mayor.

Sedgwick
The town or harbour.

Seymour
A corruption of St Maurus.

Shannon
A tranquil, gentle river.

Shaw
A plain surrounded by trees, or an open space between woods.

Sheldon
The spring in the valley. From 'schell', a spring, and 'dene', a small valley, in original Cornish.

Sherman
One who used to shear cloth.

Sherwood
Of Saxon origins meaning a clearing in the wood.

Simmons
A corruption of Simeon or Simon.

Sinclair
A corruption of St Clair, from the Latin 'clarus', meaning

pure, renowned and illustrious.

Skelton
The hill of separation or boundary.

Somerville
The village near a marsh or lake.

Southwell
The south well or plain.

Spalding
A ravine, from the German word 'spalte'.

Spencer
From the Normandy French Le Despenser, a steward. The ancestor of the family assumed the name Le Despenser from being steward to the household of William the Conqueror.

Stanton
From 'stan', a stone, and 'ton', a hill or town.

Stapleton
A town enclosed or fenced round with stakes.

Stead
'Stad' and 'stede', in Dutch, signifies a town.

Steele
A name given, in all probability, to a person who was inflexible, hard, firm, or enduring.

Stevens
From Stephen.

Stewart
An estate manager.

Stirling
From the Gaelic name 'Strila', by some supposed to signify 'the place of strife'.

Stokes
The name signifies a place, a settlement. Possibly from 'stuge', the Danish for ravine.

Stone
The name was probably given to an individual who resided near or by some remarkable stone.

Sullivan
Of Celtic origin meaning the fair eyed.

Sutton
The south town.

Taggart
Either from the Welsh 'tycwrdd', a meeting-house or the Gaelic 'tagair', to reason, to debate.

Taite
Pleasure, delight.

Talbot
A mastiff.

Taylor
A name of trade.

Temple
From the manor of Temple, in Wellesborough, Leicestershire, which name was given by the old Earl of Leicester, one of the Knights Templars.

Tennant
A person holding lands under another, from the Latin 'teneo', to hold.

Theobald
God's power or a powerful hold over the people. Of Saxon origins.

Thomas
From Hebrew, a twin.

Thompson (Thomson)
Son of Thomas

Thorpe
A village from the Dutch 'dorp'.

Tilman
One who works a farm.

Todd
An old Scottish word for a fox.

Towers
A place of defence. Tower is derived from 'tor', Gaelic and Saxon, a heap or pile and applied to conical hills or to round buildings erected for strength or security.

Townsend
One who lived at the end of the town.

Trelawney
The open town near the water; from 'tre', a town, and 'ey', water.

Trowbridge
The name signifies 'through the bridge', perhaps given for some feat of daring, or bodily courage.

Truman
A trusty, faithful man.

Tucker
A fuller, who cleaned and thickened freshly woven cloth.

Tully
From the Gaelic for 'peace loving'.

Turner
A wood turner.

Tyler
A variant of the English occupational name Tiler, a man who made and laid tiles in floors and pavements. Derived from the Old English 'tigele' meaning 'to cover'.

Underhill
Under the hill.

Underwood
Under the wood.

Unwin
Invincible.

Upton
The high hill, or the town on the height.

Urquhart
From the barony of this name on Loch Ness.

Valdez
Spanish habitational name from either of the two places called Valdés in Málaga and Asturies.

Vaughan
Of Welsh origin meaning little, small in stature.

Venables
From the French, meaning 'hunting ground'.

Vickers
From the Cornish meaning a sovereign lord.

Vincent
From the Roman given name Vincentius, from the Latin 'vincens', meaning conquering or victor.

Vine
Taken from the plant that bears the grape; a vineyard.

Wade
Derived from 'weide', a meadow or pasture.

Wadsworth
The same as Woodsworth, the farm or place in the wood.

Waite
The same as Thwaite, a piece of ground cleared of wood, a meadow.

Wagner
A wagon-maker or wagon driver.

Wagstaff
A functionary who wielded a staff of office.

Wakeman
A title given to the chief magistrate of Rippon, in Yorkshire; a watchman.

Walker
This name may signify either a fuller or an officer whose duty consisted in walking or inspecting a certain space of forest ground.

Wallace
The same as Wales or Welch and derived from the word Gaulish. A name given to the Britons by their Danish and Angles invaders, because they originally came from Gaul.

Walsh
A Welshman.

Walton
From 'wald', a wood, and ton.

Ward
A keeper, one who guards or defends.

Warren
Of French origin. The primary sense of the word is to stop, hold, or repel.

Watkins
The son of Wat or Walter.

Watson
The son of Walter.

Webster
A maker of webs, a weaver.

Wendell
From the Dutch Wandelaar, a walker, hence a traveller.

Wesctcott
From the Saxon for a banker, a money lender.

Wheaton
From the Saxon 'Whitton', the white hill or Cornish 'Whiddon' meaning white.

White
A name given from the colour of the hair, or complexion.

Whitbread
A baker, or nickname for a man with a white beard.

Whittaker
A place of burial for criminals. The north part of a graveyard allotted to the poor was called whittaker, from 'wite', a penalty, and 'acre'. A culprit who could not discharge the penalty became a 'witetheow' and was buried in the 'wite-acre'.

Wilcox
From Will, and cock, which signifies little. A 'willcock' is one who is rather obstinate.

Wilkins
From 'Wil', and the patronymic termination 'kins', the son of William.

Wilson
A descendant of William, meaning 'willpower' and 'protection'.

Wiseman
A name given for the quality of wisdom.

Witherspoon
A grazing-place in the spur of a mountain or hill.

Wyman
From the Dutch 'Weiman', a huntsman; one who shoots the game.

Yale
From a lordship of the same name in Wales.

Yarrow
A plant of a thousand leaves.

Yates
An old word for gate.

Young
Derived from the Old English word 'geong' meaning young, this surname was used as a descriptive name to distinguish father from son or to the younger of two relatives with the same first name.

York
A retreat from the wild boars which were in the forest of Gautries.

Ziegler
From the German for a tile maker.

Zimmerman
From the German for a carpenter.

Zuckerman
Of German origin: a sugar seller.

20 Famous Surnames and Their Origins

NEIL ARMSTRONG
Nickname for a strong man.

CLEMENT ATTLEE
From the old English word 'lear' meaning 'dweller at the pasture or meadow'.

TONY BLAIR
From the Gaelic 'blar', meaning battlefield.

IAN BOTHAM
Someone who lived in a broad valley.

EMILY BRONTE
From a Gaelic name meaning bestower, a generous person.

CHARLIE CHAPLIN
The servant of a clergyman.

DAVID/JONATHAN/RICHARD DIMBLEBY
Settlement near a ravine.

CLINT EASTWOOD
From a wood to the east of a settlement.

IAN FLEMING
Descendant of someone from Flanders.

PAUL GASCOIGNE
Someone from Gascony, south-west France.

GERMAINE GREER
A variant of the Scottish name MacGregor.

GERI HALLIWELL
Someone living near a holy spring.

EDDIE IZZARD
Descendant of Isolde, meaning ice and battle.

JOHN F KENNEDY
Helmeted, or having an ugly head.

NICOLE KIDMAN
A goatherd, or as frisky as a young goat.

ABRAHAM LINCOLN
Lake settlement.

PAUL NEWMAN
Newly arrived in an area.

MARY QUANT
Finely dressed or clever.

WILLIAM SHAKESPEARE
A quarrelsome soldier.

TERRY VENABLES
From the French, meaning 'hunting ground'.

INDEX

ACKNOWLEDGEMENTS

Anton Gill would like to thank the following people for their contribution to this book: Marji Campi, my wife, for help-ing hugely with the research, reading and correcting the ms, feeding me and generally being patient and kind; Nicci Crowther for ideas and lending books; Lt. Col. Joseph 'Joe' Steeples for advice on bloodstock and the St Leger; Alison Harris; Sophia Wickham for kindly helping with additional research; John de Falbe and all the staff at John Sandoe's bookshop for their usual help and advice; Patrick Dillon for letting me read his excellent new book *The Last Revolution* (Cape, 2006) before publication, giving me valuable insight into the Year of Revolution, 1688; the staffs of the British Library, the London Library, and the Bibliothèque Nationale de France; Carlton Wallace (a very big thank-you here); Dan Waddell for giving me footsteps to tread in; Trevor Dolby and Kate Latham of HarperCollinsEntertainment; the WHO DO YOU THINK YOU ARE? production team at Wall-to-Wall, especially Sarah Mould; Sheila Ballantyne; Sir John Hammerton (another massive thank-you, John!); Dr Nick Barratt, genealogist extraordinaire; and last but not least my literary agents Julian Alexander and Araminta Whitley of the LAW Writers' Agency.

PICTURE CREDITS

AKG Images: p12, p15 (br) (British Library), p17 (Rabatti-Dominge), p91, p111 (Sotheby's), p116, p118 (Sotheby's), p119, p134 (Sotheby's), p136, p138 (Sotheby's), p146, p152, p166, p175, p177 (Sotheby's), p183, p191 (Nimatallah), p194 (Sotheby's), p207, p208; Art Archive: p7 (Culver Pictures), p14 (Bodleian Library, Oxford), p16 (t) (National Archives), p16 (b) (Cava dei Tirreni Abbey Salerno / Dagli Orti), p68 (Private Collection MD), p73 (Private Collection MD), p83 (Musée du Château de Versailles / Dagli Orti), p84 (Musée Carnavalet, Paris / Dagli Orti), p85 (Eileen Tweedy), p88 (t), p88 (b) (Courage Breweries / Eileen Tweedy), p90 (Musée Jacquemart-André Fontaine-Chaalis / Dagli Orti), p99 (t) (Usher Art Gallery, Lincoln / Eileen Tweedy), p101 (r) (Musée du Château de Versailles / Dagli Orti), p112 (Musée du Louvre, Paris / Dagli Orti), p115 (Handel Museum, Halle / Dagli Orti), p120(b) (Thomas Coram Foundation / Eileen Tweedy), p135 (Army and Navy Club / Eileen Tweedy), p139 (Museo Tosio Martinengo, Brescia / Dagli Orti), p149 (Musée du Château de Versailles / Dagli Orti), p170 (Galleria degli Uffizi Florence / Dagli Orti), p173 (Palazzo Pitti, Florence / Dagli Orti), p174 (Burnley Art Gallery), p192 (t) (Civiche Racc d'Arte Pavia, Italy), p192 (b) (Nationalmuseet Copenhagen, Denmark / Dagli Orti), p197, p203 (l) Dagli Orti, p206 (San Carlos Museum, Mexico City / Dagli Orti), p209 (National Maritime Museum London), p210 (Galleria Sabauda Turin / Dagli Orti); Bridgeman Art Library: p13 (British Museum, London), p15 (br) (Musee du Louvre, Paris), p18 (bl) (Private Collection), p18 (br) (British Library, London), p19 (City of Westminster Archives, London),p23 (l) (Warden and Scholars of New College, Oxford), p23 (r) (Lambeth Palace Library, London), p30 (Private Collection), p31 (t) (Society of Antiquaries, London), p31 (b) (Trustees of the Weston Park Foundation, UK), p32 (Hatfield House, Hertfordshire), p44 (Private Collection), p54 (Private Collection), p55 (Private Collection), p71 (Scottish National Portrait Gallery), p86 (Marylebone Cricket Club, London), p92 (Private Collection), p96 (Guildhall Art Gallery,London), p98 (Private Collection), p100 (Private Collection), p101 (Victoria and Albert Museum, London), p137 (Private Collection), p140 (Royal Society of Arts, London), p161 (Private Collection), p164 (British Museum, London), p165 (Private Collection),p169 (Trustees of the Weston Park Foundation,UK), p171 (O'Shea Gallery, London), p202 (r) (Guildhall Library, London); Corbis: p15 (Stapleton Collection), p20 (Michael Nicholson), p22 (Dean Conger), p35 (Bettmann), p53 (Philippa Lewis/Edifice), p62 (Hulton-Deutsch Collection), p63, p66 (Hulton-Deutsch Collection), p89 (Patrick Ward), p93 (National Gallery,London), p109 (Arte & Immagini srl), p114 (Historical Picture Archive), p144 (Stapleton Collection), p160 (Christie's Images, London), p162 (Bettmann), p167 (t) (Bettmann), p167 (b) (Hulton-Deutsch Collection), p195 (Bettmann), p203 (r) (Stapleton Collection), p204 (Michael Nicholson), p205 (Francis G. Mayer), p213 (Angelo Hornak); Mary Evans Picture Library:p9 (Barnaby's Studios), p36, p48, p82, p99, p122, p126 (Bruce Castle Museum, London), p168, p180; Getty Images: p8 (Image Bank), p13 (National Geographic/Sissie Brimberg), p64 (Hulton Archive), p95 (Hulton Archive), p108 (Hulton Archive), p120(t) (Hulton Archive Three Lions), p123 (Hulton Archive), p145 (Hulton Archive), p171 (Hulton Archive), p190 (Hulton Archive), p196 (Hulton Archive); London Topographical Society: p212 (The A–Z of Elizabethan London/ Adrian Prockter and Robert Taylor); National Archives: p4, p42, p52; National Trust Photo Library: p202 (l) (Angelo Hornak); Society of Genealogists: p45 (Boyd's Marriage Index); Somerset County Council: p52; University of London: p67 (Estate of Charles Booth).

Barbara Windsor: page 156 (right), page 158 and page 159
Colin Jackson: page 132
David Dickinson: page 186 (above and above right), page 187 and page 188 (top)
David Tennant: page 60
Felicity Warren: page 104
Gerald and Joan Bailey: page 156 (far right) and page 157
Helen MacDonald: page 58 and page 61
Jeremy Irons: page 106 (above right)
John McLeod: page 59
Julia Sawalha: page 78
Liz Gried: page 105
Marie Smith: page 188 (above)
Nigella Lawson: page 216, page 217 and page 219
Ossie and Angela Jackson: page 130, page 131 and page 133
Pip Sharpe: page 106 (top and above) and page 107
Robert Lindsay: page 26 (above and right), page 27, page 28 (above and right) and page 29
Roberta Sawalha: page 76 (above and top), page 77 and page 79
Veronica Cohen: page 218
Wall to Wall/ Andrew Montgomery: page 24, page 56, page 74, page 102, page 128, page 154, page 184, page 214

All celebrity family photographs are the copyright of the respective families